DOUBTS ABOUT CREATION? NOT AFTER THIS!

1997, 1998, 2000, 2003

BRIAN YOUNG

CREATION INSTRUCTION ASSOCIATION

Copyright 2003 by Creation Instruction Publishing

All Rights Reserved. No part of this book may be reproduced or transmitted in any form or by any means, electronic or mechanical including photocopying, recording, or by any information storage and retrieval system without permission in writing form the publisher.

ISBN 1-928765-00-9

Library of Congress Catalog Card Number:

Any questions or comments may be directed to:

**Creation Instruction Association
1770 S. Overland
Juniata NE 68955
Or visit our website at**

www.creationinstruction.org

Other resources available through CIA:

For a free newsletter, "From the Beginning" write to the address shown. Also, CIA has videos dealing with various areas of the creation -- evolution debate that can be ordered directly through them. For a more dynamic approach, contact Brian Young to speak personally at conferences, local churches, or for seminars today.

**Printed by Maverick Publications
PO Box 5007
Bend, Oregon 97708**

Chapter 1 -- Why The Creation Ministry Is Important
    Personal Testimony
    Genesis-A Foundation for Church Doctrine
    Evolution and Abortion
    Genesis - A Foundation for Christ
    Evolution and Humanism

Chapter 2 --How to preach the Gospel "Creation - Wise"
    Fear of the Great Commission
    A Need for Creation Evangelism
    Creation Debates

Chapter 3 --Biblical Times and Cave Men
    Scientific Pangea
    Biblical Pangea
    Origin of Cave Men
    Origin of Races

Chapter 4 --Six Literal Creation Days
    "Yom:" A Literal Day
    Happy ___?___ Birthday Planet Earth

Chapter 5 --Results of a World Wide Flood
    View of Catastrophic Events Today
    Catastrophism and the Formation of Coal
    Catastrophism and the Ice Age
    Catastrophism and Fossil Forests
    Catastrophism and carbon Dating
    Catastrophism and Fossilization

Chapter 6 --Evolution By-laws
    Second Law of Thermodynamics
    Ontogeny Recapitulates Phylogeny
    Law of Biogenesis

Chapter 7 --Fossil Record
    No Transitional Forms
    Grand Canyon
    Archaeopteryx
    Why Humans & Dinosaurs Not Found Together

Chapter 8--Dinosaurs
    Are Dinosaurs Really Extinct
    Did Dinosaurs and Man Live at the Same Time
    Dinosaurs or Birds
    What Really Happened to the Dinosaurs

Chapter 9--Fossils: "Humanly" Speaking
    Examining the Evidence
    Genetic Similarities
    Why Are So Few Human Bones Found
    Did Life Originate on Mars?

Chapter 10--Dating Methods
    Sedimentary Rocks
    Radioisotope
    Carbon 14
    Radio Halo

Chapter 11--"Universal" Problems for Old Earth Theory
    Meteoric Dust From Space
    Comets
    Winding of the Galaxy
    Atmospheric Conditions
    Earth's Magnetic Field
    An Orderly Universe
    The Sun

Chapter 12--"Down to Earth" Problems for the Old Earth Theory
    Salt in the Sea
    Preservation of Fossils
    Geophysics Computer
    Soil Erosion
    Where Are the Soil Layers
    Stalactites
    Archaeology
    Population Crunch. . .Not

Chapter 13--The "Very Good," Pre-Flood World
    Firmament
    Longevity of Man

Chapter 14--Noah's Ark
    What Happened?
    17th Day of Nisan Not a Coincidence
    Did Giants Really Roam the Earth?
    What About All That Water?
    The Ark Itself
    The Mountain of Ararat
    Eyewitness Accounts

Chapter 15--Human Beings by Chance or Design

Chapter 16--The Bible: Divinely Inspired and Authority
    Archaeology
    Historical Records
    Scriptural Evidence
    The Bible is Inspired by God
    Conclusion

Chapter 17---Updates
    I Do Believe in Evolution
    Evolution is not Even a Theory
    2nd Law Buries Evolution
    Evolution and Similar Characteristics
    A Common Textbook Lie
    Which Came First, The Chicken (DNA) or the Egg (RNA)
    Food for Thought
    Our God is an Awesome God
    Creation Puts and End to Pro-Choice
    What Makes a Right Choice
    Genesis: Revelation Foretold
    What if Heaven Wasn't That Great
    Outdated Information
    Further Evidence of Dinosaur Living with Man
    Trees Show Evidence of Noah's Flood
    Geological Column
    Fetus Similarity with Animals
    Can Creation be Taught in Public Schools
    The Importance of Creation as a Foundation for Morals

CHAPTER 1
WHY IS CREATION EVANGELISM IMPORTANT?

Personal Testimony

My childhood curiosity always had to find out how things worked; even if that meant taking everything apart so that it would never work again. But confusion always begins when a person discovers something which cannot be torn apart and examined. Christians and others often question the validity of religious beliefs; after all, many non-Christian religious groups fought diligently also to evangelize for their own sects. We all can't be right; yet all of us think we are. Unfortunately, the philosophical world is not made up of the familiar mechanics, but is something much bigger and more complex than my feeble young mind could handle. At the risk of sounding like a heathen, I mustered the courage to ask my parents how we could be certain of our beliefs. The reply, "we just have to accept it by faith." Many times we are given superficial answers because we lack knowledge in both Scripture and Science. I believe faith in the supernatural powers of the Triune God is vital, but I also believe God did not leave us to accept these things by blind faith alone. As a young child, this partially answered question haunted me periodically into adulthood. Whenever there was something I had to accept by blind faith, I wondered if possibly someone else's answer could be the right one. After all, they were also accepting things by faith.

A few years later, while attending a secular university, my faith in Jesus Christ was finally put to an ultimate test, challenged at its foundation. . . Genesis! After taking various science courses I noticed a unifying theme throughout all my classes - - the earth was billions of years old. These wise professors, I thought, were now showing me the concrete evidence which my mind had craved since early childhood. It now seemed my acceptance by faith, an earth only 6,000 years old, was proved emotionally incorrect. I knew we all couldn't be right; I must have been wrong about the age of the earth. It all made sense now - - the TV, newspapers, radio, magazines, high-school, friends - - they were right after all. The earth was old. A campus pastor even confirmed my previous ignorance when he showed me how evolution and God fit together into something called Theistic Evolution. He explained how God could have used evolution to create man and how each of the six days of creation could have been millions of years. One can imagine the joy I had as the complex question I had as a child now became so simple and I could still have faith in God's Word (Provided I could tell what should be taken literally now).

My newly acquired intellectual high was short-lived, since many other questions began to pop into my mind. Did God really stop the sun for Joshua? Did Christ really rise from the grave? Did Noah really take all those animals on board? Now that I had the freedom to make Scripture reasonable, many other unreasonable events had to be explained. No longer could I take Scripture at face value if it didn't fit into the scheme of human reason and experience.

I am now truly ashamed that I needed such "evidence" to support Scripture and that I let that evidence falsely interpret Scripture. I should have let Scripture interpret the evidence. I give much credit to God's servant, Alfred M. Rehwinkel, for bringing me back to true faith in God's promises. It was Rehwinkel's book, The Flood, which first set my feet back on the right path. In this book I learned for the first time things the public school did not teach me. The evidence I once needed was all there and it supported a young earth as Scripture had always said. Much of this evidence and more will be presented in this book. Even so, evidence is not the key. Faith is! "I tell you the truth, unless you change and become like little children, you will never enter the kingdom of heaven" (Matthew 18:3). It is through God's Holy Word that the Holy Spirit works faith in us; and from this Spirit comes true wisdom. "If any of you lacks wisdom, he should ask God, who gives generously to all without finding fault, and it will be given to him." (James 1:5; see also Ex. 31:3; Prov. 9:10; 1 Cor 1:20).

I have visited others who have experienced a similarly weakened faith caused by the destructive devices of evolution and Satan, the "father of lies" (John 8:44). What can we do to protect children from a bombardment of millions of years here and billions of years there? To begin with, the Bible teaches parental responsibility : "Fathers, do not exasperate your children; instead, bring them up in the training and instruction of the Lord" (Ephesians 6:4). Concerning God's Word, "Impress them on your children. Talk about them when you sit at home and when you walk along the road, when you lie down and when you get up" (Dueteronomy 6:7).

Genesis: A Foundation for Christian Doctrine

Many people think the creation/evolution debate is simply an interesting side issue compared to "more important" things such as homosexuality, pornography, and abortion, when in fact, evolution is the cause of many of these societal problems. Evolution cannot really cause moral values to diminish. After all, its only science isn't it? Before we can answer this question we must first look at what science really is. Science can be summed up as, "the total collection of knowledge gained by man's observations of the physical world, using one or more of his five senses, taste, smell, sight, hearing, or touch, to investigate the world that only exists in the present, and observations can be repeated" (Ham, Relevance p. 5). The average high-school student defines science as cutting up animals, mixing chemicals, or torture. However, without the proper understanding of what science really is children cannot actually know which learning is scientific. Scientists claim "scientifically" that the earth is very old. Is this true or just a conjecture of a biased religion? What about fossils? Do fossils tell us about the past or the present? Ask your child that question and see if the answer is correct.

With opinions and conjectures flying around the scientific community we simply can't tell fact from fiction, or creation from evolution. Scientifically, fossils tell us about the present because they can only be observed and tested in the present. Dry bones only tell us that this animal once existed. Unless the skin has been fossilized or other rare circumstances occur, bones cannot tell us what the creature looked like exactly, what it ate, if it had hair, etc. When a paleontologist finds a fossil, he takes it back to his lab where he examines it and forms his own opinions about that bone. Once his theory is complete he has an artist draw a picture of what he feels this animal and the landscape around it looked like. From an unscientific background, we see these murals on the museum walls and our brain registers this information as fact, when it is merely artistic license.

Evolution is a belief system, not a science. We cannot test evolution in the present because it doesn't take place today, although some try to claim it does. Today, we do not observe animals turning into people. Again, if real science is what can be tested in the present, evolution is not science. Creation is a belief system, but contrary to popular belief, it <u>does</u> hold some scientific value, as even some evolutionists admit. Dr. Lipson, a professor of Physics at the University of Manchester, admits, "If living matter is not caused by the interplay of atoms, natural forces and radiation, how has it come into being? There is another theory, now quite out of favor, which is based upon the ideas of Lamarck: that if an organism needs an improvement it will

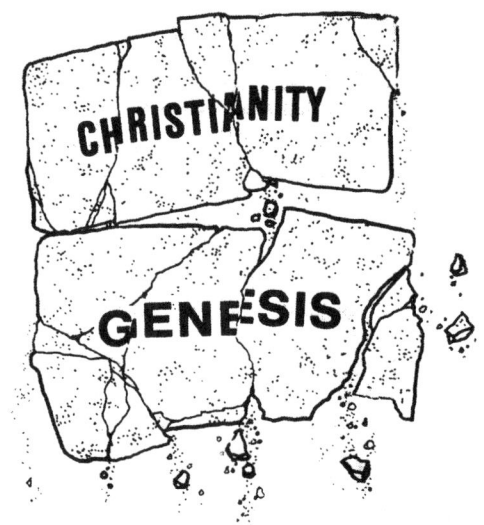

Figure 1: Christianity can not stand without Genesis as literal truth. (Reprinted by permission of *Answers in Genesis*, PO Box 6330, Florence, Kentucky, 41022, from the book <u>The Lie:Evolution,</u> by Ken Ham).

develop it, and transmit it to its progeny. I think, however, that we must go further than this and admit that the only acceptable explanation is creation. I know that this is anathema to physicists, as indeed it is to me, but we must not reject a theory that we do not like if the experimental evidence supports it" (Lipson, p. 138). Also, Dr. Edward Tryon of City University of New York writes, "In 1973, I proposed that our Universe had been created spontaneously from nothing (*ex nihilo*) as a result of established principles of physics. This proposal variously struck people as preposterous, enchanting, or both. The novelty of a scientific theory of creation *ex nihilo* is readily apparent, for science has long taught us that one cannot make something from nothing" (Tryon, p. 14).

How can we be sure about information we receive about the earth's origin? According to the scientific practice, we must either be omniscient or have been there to observe its beginnings. For scientists this is dismal, but for Christians inspiring, because we know Someone who was there and is omniscient - - God our Creator. With God as our foundation for truth, science, and history, we can be sure of our beliefs.

A good example of how the pseudo facts of evolution are formed can be seen in a murder mystery on television. Shortly after the program begins we think we know who is guilty. Half way through the program we know the guilty one and are waiting for the show to end so we can tap ourselves on the back for such skill. But just before the show is over, our pride is squelched as we realize

Figure 2: Bible as truth is foundational for life and society.

we were wrong. Why were we led to this wrong conclusion? Because we did not have all the evidence. This is the same problem we have with science because all the evidence is not there for us to see or understand; hence, as history teaches, we draw premature and inaccurate conclusions. Science has changed many times in the past and reputable men have had to recant their beliefs because new evidence proved old evidence incorrect. Accordingly, we can also suspect that science will continue to change because of emerging, new evidence. However, to an evolutionist, new evidence disproving evolution elicits the likely answer, "Oh no, Evolution is fact." Unfortunately this is the mind-set we are dealing with today. Ken Ham comments on this mindset: "No matter how much you know there is always an infinite amount more to know; which means no matter how much you know, you don't know how much more there is to know anyway; which means you don't know how much you do or don't know, which means you just don't know much at all" (Ham, Creation video).

Today we tend to form opinions based upon human wisdom. We must abandon this opinion-oriented philosophy of life and "start with the One who was there and who does know everything, not with the words of man who wasn't there and doesn't know everything" (Ham, Creation Video). Only when we admit human fallibility can we be sure about anything.

The premise from which to begin is that Scripture is the foundation for truth. Many people are ignorant of Genesis as the foundation for much of our Church Doctrine. Over 165 times Genesis is quoted in the New Testament alone. In fact, every New Testament author quotes it at least once and, therefore, it must be a book of high standing and importance. Why, then, is Genesis the most attacked book we have today? Christ's words in John 5:45-47 provides the answer, "Do not think I will accuse you before the Father. Your accuser is Moses, on whom your hopes are set. If you believed Moses, you would believe me, for he wrote about me. But since you do not believe what he wrote, how are you going to believe what I say?" Again, in Luke 16:31, Jesus quotes Abraham as saying, "If they do not listen to Moses and the Prophets, they will not be convinced even if someone rises from the dead." These verses become so much more meaningful when we realize that it was Moses who wrote Genesis; therefore, our warning is made clear. If we do not believe Moses (Genesis) how can we believe Christ's Words, let alone his resurrection from the dead? For this reason the devil certainly knows Psalm 11:3 by heart. It reads, "When the foundations are being destroyed, what can the righteous do?" Today our foundation (Genesis and God as Creator) is being destroyed and we have little, if any, support left to stop the demise of our society.

To illustrate this further, consider the parable of the wise and foolish builder in Matthew 13. Taking the parable slightly out of context, we see that a house built on a solid foundation will stand firm, but if our foundation is weakened or shaken for some reason, the structure will collapse. Today our foundation, God as Creator, is being shaken by evolution, leaving us a crumbling society filled with divorce, homosexuality, pornography, and various other forms of godlessness. Our Christian framework can only stand when a foundation exists, but it has been slowly removed by the evolutionary termites who eat away at it without being noticed. Though our weak foundation goes unnoticed, the effects of it speak loudly through our lifestyles. Not to worry, however; we are not left foundationless, because the public education system, in many cases, is replacing it with the theory of evolution. (As mentioned at the start of this chapter, I have personally felt the detrimental effects of this teaching).

Often we don't realize what Christ as Creator means for us. If God is our Maker, He owns us and therefore sets the rules for our lives; nothing depends upon human opinion. On the other hand, if evolution is true, the belief that we are a product of chance resulting from lightning striking some primordial soup billions of years ago, then we make our own rules and have no one to answer to. When this happens we become like the Israelites in the book of Judges when, "In those days Israel had no king; everyone did as he saw fit" (Judges 17:6). For many, our king is being dethroned and we are all doing what is right in our own eyes as we practice homosexuality and perform abortions. The new god is that of human wisdom and tolerance of all opinions, provided it's not the Christian opinion because of its intolerance - - (something society refuses

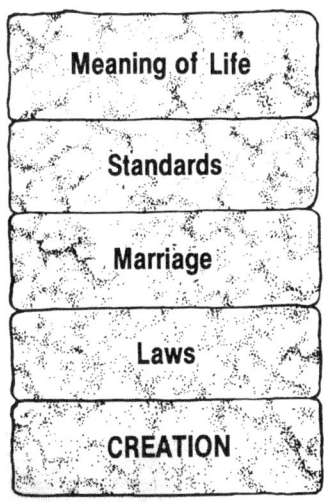
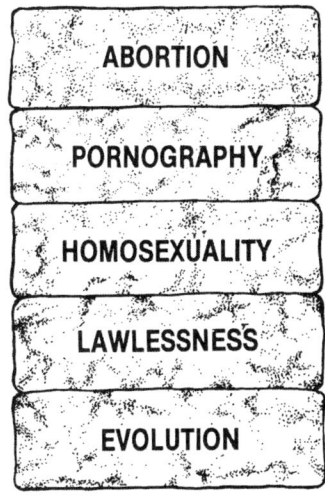

Figure 3: If Adam is not our ancestor, we make our own rules and morality. (Reprinted by permission of *Answers in Genesis*, PO Box 6330, Florence, Kentucky, 41022, from the book <u>The Lie: Evolution</u>, by Ken Ham).

to tolerate).

The fundamental issue is church doctrine. If a person wants to find the true meaning of something, the primary source is paramount. For example, the meaning of the word "door" requires its use in an initial context. Simply put, "The meaning of anything is tied up in its origins." I believe Christ understood this principle, because in Matthew 19:4-5 the Saduccees and Pharisees were questioning Jesus about divorce. To answer their question Christ took them all the way back to the origin of marriage, Genesis. Here Jesus pronounced, "Haven't you read that at the beginning the Creator 'made them male and female,' and said, 'For this reason a man will leave his father and mother and be united to his wife, and the two will become one flesh?'" Jesus quoted Genesis to set the standard for marriage and give it its foundation. First of all, this passage gives us the spiritual meaning of marriage. The husband and wife became one flesh; therefore, divorced persons are incomplete, only half of what used to be a whole. If one rejects this oneness, what is to stop us from living together before we are married? After all, we are just two individuals living our lives independently, and after divorce we may go on as if nothing ever happened. Second, we find the origin of the family unit tied up in this passage. God created one woman for one man, not two men or two women. Again God set the standard, but homosexual couples continue to claim themselves a family despite this sanction. Finally, we learn about the roles of a husband and wife. In today's marriages there has been a breakdown in the family roles, but for a marriage to be truly successful, I believe a man and a woman must enter into the marriage with a proper understanding of those roles. The woman's role is to be submissive to her husband, yet many woman don't want to be obedient; but again, its not a matter of our opinion but rather what God has ordained. As Scripture points out, submission is not a matter of equality but rather a matter of roles for, "There is neither Jew nor Greek, slave nor free, male nor female, for you are all one in Christ Jesus" (Galatians 3:28). On the other hand, the husband's role is to love his wife as Christ first loved the church and gave Himself for it. How many husbands love their wives like that today?

Husbands and wives are to procreate, which also ties directly into parenting. The role of the father is made clear in Ephesians 6:4 where we read, "Fathers, do not exasperate your children; instead, bring them up in the training and instruction of the Lord." Or Isaiah 38:19 which states, "Fathers tell their children about your faithfulness." It's obvious that the role of a father is to be the spiritual head of the house. How many fathers are abandoning this role? It often seems to be the mother who gets the children out of bed on Sunday morning to make sure they get to church and Sunday school. Sometimes they must even get their husbands out of bed so they go to church rather than going golfing. Or if there is a Christian school in your area, how many fathers make sure their children are enrolled? Again, it's not a matter of what we feel like doing, rather it's our God-given responsibility and we must follow it.

Why do we wear clothes? The meaning of clothing also looks at origins. Here, we must go all the way back to Genesis and the fall of man in the

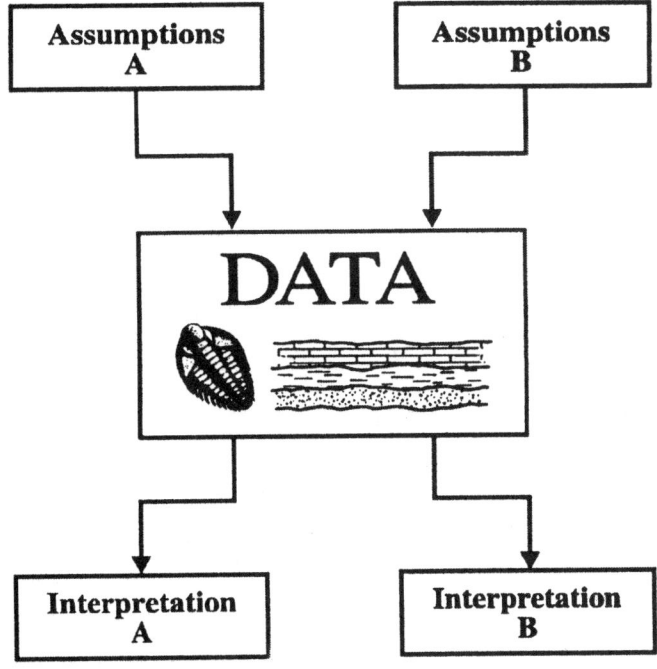

Figure 4: Our belief in Creation is our starting point for the rest of our values.

Garden of Eden. We see Adam and Eve sinning and becoming aware of their nakedness. God then killed the first animal as a blood sacrifice and a covering for their sins. There it is - - sin is why we wear clothing today - - and consequently, a man and woman can no longer look at each other in the perfect way they once could because sin has distorted their relationship. Therefore, what we wear can put a stumbling block in another person's path, thereby causing them to sin. We are told that if a man lusts after a woman's body he commits adultery. Why are men singled out? I would probably get little argument from males when I declare that a man responds very easily to a woman's body sexually and, therefore, what she wears can put a stumbling block in a male's path, causing him to sin. Matthew Henry, a popular Bible commentator, once said, "Men sin but devils tempt to sin." How true this is. We are all sinners and need the support and guidance of others to help us along. When a woman wears clothes that are indecent she is tempting the male into sin, maybe not intentionally, but nonetheless she is tempting. This does not relieve the male from his responsibility to keep his eyes from wandering. Nor does it relieve the female from her responsibility of dressing decently.

As fathers, we need to explain to our children what men are like so they may have a better understanding of the importance of dressing decently. This very argument often becomes a battle of opinions when one's daughter wants to leave the house in a revealing outfit. The father objects to her attire followed by the daughter asking "why?" Father responds, "because it's not right." "Why not?" asks the daughter. "Because it's wrong," answers the father. "Why is it wrong?" "Because it's not right," announces the father as it starts all over again. Rather than fighting battles based on opinions, we must turn the table and fight at a foundational level, with God as the ultimate authority. Set your daughter down and show her in Scripture why we wear clothing and what the effects of indecent clothing are. Show her how God has commanded you to raise her in a Godly fashion and whether you, as a father, like it or not, must step in and obey God rather than your own emotions. In doing so the battle of opinions becomes a battle of God's Word verses your daughter's opinion. "But who are you, O man, to talk back to God?" (Romans 9:20).

Evolution and Abortion

As mentioned earlier, if Adam is our ancestor we have laws that we must abide by, because God is our Creator and He established them. For example, clothing has been given to us because of our sin and, therefore, we must dress decently. Marriage and life both have spiritual meaning and purpose, inducing us with joy and comfort. However, if ape is our ancestor then our laws are mere human opinions and we may do what we please. Clothing depends on our own opinion and we can wear what we want, when we want, if we want to wear anything at all; marriage is an opinion and, therefore, homosexuality IS an acceptable alternative; and finally, life has NO meaning or purpose so we are filled with strife, and what is to stop us from performing abortions or committing suicide?

I hear many people say that evolution and abortion are not related; the two have nothing in common. If this is true, why then are some young, yet to be mothers, counseled before an abortion, when they are told that the fetus isn't a human being yet? Evolution plays a large part in desensitizing society toward the value of an unborn child. In Jeremiah 1:5 we hear God say, "Before I formed you in the womb I knew you, before you were born I set you apart. . ." Yet Eli Schneour, the Director of the Biosystems Research Institute in La Jolla, California states, "During development, the fertilized egg progresses over 38 weeks through what is, *in fact* (my emphasis), a rapid passage through evolutionary history. From a single primordial cell, the conceptus progresses through being something of a protozoan, a fish, a reptile, a bird, a primate and ultimately a human being" (Schneour, LA Times). Though few knowledgeable evolutionists continue to use this false evidence, it still remains in circulation today. The theory of evolution deeply affects abortion and life's purpose. Not to long ago the television news showed a picture of Susan Smith's children. Susan had strapped her children into her car and pushed the car and children into a lake, drowning them. To cover up her wrong doing she told the police they were kidnapped, but it wasn't long before they found the car with her children still strapped in. The media coverage brought forth many people who were disgusted with Susan Smith, but one man wrote into his local paper and asked people why they were getting so upset. Susan didn't do anything wrong; she simply didn't want to take the responsibility of her children so she got rid of them. Today, if we unburden ourselves before the child is born it's called abortion, but if after they are born, it is murder. According to evolution one might say that Susan was only guilty of "bad timing."

One might even add that abortion is inconsistent with evolutionary beliefs. If the natural processes of the world are what caused our existence and the "survival of the fittest," what business do we have in interfering with the natural course of birth? Why are we trying to destroy something such as the aids virus. If evolution is true we should shut down all the hospitals, stop fighting for the endangered species, and let those earthquakes come. The very fact that these statements bother us suggests we are not a product of evolution, because evolution does not have a conscience. Has anyone ever seen a sympathetic virus or hurricane? Should nature be left alone to run its course because evolutionary logic concludes that survival of the fittest is how it all works, so don't stop the *progress* of evolution?

Genesis: A Foundation for Christ

By far the most calamitous outcome of evolution is destroying Christ as Savior. Evolution claims that death and disease resided for millions and billions of years before man ever existed and, therefore, death is not a direct result of sin as Scripture clearly points out. To an evolutionist, the fossils are a record of death and disease that occurred long before man. However, the Bible states, "Therefore, just as sin entered the world through one man, and death through sin, and in this way death came to all men, because all sinned-- " (Romans 5:12). Also, "For the wages of sin is death, but the gift of God is eternal life in Christ Jesus our Lord" (Romans 6:23). If we believe these promises are true, death could not have existed before man; however, the fossil record, according to evolutionists, was laid down before man existed. If death is not the payment or wages of sin, Christ's death on the cross is meaningless and has no power or purpose. Unfortunately, evolutionists understand this concept much more than Christians. Richard Bozarth, an evolutionist writes, "Christianity has fought, still fights, and will fight science to the desperate end over evolution, because evolution destroys utterly and finally the very reason Jesus' earthly life was supposedly made necessary. Destroy Adam and Eve and the original sin, and in the rubble you will find the sorry remains of the Son of God. Take away the meaning of his death. If Jesus was not the redeemer who died for our sins - - and this is what evolution means - - then Christianity is nothing!" (Bozarth, pp. 19,30). Evolution and Scripture are in total conflict; one says death and disease caused man's existence, but Scripture shows that it was man's existence (sin) that caused death and disease.

I pray that Christians who are out spreading the Good News of Christ crucified do not take evolution in any way, shape, or form, because in so doing, one destroys the very Gospel message. God Bless all of you in His service as creationists, not theistic evolutionists.

Evolution and Humanism

To grasp the relation between evolution and humanism we first examine the typical humanistic belief. The following is a statement of the British Humanist Association: "I believe in no god and no hereafter. It is immoral to

Figure 5: Evolution and Humanism depend upon man's wisdom, not God's.

indoctrinate children with such beliefs. Schools have no right to do so, nor indeed, have parents. I believe that religious education . . . should be abolished. . . I believe that children should be taught religion as a matter of historical interest, but should be taught about all religions including Humanism, Marxism, Maoism, Communism, and other attitudes of life. I am as yet unsure whether the grossly handicapped are people in the real sense. . . I believe in no sin to be forgiven, no life beyond the grave but death everlasting" (Sippert, Evolution, p.336).

People have told me that humanism and evolution are two separate things. However, evolution, as we have seen, trumps humanistic philosophies. Even Julian Huxley, a world renown evolutionist and *founder* of the Humanist

Association remarked, "I use the word "humanist" to mean someone who believes that man is just as much a natural phenomenon as an animal or plant, that his body, mind and soul were not supernaturally created but are the products of evolution, and that he is not under the control or guidance of any supernatural being or beings, but has to rely on himself and his own powers" (Sippert, Evolution, p.337). Again prevalent is the idea that God is nothing and man is the all powerful savior. Evolution, too, states that man is evolving into superior forms and God is nothing. While some evolutionists entertain the thought of God, He *is* the all powerful, all knowing, Creator God that the Bible talks about.

Why are so many people upset when God as Creator of the universe is presented in our schools? They say that religion does not belong in schools, so why is the opposite allowed; the religious belief that there is no God or Creator. John Dunphy answered this question in *The Humanist* by stating, "I am convinced that the battle for humankind's future must be waged and won in the public school classroom by teachers who correctly perceive their role as the proselytizers of a new faith; a *religion* [emphasis mine] of humanity that recognizes and respects the spark of what theologians call divinity in every human being. These teachers must embody the same selfless dedication as the most rabid fundamentalist preachers, for they will be ministers of another sort, utilizing a classroom instead of a pulpit to convey humanist values in whatever subject they teach, regardless of the educational level -- preschool day care or large state university. The classroom must and will become an arena of conflict between the old and the new -- the rotting corpse of Christianity . . ." (Sippert, Evolution, p. 338).

The evolutionary scientists indeed are following a religion. I dare call them scientists, but rather philosophers. I can only pray they will become theologians!

CHAPTER 2
HOW TO PREACH THE GOSPEL "CREATION-WISE"

Fear of the Great Commission

One of the most asked evangelistic questions reflects a fear of failure. "What is the best way to reach people with Christ's love, without chasing them away?" Often well-meaning Christians direct others to speak in a certain tone of voice, to present oneself favorably, and to make sure to use right words at a proper time. To some it seems as if the Gospel can be spread by only those who have "the skill," driving many evangelists away from the Great Commission (Matthew 28). Is it really necessary to be an eloquent, persuasive speaker to share Christ crucified?

Again, to fully respond to this question we must go to Jesus, the Master Teacher, and those who learned directly from Him. The Great Commission instructs us to, "Therefore go and make disciples of all nations, baptizing them in the name of the Father and of the Son and of the Holy Spirit, and teaching them to obey everything I have commanded you. And surely I am with you always, to the very end of the age" (Matthew 28:19-20). To first alleviate the fear and unworthiness many feel at the sound of these words, I offer Jesus' comforting words: "lo, I am with you always." We can take this promise with us as we go out to preach, thereby having complete confidence in the power of the Holy Spirit. The disciples were told not to put their confidence in themselves, but rather in God, "When you are brought before synagogues, rulers and authorities, do not worry about how you will defend yourselves or what you will say, for the Holy Spirit will teach you at that time what you should say" (Luke 12:11-12). Evangelistic problems among Christians today occur when we feel as if the salvation of those to whom we are ministering is dependent upon our words and how we say them. Rather, we really need only to share the words of Scripture. God tells us in Isaiah 55:11, "So is my word that goes out from my mouth: It will not return to me empty, but will accomplish what I desire and achieve the purpose for which I sent it. ." How can one argue with that? "What, then, shall we say in response to this? If God is for us, who can be against us?" (Romans 8:31).

Second, the commission is to "make disciples of ALL nations." For many Christians, evangelism means welcoming the new visitor to your church and giving an occasional reprimand to a straying lamb; however, "all nations" include those souls inside and outside of the church body, both saved and unsaved. As Christ proclaimed, "It is not the healthy who need a doctor, but the sick. I have not come to call the righteous, but sinners" (Mark 2:17). Similarly we must be careful not to be quick to judge, for "why do you look at the speck of sawdust in your brother's eye and pay no attention to the plank in your own eye?" (Matthew 7:3). It is easy to eye neighbors across the street and question their reputation and believe the rumors that have rampantly been spread about them. It is much more difficult to invite neighbors over for dinner, welcome them with loving arms, and witness to them by verbalizing Christ in YOUR life, not pointing out the lack of Christ in THEIRS. Just as Christ in bodily presence welcomed and loved the sinner, we too learn from His example as we share Christ crucified present in our lives. As the Master Teacher has shown, He loved us sinners so much that He gave His time, words of comfort, and His life so that we may live in Him and with Him forever.

A Need for Creation Evangelism

We are to "teach them ALL things [Jesus] has commanded." Our example is Peter and Paul's preaching. When Peter or Paul preached to the Jews, people who knew of God as their Creator, they taught Christ crucified, died, and resurrected. For example, when Peter had his vision of the clean and unclean animals being lowered down from the four corners of the earth, he is called to the house of Cornelius who, though a Gentile, was a righteous man who served God and knew of His mighty works. In keeping with the "all nations" aspect of the commission, Paul immediately explains Christ to this Gentile (Acts 10). Again, when Paul goes to Antioch in Pisidia and preaches to the Jews in the synagogue, he goes directly to tracing the line of Jesus, leading all the way to the cross (Acts 13). Also, among those in Thessalonica, Paul preaches in the synagogue of the Jews, where, "As his custom was, Paul went into the synagogue, and on three Sabbath days he reasoned with them from the Scriptures, explaining and proving that the Christ had to suffer and rise from the dead. 'This Jesus I am proclaiming to you is the Christ'" (Acts 17:2-3). The same "Christ centered" style of preaching occurs at Jerusalem (Acts 15:1-10) and everywhere else in which the listening audience already had the background of Scripture and God as Creator.

On the other hand, if those listening were Gentiles, who had little knowledge of Scripture, Paul first spoke of God as Creator of the universe. For example, in Lystra when Paul healed a cripple, the Gentiles who saw this miracle, cried out, "The gods have come down to us in human form! Barnabas they called Zeus, and Paul they called Hermes because he was the chief speaker. . .. But when the apostles Barnabas and Paul heard of this, they tore their clothes and rushed out into the crowd, shouting: 'Men, why are you doing this? We too are only men, human like you. We are bringing you good news, telling you to turn from these worthless things to the living God, who made heaven and earth and sea and everything in them'" (Acts 14:11-15). Once more, while in idol-filled Athens, Paul stood in the midst of the Areopagus, a rocky hill west of the Acropolis where the council met, and said, "Men of Athens! I see that in every way you are very religious. For as I walked around and looked carefully at your objects of worship, I even found an altar with this inscription: TO AN UNKNOWN GOD. Now what you worship as something unknown I am going to proclaim to you. The God who made the world and everything in it is the Lord of heaven and earth and does not live in temples built by hands" (Acts 17:22-24).

"God as Creator" style of preaching among the Gentiles is essential because "we preach Christ crucified: a stumbling block to Jews and foolishness to Gentiles" (I Corinthians 1:23). The Gentiles did not have the knowledge of the Old Testament as the Jews had, and therefore, this Christ who rose from the dead seemed foolish because they were unaware of the coming Messiah or the deliverance He was to bring. The Jews, however, had Moses and the prophets, all of whom spoke of the coming deliverer who, in their minds, was to set up an earthly kingdom. When Christ did not establish their earth-bound kingdom He became a stumbling block to them. As a result, when Paul was among Jews he needed to open their eyes to the prophecies of the Messiah and His deliverance. But when among the Gentiles, Paul had to establish a foundation, one which the Jews already had, that the one and only God created the universe and that this same God has provided a Redeemer for our sins.

When we examine these different evangelistic styles we need to apply them to our mission today. Ken Ham, of Answers in Genesis, grew up in Australia and observed the much needed missionary outreach which took place in his country. Ken Ham once noted the huge success of bringing people to

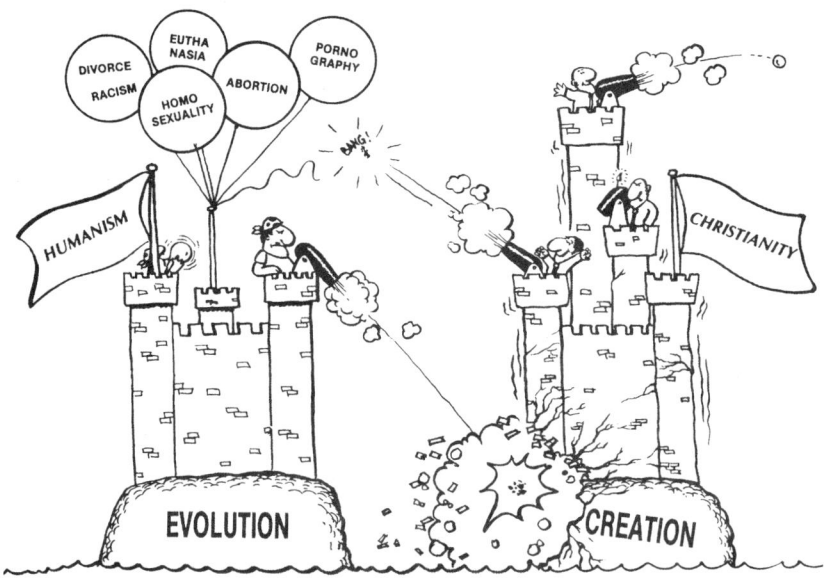

Figure 6: To win this battle we must fight at a foundational level as well as at the issues. Also, we must stop fighting among ourselves. (Reprinted by permission of *Answers in Genesis*, PO Box 6330, Florence, Kentucky, 41022, from the book The Lie:Evolution, by Ken Ham).

Christ which Billy Graham had in Australia in the early 1950's. Unfortunately, the evangelists in Australia today do not have nearly the success that Billy Graham had preaching the Gospel, because today's society has become more like the Gentiles and less like Jews, lacking Biblical knowledge, especially that

Figure 7: **We must prepare the ground by ridding it of evolutionary philosophies before the Gospel seed can take root.** (Reprinted by permission of *Answers in Genesis*, PO Box 6330, Florence, Kentucky, 41022, from the book <u>The Lie:Evolution,</u> by Ken Ham).

of Old Testament. Despite this lapse, we continue to preach to them as if they were of Jewish background, knowing Scripture in both heart and mind. The information contained in the Old Testament is vital to the Gospel. If we do not understand the bad news (fall into sin) in Genesis, how can we comprehend the good news (means of salvation) in the New Testament?

There has been a change in the attitude and Biblical knowledge of society. Church and Sunday School attendance have dropped for young and old alike; school prayer has been taken out of the public schools; sexual perverseness has grown; Adam and Eve have become mythical characters and Christianity as a whole has become a quick Sunday fix for the guilty conscience. Even our laws show signs of a wicked generation. We have the same constitution that we had before abortion. Did the constitution change? No, rather the hearts of men changed.

Our once prepared ground was ready for the Gospel seed to be planted and take root, but the societal grounds are now overtaken with weeds and thorns, choking the message, sometimes before it can sprout. We must, therefore, go forth and clear the ground and prepare it, once again for the Gospel. "This is what the LORD says to the men of Judah and to Jerusalem: 'Break up your unplowed ground and do not sow among thorns'" (Jeremiah 4:3).

Likewise we see in the Parable of the Sower how important prepared ground is. "As he was scattering the seed, some fell along the path, and the birds came and ate it up. Some fell on rocky places, where it did not have much soil. It sprang up quickly, because the soil was shallow. But when the sun came up, the plants were scorched, and they withered because they had no root. Other seed fell among thorns, which grew up and choked the plants. Still other seed fell on good soil, where it produced a crop--a hundred, sixty or thirty times what was sown. He who has ears, let him hear" (Matthew 13:4-9).

Jesus later explained this parable to the Apostles, telling them that the Gospel must be received by people who have been prepared for it. No longer are we preaching to a society of Jews, but rather to Gentiles. Until our fields are prepared for planting, the Gentile society will not be able to accept the message we have to share; therefore, Creation Evangelism is of utmost importance, not to replace the Gospel but to prepare human hearts for It.

Creation Debates

I am not recommending that everyone debate with evolutionists, especially if one is not well-qualified. In fact, debating at the "evidence" level doesn't seem to have great success in changing the minds of evolutionary scientists anyway. But I feel it necessary to share the attitude among the scientific community regarding Creationism.

Niles Eldridge, in his book *The Monkey Business* writes, "Creationists travel all over the United States, visiting college campuses and staging 'debates' with biologists, geologists, and anthropologists. The creationists nearly always win. The audience is frequently loaded with the already converted and the faithful. And scientists, until recently, have been showing up at the debates ill-prepared for what awaits them. Thinking the creationists are uneducated, Bible-thumping clods, they are soon routed by a steady onslaught of direct attacks on a wide variety of scientific topics. . . .Creationists today -- at least the majority of their spokesmen -- are highly educated, intelligent people, skilled debaters who have always done their homework. And they are usually better informed than their opponents who are reduced too often to a bewildered state of incoherence. . . . their arguments are devoid of any real intellectual content. Creationists win debates because of their canny stage presence, and not through clarity of logic or force of evidence. The debates are shows rather than serious consideration of evolution" (Eldridge, pp. 17-18).

Lacking "real science," evolutionists often fail at these debates. It must be remembered, however, that creationists do not have real science either because Creation is something of the unobserved past and, therefore, cannot be scientifically proven. However, when these assumptions are exposed, Creation always comes out ahead.

Dr. Morris informs us that, "All but one voice at the N.A.S. (National Academy of Sciences) gathering agreed that debating with creationists should be avoided" (Morris, Christian p. 102). The March 1987 *Acts and Facts*, also points out that three of the world's top evolutionists (Dr. Carl Sagan, Dr. Isaac Asimov, and Dr. Stephen Gould) had turned down debates with Creationists. Why is this? What are they afraid of? The remainder of this book will address this question in detail. I believe that when all the facts are laid out and the assumptions behind them are understood, God as Creator, Sustainer, and Savior is exalted to His proper position -- Jesus is Lord!

CHAPTER 3
BIBLICAL TIMES AND CAVEMEN
Scientific Pangea

Much talk has surfaced in recent years about the Pangea continent which may have existed at the beginning of creation (one large continent). Of course, evolutionists believe this super continent existed millions of years ago, even before the Ice Age. From a Biblical perspective, however, Pangea must have existed only a few thousand years ago. Genesis 1:9 reads, "And God said, 'Let the water under the sky be gathered to one place, and let dry ground appear.' And it was so.'" With the waters being gathered together in **one** place, we have an indication that Pangea did indeed exist. Understanding this concept better may help us to understand how the many nations and races we have today first came into being. Evidence for Pangea include sea floor spreading, magnetic fluxes, subduction zones, and similar rock patterns on different continents and that the continents today seem to fit together like a puzzle.

Evolution states that the continents are continuing this spread today at a very slow rate, from two to 18 centimeters per year. At this rate, it would take 100 million years to form the present geographical scarring. At a 1989 conference, David Smith of NASA reported that data collected since the 1970's, by space geodetic techniques of laser ranging to satellites and very long baseline interferometry (VLBI), showed a 15mm/yr. movement across the Mid-Atlantic Ridge; 170 mm/yr. across the East Pacific Rise; and 28mm/yr. across the San Andreas Fault. Smith does not say exactly how far these plates have moved or in what time period. Also problematic is that these figures are only an extension of the same NASA recordings as reported in *Scientific American* and *Science News* in 1983, where it was said by the latter that no one had yet measured any movement (Snelling, pp.55-56). The authors of the article in *Scientific American* even stated, "The baseline lengths are increasing at a rate of between one centimeter and two centimeters per year. On the other hand, the baseline lengths also exhibit equally large random fluctuations; hence, from these data alone we would be reluctant to conclude that we had really measured plate motions" (Carter, p. 51). We see that "evidence" is lacking to show movement of these plates today.

Indications suggest movement of the continental plates in the past, but all of them present certain problems, at least when slow and gradual theories are applied to these evidences. We have already mentioned that drift measurement is not objective, but convincing evidence exists telling of a movement in the past. Sea floor spreading along mid-oceanic ridges is one such evidence. The continental plates seem to be separating slowly at a continuous rate, driven by a force of molten lava injected up between the plates, pushing them outward. Eventually these plates then either collide, causing them to buckle and form mountains, or one plate slides under the other and is subducted back down into the molten magma, creating volcanoes. The subducted plate, compressing and breaking up, is also said to cause earthquakes. Answering concerns about subduction, Snelling writes, "First, if subduction occurs, there should be compressed, deformed, and thrust-faulted sediments on the floors of the trenches. However, the floors of the Peru-Chile and East Aleutian Trenches are covered with soft flat-lying sediments devoid of compressional structures. Second, seismic first-motion data indicate that modern earthquakes occurring approximately under trenches and island arcs are often tensional, and only rarely compressional" (Snelling, p. 49).

Also, according to theory, the molten material which is injected up from the mid-oceanic rifts eventually cools, creating new oceanic crusts; we should expect the material closest to the ridge to be younger and the further away, older. A claim for Potassium-Argon dating has proved that older rocks exist further away from the ridge and a definite magnetic pattern in a positive/negative, striped fashion exists with the positives/negatives corresponding on either side. Concerning dating methods, Snelling writes, "As to the 'successful' dating of the sea-floor magnetic anomalies, such a claim is doubtful. . . .others have found that the greater argon content (giving older apparent age) of the ocean-floor basalts on the flanks of the mid-ocean ridges can be easily explained by greater depth and pressure at the time of solidification, incorporating original magmatic argon (not derived by radioactive decay)" (Snelling, p. 48). More about Potassium-Argon problems later; however, many assumptions are involved which can not be accepted by objective, scientific creationists.

The direction of the earth's magnetism has reversed a number of times

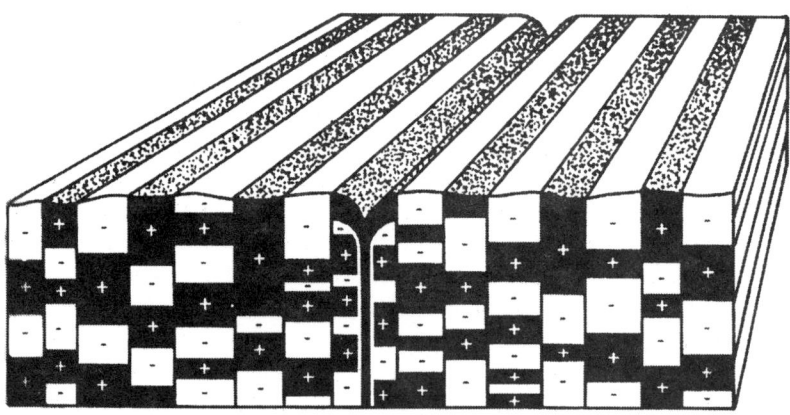

Figure 8: Drilled cores show chaotic paleomagnetic patterns, providing evidence for rapid spreading and rapid reversals along the rift.

in the past, shown in the rocks as they cooled from a molten state. Therefore, we would expect to see the presence of past magnetic reversals in those rocks which have moved away from the ridge from sea floor spreading. The pattern for these reversals should be the same on both sides of the ridge as the new material is pushed further away. One problem with the magnetic reversal theory is the presumed source of reversal, which some scientists question. Doell and Cox testify, "the reversed magnetization of some rocks is now known to be due to a self-reversal mechanism" (Doell, p.452). Therefore, as Jacobs admits, "such results show that one must be cautious about interpreting all reversal as due to field reversal and the problem of deciding which reversed rocks indicate a reversal of the field may in some cases be extremely difficult" (Jacobs, p. 106). Core samples from the ocean floor show an erratic pattern of positive and negatively polarized areas. Dr. John Morris writes, "Problems in the theory of spreading along the rift zones are compounded by studies showing that reversals are not only found in parallel zones perpendicular to the mid-ocean rifts, but vertically in each rock zone, as drill cores have displayed for years, a fact seldom admitted by my uniformitarian colleagues. In my opinion, these zones are best understood as resulting from rapid reversal coupled with rapid spreading, and go hard against the slow and steady spreading hypothesis" (Morris, Young, p. 78-79).

Information from the First International Conference on Creationism examines magnetic reversals and Noah's Flood. Snelling explains, "The Flood model for the development of many of the earth's crustal strata can account for the magnetic stripes in some layers that appear to record past countless reversals of the earth's magnetic field. If we apply the Barnes mechanism for generation of the earth's magnetic field (which is superior to the so-called dynamo hypothesis), the earth's magnetic field could well have flipped many times during and soon after the Flood" (Snelling, p. 58).

A final uncertainty dealing with the uniformitarian theory of plate tectonics deals with the driving mechanism. What energy source could move an entire continent of several thousand square miles and over 60 miles thick. It's easy to provide a catastrophic source (Noah's Flood) with enough energy to do such a thing quickly. But what kind of energy could move this large mass slowly over millions of years and provide necessary momentum to create mountains? One popular theory is that the circular convection currents of the earth's mantle, much like boiling water, cause the plates to move outward. However, the large scale convection currents needed are impossible with the earth's mantle (Snelling, p. 51). Other theories involve gravity, chemical phase changes caused by melting, and slow injection of magma into vertical cracks. A combination of these forces would not be enough power to overcome the friction and drag caused by such a mass. These theories neither explain differences in elevation throughout, nor how the present plate boundaries began (Snelling, pp. 51-52).

This matter is far from settled. The present consensus among evolutionists is that continental drift occurs today at a slow and gradual rate. As these plates continue to collide the mountains slowly rise. All this conjecturing despite controversy among the sheep of their own flock, because to deny the uniformitarian approach is to admit failure and put the entire theory of evolution at stake. For the creationist, evidence points strongly to a super continent at one time, but seems to deny the uniformity of the slow drifting of plates. We will examine this theory further in the following section.

Biblical Pangea

At Creation, God said, "Let the water under the sky be gathered to one place, and let dry ground appear. And it was so" (Genesis 1:9). The singular "dry land" gives Biblical support for a super continent at the time of Adam and Eve. This Pangea, as it is called among the secular world, is generally accepted by Creationists as a certain part of our history. Creationists believe that once Pangea split it began moving and, for the most part, has stopped moving today; although a little disagreement exists regarding when and how this drifting took place.

Among the creationists, one theory as to the timing of the split of Pangea is that it occurred in the late stages of Noah's Flood (it may have helped get rid of the mountain-covering waters). John Morris, a scientist at the Institute for Creation Research, explains, "There is plenty of water available to cover the earth. If the earth were completely smooth, the water would stand over a mile and a half deep. Evidently, before the Flood, the world's topography was much less pronounced--the oceans weren't so deep and the mountains weren't so high, . . .But how did the Flood end? Where is the water now? Obviously, the water is now in the ocean basins, which are much deeper than the continents are high, and cover over two-thirds of the globe. . . Somehow the oceans must have been deepened and widened, allowing the water to drain into them. . .Continental separation may have been one of the physical mechanisms involved. This partially explains why no oceanic crust has been discovered dating from the early earth. It was formed late in the Flood" (Morris, Young, p.78). Regarding the mid-oceanic ridge, this 40,000 mile long mountain range goes completely around the globe and is roughly parallel to the major mountain ranges like the Alps, Rockies, Appalachians, Himalayas, and Andes. This ridge may be the scar of a broken Pangea that slipped outward at great speeds, later colliding to form the land mountain ranges. Other Biblical evidence which may support this theory comes from Genesis 7:11, where one of the sources of water for the Flood comes from underground where "the fountains of the great deep were broken up." Regarding this possibility, Dr. Clark writes, "Vast quantities of pressurized waters and magmas had broken forth and tremendous readjustments of continents and oceans may well have taken place after the Flood. . . .The velocity of drift would gradually decrease with the passing of time, eventually becoming essentially imperceptible, as it seems to be at the present" (Clark, p.124). Furthering support of the fact that the mountains may have been raised and the oceans made deeper, Psalm 104:6-9 reads, "Thou didst cover it with the deep as with a garment; the waters stood above the mountains. At thy rebuke they fled; at the sound of thy thunder they took to flight. The mountains rose, the valleys sank down to the place which thou didst appoint for them. Thou didst set a boundary which they should not pass, so that they might not again cover the earth" (RSV). Finally, as mentioned earlier, the Ice Age would then begin rather abruptly as a result of the Flood and would last perhaps 500 or more years, taking up additional water and exposing various land bridges, connecting the continents.

Another popular theory based upon Genesis 10:25 reads, "And unto Eber were born two sons: the name of one was Peleg; for in his days was the earth divided." Some interpret this division of people at the Tower of Babel as political, not a physical land separation. Further examination pinpoints the time of Peleg in relation to the Tower of Babel. Assuming there are no gaps in the genealogies around this time, Peleg would have been the great-great-great-great grandson of Noah and lived to be 239 according to the Massoretic text, or 339 years LXX text. This also means, according to the Massoretic text, that Noah would still be living at the time of Abram. This interpretation, however, is strongly rejected by those who believe gaps occur in the genealogies. Dr. Erich Von Fange writes concerning these possible gaps, "Some students of the Bible believe that the scattering of the people at Babel is the Peleg event. If this is so, we have another good argument for a long period of time between the Flood and Abram. Traditional chronology had Noah, Shem, and other forefathers of Peleg living through the lifetime of Peleg. How could the division then be linked to Peleg when much more prominent patriarchs were living at the time. The only reasonable conclusion is that 'begat' is used in an ancestral manner here. Thus Peleg must have been a distant descendant of those named as his father and other forefathers. This is supported also by the fact that a sharp drop in life span occurred between the time of Eber and the time of Peleg. There is further support for extending the period of time between Flood and Abram. At the time of Babel the people were still unified geographically. . . . All this is in sharp contrast to Abram's day when there were already long established kingdoms, such as Egypt" (Von Fange, pp. 291-292).

In a similar fashion, it is also proposed that the division at the time of Peleg in Genesis 10:25 was a physical land separation. Genesis 10:4-5 records, "The sons of Javan: Elishah, Tarshish, the Kittim and the Rodanim. (From these the maritime peoples spread out into their territories by their clans within their nations, each with its own language)." These verses are obviously talking about the Tower of Babel because of the separation of people and languages; however, Peleg is not mentioned until verse 25, twenty verses later, where the earth is divided. If the Tower of Babel and Peleg were at the same time why would they be listed so far apart in the genealogical record? Therefore, an alternate view states that at the time of Babel there was a political and language division, and once these people were sufficiently spread out, God divided the land physically (Von Fange, p. 293). I believe it is also important to note that the two Hebrew words used for division in verses 5 and 25 are different, suggesting a possible difference in usage. However, some reject this as evidence, as Dr. Clark shows in writing, "Even though the Hebrew word for 'divided' in Genesis 10:25 is a different word than the one used in 10:5 and 10:32 (owing to the different type of subject in view), they are sufficiently synonymous in meaning and usage to justify assigning them to the same basic event. In the one case, the division was linguistic; in the other, it was the geographical division which ensued as a result of the migrations forced by the linguistic division" (Clark, p. 124).

One more problem is that of how the land was divided; by actual splitting of continents or simply by the meltdown of glaciers covering the once existing land bridges, a scientific possibility. Both divisions could be possible, making it just a matter of timing. If John Morris is correct about the continents splitting near the end of the Flood, providing a reservoir for the water, then the energies needed for such an event are apparent. Meanwhile the Ice Age would have exposed land bridges which would allow for people to separate at the time of Babel. (Note: The sin at the tower of Babel was direct disobedience to God's command to spread out and fill the earth. The people were building a city out of sun dried bricks, something used for permanent settlements.) Later, the separation was completed at the division in the days of Peleg, near the end of the Ice Age when land bridges were covered up by melting ice (as the geological evidence suggests), ensuring they would not reunite. Regarding the division at the time of Peleg, Dr. Clark writes, "It is very doubtful that this refers to an actual physical division of an original single continent, especially in light of Genesis 10:5, which states that the primary intent of chapter 10 is to show how mankind was divided by languages, by families, and by nations" (Clark, p. 122).

Some believe, as the Bible states, that the Flood had three sources of water: 1) waters already in existence, 2) fountains of the great deep opening, and 3) windows of heaven falling (firmament collapsing). Scientists now claim that the earth has an internal temperature over 12,000 degrees Fahrenheit, twice the temperature of the sun's surface (Williams Q., p.345). The main cause of this great temperature is known as radioactive runaway, or great radioactive decay

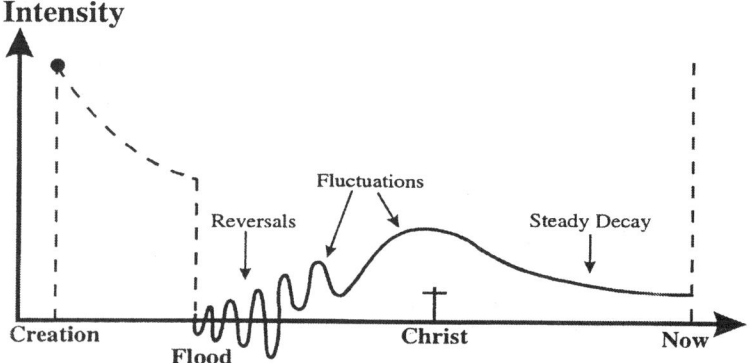

Figure 9: Magnetic field intensity increase from Creation to present, as recorded in the rocks. Note an increase in the field when Christ was on earth.

(Powell, 1991). In addition, the earth is similar to an egg, in that it has an outer shell and much liquid on the inside (Weiner, p.31). In fact, secular scientists note vast quantities of water pockets beneath the surface (Zimmer, p. 20). Just as when an egg is put in a microwave, it cracks; likewise the earth, being bombarded by the high levels of background radiation, was ruptured (not completely separated) at the time of the Flood (Klenck, p. 78). During experiments of bombarding an egg with energy, the egg will crack where the energy enters and will bulge or blow out on the opposite side. The earth exhibiting these cracks and bulges suggests a high amount of energy entering near the Mesopotamian Basin. Other evidence from the secular world notes two great surges of volcanic activity, an older and a younger one (Meyerhof, p.309). Perhaps the older results from the Flood and the younger from the time of Peleg.

A composite of this information pictures the Flood beginning in some supernatural way, (only God can know for sure), with perhaps background radiation cracking the earth's surface, as some creationists have proposed (Brown, p. 70). This cracking caused the continents to push down on the water below, shooting pressurized water streams up to 70 miles high. The high pressure being shot from the ground pushed away the water lubricated continents forming the mid-oceanic ridge. These streams also broke through the firmament (10 Miles high) causing it to collapse (Brown, p. 32). This fits well with Genesis which states, "the fountains of the great deep were broken up, and the windows of heaven were opened." This vast amount of water may have contributed to the ice-age, since at about 60,000 feet above the earth temperatures are as cold as -110 degrees Fahrenheit and at 100,000 feet, -200 degrees Fahrenheit. As a result, the streams of water shooting up near the poles came down as ice, initializing the ice-age, and then continued as described above with the warmer waters evaporating and coming down as rain, ice and snow, freezing animals such as mammoths within minutes. Runaway subduction occurred just as John Morris suggests. The primary source of the water coming from the fountains of the great deep covered the mountains and left sedimentary deposits all over the world. Again, at this time the continents had been ripped apart and altered a great deal but were not completely separated yet, nor will they be until the time of Peleg when the earth is divided. Meanwhile, the Ice Age could certainly be taking up vast quantities of water, exposing land bridges. Science is now telling us that the earth has greatly increased in diameter; (Baugh, Symphony); therefore, after the dispersion at the Tower of Babel, in the days of Peleg, the earth bulged because of a "nuclear meltdown," quickly spreading out the ridges formed by the Flood, ramming mountains together, etc. . . . This era is evidenced by what one secular scientist in the 1995 *Scientific American* calls the "Mid-Cretaceous Super Plume Episode," when a great bulging of the earth occurred (Larson, 825-885). On the Eastern seaboard of the United States, the sedimentary rock matches up with those of the neighboring continents and, therefore, must have been separated after the Flood. Finally, the earth's magnetic reversals could also be caused by the Flood and the expulsion of magma at the time of the great bulge rapidly taking place on local scales, rather than slowly on global scales. Secular scientists are proposing that these rapid (perhaps within 15 days), local magnetic changes, have taken place because of expulsive magma (Roberts, *Nature*). Other scientists have reported that lightning strikes can also cause these reversals (Aerate, pp. 170-181). Both lightning and magma expulsion would be expected during the Flood and post-Flood era. As the record shows, the earth's magnetic field dropped rapidly around the time of the

Flood and again at the time of Peleg. There was an increase in magnetic energy around the time of Christ, and then another decrease after His ascension (Humphries, p. 2).

We simply do not presently have all the information needed to form an objective conclusion. I believe it is clear that the Bible does give sufficient evidence for the continental drift; that is, provided we understand continental drift in the confines of a quick catastrophic event, not a slow and gradual process. God has the power to do the above mentioned, outside of our scientific explanations but, nevertheless, science supports what Scripture surely teaches.

Origin of Cave Men

I am often amazed at the foolishness of evolutionists today, who stand in awe of the many technological advances made in the past few decades. Because of the latter, it seems that we can watch our heads get bigger by the minute as our pride grows to excess. But lest you fall, take heed to Proverbs 16:18: "Pride goes before destruction, a haughty spirit before a fall." Most of this attitude stems from the evolutionary belief that man evolves in an upward manner, until finally reaching a heightened intellect. The new age belief is that man has reached his highest physical evolution and is now moving toward freedom of the mind, enabling him to explore the world of the subconscious and the spirits. However, when we honestly view the past, we see the steady decline of both our physical and intellectual nature.

According to evolutionary theory, cave men arrived during the Stone Age (Paleolithic Era) when biologically these people had reached their peak and worked toward cultural enlightenment. During this time, cave men led a simple life of "hunting and gathering," without concerning themselves about agriculture or domesticating animals because of their nomadic practices. Metallurgy was not around, nor was any system of writing and, therefore, tools consisted of chipped stone. For protection from the elements they lived in caves, provided they were available, or stayed out in the open.

Next came the New Stone Age (Neolithic era) during which broken stones gradually became sharpened tools, animals were domesticated, there was a development of agriculture as the knowledge of it was acquired, and metallurgy and pottery were slowly becoming useful. The development of metal tools naturally took them into the Bronze age, followed by the Iron Age.

The above theory is once again based upon vast periods of time as interpreted by the geological record with an evolutionary bias. Now let us look at what the same evidence looks like from a scientific creationist point of view with a Biblical bias. In order to comprehend what seems to be a somewhat primitive culture, we need to first find out where cave men came from and what their background was. Biblically speaking, the Tower of Babel provides an excellent answer to almost all our questions. When Noah and his family left the Ark, God gave them an important command to spread out and fill the earth (Genesis 9:7). However, not too long after this command, we find one of the earliest post-Flood, larger settlements beginning to take root at Babel (Babylon), a direct defiance of God's command to spread out. God threw the people into confusion and upset their common language, stopping their building and communication. This naturally makes most of the individuals more primitive than their society was as a team with their combined talents and ideas.

Separation from today's society would leave many without knowledge of metals turned into tools. Such lifestyles would most likely consist of hunting and gathering available food, because vast agriculture would be useless for a small population. Homes of nomads would probably be very simple and temporary since they followed animal herds. Rather than taking the heavy, quickly made stone tools in the move, new tools would be fashioned in new settlements. Now years later, when archaeologists dig up these camps, primitive, muscle-head images come to mind.

Problems continue to flood this "cave man mentality" presupposition of ancient man, as more and more archaeological evidence is uncovered. One mural painting in the cave of Lascaux in France has been called by *National Geographic* as the Ice Age Leonardo da Vinci (10/1988, p. 434). *Time* magazine describes amazing feats of so called primitive stone age people: "Stored in memories of elders, healers, midwives, farmers, fishermen and hunters in the estimated 15,000 cultures remaining on earth is an enormous trove of wisdom. . . Over the ages, indigenous peoples have developed innumerable technologies and arts. They have devised ways to farm deserts without irrigation and produce abundance from the rain forest without destroying it; they have learned how to navigate vast distances in the Pacific using their knowledge of currents and the feel of intermittent waves that bounce off distant islands; they have explored the medicinal properties of plants; and they have acquired an understanding of the basic ecology of flora and fauna. . . guided by their conceits, scientists have often failed to notice traditional technologies even, for instance, when they are on display. . . Andean artifacts revealed that they had been gilded with an incredibly thin layer of gold using a chemical technique that achieved the quality of modern electroplating. No one had previously suspected that these Indians had the know-how to create such a subtle technology... During the Gulf War, European doctors treated some wounds with a sugar paste that traces back to Egyptian battlefield medicine of 4,000 years ago . . . In central Africa a man's chest was being eaten away by an amoebic infection. It did not respond to drug treatments. A healer applied washed and crushed soldier termites to the open wounds. The patient made a remarkable recovery. The secret of this treatment had been passed down in the tribe for untold generations" (9/23/1991, pp. 46-56). In caves near Beer-sheba, pottery and stone vessels were made but so were intricate figurines carved out of ivory and bone, displaying their advanced craftsmanship. From the excavations of Ur (Abraham's city) clay tablets outlining the principle of Pythagoras' Theorem were found. Though the name Pythagoras' Theorem does not appear, it demonstrates that in a right-angled triangle the square of the hypotenuse is equal to the sum of the squares of the other two sides. All this 1,500 years before the time of Pythagoras. Also at Ur, iron chariot rings were found more than 1,000 years before iron was supposedly being used (Wilson, p.105, 73, 65). In France successful brain surgery took place almost 7,000 years ago, say secular scientists (Oregonian, 6/4/97 p. C12). These are just a few of the hundreds of examples showing early man as intelligent. Von Fange writes, "Over and over scientists are amazed at the sophistication of what they have found. The so-called cave man period of savagery is repeatedly contradicted by what is actually found in Ice Age sites (Von Fange, pp. 188-189).

    A possible explanation is that the stone age may simply be a period of spreading out and resettling when stone tools were accessible and expendable. Rather than the stone age being a period of geological time, it could be a period of adjustment and repopulation. (I know when my wife and I are moving, the house we move into looks like a tornado ran through it for a few months until we slowly get settled in. Sometimes things remain in storage for a while until they are needed). Likewise, when the Babel event dispersed individual groups, a period of cultural chaos occurred and their houses were in shambles. Just as a single checking account does not need a computer to keep track of all transactions, some of the technologies had no use among such a small group and, therefore, were not "unpacked" from memory until a further date. Clark adds, " Wherever one looks around the world, at each site suitable for human cultural habitation, there is nearly always evidence of a 'Stone Age' culture when that site was first occupied. Later occupations (or later periods in the original occupation) indicate higher cultures, not because of slow evolutionary development, but because of rapid growth of population, development of specializations, locations of sources of metal and building material, and establishment of stable supplies of food and clothing. When a culture was interrupted by an outside invasion, the latter (if successful) had usually come from a center of a still higher culture, which is then transplanted to the new site" (Clark, p. 129). In addition, progress would be severely hindered because of the language barrier created at Babel. Today we gain much knowledge from sharing ideas and relating them with each other; however, without communication this would not be possible. Great Ice-Age hunters, whom archaeologists are now noting, may have used caves when they traveled great distances north to hunt the huge mammoths and other Ice-Age animals (Von Fange, p. 30).

    Many other archaeological finds suggest that man was intellectually prosperous and perhaps had information that we still do not possess today. Such finds include the ancient batteries found in Egypt which, for the longest time, nobody knew how or why they were used. Some felt the electric current may have been used for electroplating, but much more than simple low voltage is required for this process. Recently however, Dr. Paul Keyser of the University of Alberta, Canada has come up with a possible alternative, that being medicinal purposes. Keyser notes that the Greeks and Romans used electric eels to treat headaches and gout. It was also pointed out that in Sumeria, Akkad, and Babylon, the physicians known as the Asu may have used electric currents for certain ailments (Down, pp. 11-13). This electricity seems to be a strange and rather unconventional form of treatment, but many doctors today are re-discovering the use of electric shock treatment for venomous snake and spider bites. These devastating and sometimes life threatening bites have been cured almost immediately by electric currents (Osborn, p. 9). The electro magnetic current will be discussed further in the chapter on the Pre-Flood World.

Just because people happened to live in caves did not mean they were intellectually challenged. In fact, today in other parts of the world there are people who still live in caves by choice. Obviously this minority is not ignorant, rather the caves fit their needs. The people in Bible times seem to have been

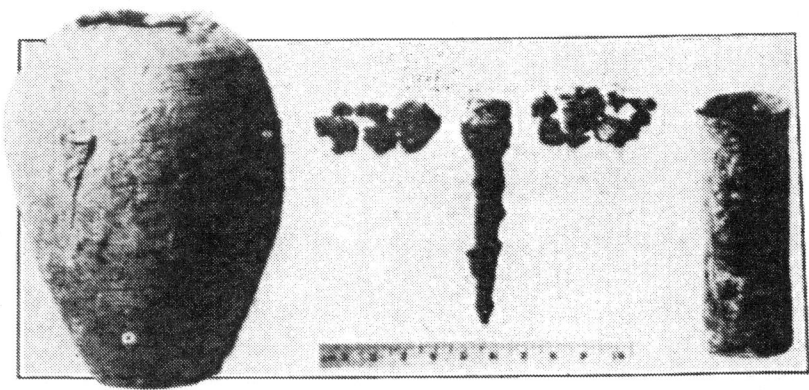

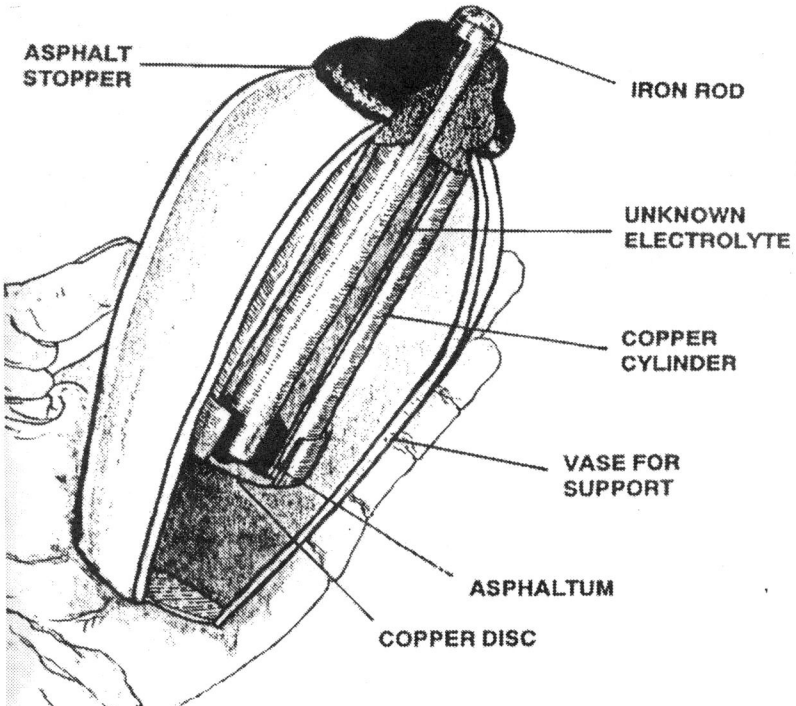

Figure 10: Battery-like artifact found in Egypt

familiar with cave men, not as ape-like creatures but rather as social outcasts and fugitives: "Of what use was the strength of their hands to me, since their vigor had gone from them? Haggard from want and hunger, they roamed the parched land in desolate wastelands at night. In the brush they gathered salt herbs, and their food was the root of the broom tree. They were banished from their fellow men, shouted at as if they were thieves. They were forced to live in the dry stream beds, among the rocks and in holes in the ground. They brayed among the bushes and huddled in the undergrowth. A base and nameless brood, they were driven out of the land" (Job 30:2-8); "Lot and his two daughters left Zoar and settled in the mountains, for he was afraid to stay in Zoar. He and his two daughters lived in a cave" (Genesis 19:30); "Because the power of Midian was so oppressive, the Israelites prepared shelters for themselves in mountain clefts, caves and strongholds" (Judges 6:2); "When the men of Israel saw that their situation was critical and that their army was hard pressed, they hid in caves and thickets, among the rocks, and in pits and cisterns" (I Samuel 13:6); "Say this to them: 'This is what the Sovereign LORD says: As surely as I live, those who are left in the ruins will fall by the sword, those out in the country I will give to the wild animals to be devoured, and those in strongholds and caves will die of a plague'" (Ezekiel 33:27); "The world was not worthy of them. They wandered in deserts and mountains, and in caves and holes in the ground" (Hebrews 11:38). These were not people who had yet to evolve into complete human beings, but lived in caves because of social circumstances. These cave men did not live in a separate time frame but simultaneously with intelligent people, explaining the mysterious, "out of place" artifacts which saturate both early and late Stone Age periods.

The cave men were probably close descendants of those dispersed at Babel who settled in small villages, with some going off on hunts or explorations, others rebelling against the villagers and becoming outcasts or criminals. Presently these village remains of the conquests made by the larger, more warlike individual groups and the nomadic following of herds have been misinterpreted by modern archaeologists as primitive, ape-like, subhumans.

Origin of Races

The origin of cave men is directly tied into the origin of races because of the common link to the Tower of Babel. As the languages were confused and small groups of people spread throughout the world, inbreeding resulted, causing different races. Not only does the Bible record this dispersion as actual history, but we also see it described in the inscriptions of tablets found at ancient Babylon (where the Tower of Babel was), which read: "Babylon corruptibly proceeded to sin, and both small and great mingled on the mound. . . . All day they founded their stronghold, but in the night God put a complete stop to it. In his anger He also poured out his secret counsel to scatter them abroad, He set his face, He gave a command to make foreign their speech" (Sayce, p. 131 & Smith, p. 143).

Many people, in desperate attempts to explain racial differences, use their active imaginations to say that black people gradually adapted to the intense ultraviolet light nearer the equator. This theory is neither scientific or logical. Why then are all people in South America not equally black? An interesting fact about race, whether black or white is that we are all the same color, some of us just have more color than others. The epidermis of our skin contains three different types of cells: melanocytes, keratocytes, and langerhans. It is the melanocytes that produce melanin, which is responsible for the diversity in skin color. Those with darker skin simply have melanocytes which are more active than those with light skin (Comptons Encyclopedia, melanin). Therefore, it is not a great evolutionary change nor a separate line of evolution that causes different skin color, rather a simple biological difference.

Though not as applicable today due to supplemental vitamins, at the time of the Babel dispersion there was a natural reason black people flourished better in warmer climates. While sunlight is needed for vitamin D, too much sun damages the skin and reduces folic acid. Folic acid is needed for reproduction. The people with more melanocytes are darker colored but they are also naturally protected from the sunlight and, therefore, their folic acid is untouched, enabling reproduction to continue very successfully. However, vitamin D enters the darker skin more slowly but in warmer climates people shed clothing and receive more direct sunlight thus receiving enough vitamin D. This is why darker skin became dominant near the equator. Those with black skin can safely be out in the sun without harm, while at the same time obtain vitamin D. Caucasians living in hot areas would become a minority quickly since their ability to reproduce is hindered by the sun's destruction of folic acid. Today, sun screen and vitamin D pills help us keep this balance "unnaturally." On the flip side, light skinned individuals living in cooler areas of the world keep their skin covered more thoroughly. Therefore, they are protected from folic acid loss while plenty of vitamin D is obtained through only a small amount of exposed skin. The darker skinned people in cooler climates would not be able to get enough sun to get the vitamin D necessary. Lack of vitamin D also lowers fertility and causes a bone disease called rickets. Therefore, darker skinned people would not reproduce as quickly and would become the minority in colder climates. (Interestingly, rickets has been found in almost every Neanderthal bone discovered. This may suggest that they had darker skin).

Technically, race is a subdivision of a given species because no matter what color, human beings are made in God's image. Anything to the contrary is atheism, evolutionism, and racism. Evolution has been the basis for racism for years. Henry Osborn, one of the leading evolutionary scholars of the 1920's, used evolution as a scapegoat to express racial discontent. In an article dealing with the past history of evolutionary philosophies, *Natural History* (April, 1980) reprinted an article written by Mr. Osborn. Osborn hypothetically suggested that if an objective scientist from Mars could come to earth, examine and classify humans into specific genera and species, the Negroes would be in a separate species all together, one in which full evolutionary development had not taken place. He stated that, "The standard of intelligence of the average adult Negro is similar to that of the eleven-year-old youth of the species *Homo sapiens*" (Parker, p. 153). Hitler too, used evolution as his justification for the mass slaying of the Jews. Hitler believed he had a Divine mission to convince the

German people that killing Jews would bring them one step closer to a perfect Aryan race of people (Feig, p. 9). Hitler's entire philosophy revolved around Social Darwinism, and he believed that "Victory is to the strong and the weak must go to the wall. She [nature] teaches us that what may seem cruel to us, because it affects us personally or because we have been brought up in ignorance of her laws, is nevertheless often essential if a higher way of life is to be attained. Nature. . . knows nothing of the notion of humanitarianism which signifies that the weak must at all costs be surrounded and preserved even at the expense of the strong" (Carr, 113-114). Osborn and Hitler are just two of many examples by which evolution and the misinterpretation of "race" has led to the heathenistic destruction of so many innocent children of God.

According to evolution, the current races today have come about by one of two possibilities: 1) Mono-phyletic process (linear)-- whereby we come from a single ancestor (pre-human) split from a larger group, which had developed from the evolutionary processes; or 2) Poly-phyletic process (branched)-- whereby we come from a parallel evolution of different groups of pre-human primates (Clark, p. 111). Both theories consist of numerous problems. The poly-phyletic theory naturally gives rise to the racist ideas discussed above, because one race can say they have been developing longer and have achieved a higher level of intelligence. The mono-phyletic theory chosen by those who wish to stay away from the sociological consequences, also have run into problems. How, then, could the sundry characteristics of culture, skin color, posture, and other physical features be explained by one evolutionary line.

Both mono-phyletic and poly-phyletic theories contradict the evolution of language. With over 5,000 separate languages in existence today, not one of them can be linked in the smallest way, to the sounds of a chimpanzee (Clark, p. 112). Worse yet for evolutionists is that languages cannot evolve into a more complex form, in fact, they can only degenerate into simpler, less complex organizations. For example, Ancient Greek is far more complex than Latin; Latin is far more complex than French etc. (Robinson, p. 47). Therefore one must turn to Scripture in order to resolve such difficult conflicts.

The Bible is clear regarding human origin and the nations thereof: "And He has made from one blood every nation of men to dwell on all the face of the earth, and has determined their preappointed times and the boundaries of their dwellings" (Acts 17:26 NKJ). Shortly after creation, however, men became evil and God sent the great Flood to destroy the earth and everything in it, including man. Only Noah and his family survived, from which we all descended, "Now the sons of Noah who went out of the Ark were Shem, Ham, and Japheth. And Ham was the father of Canaan. These three were the sons of Noah, and from these the whole earth was populated" (Genesis 9:18).

For years following the Flood, a common language kept us together in communication and as a nation (Genesis 11:1). But when men decided to disobey God's command to spread throughout the earth and instead began building a tower unto heaven, God changed their plans by confusing their languages so none could understand the other (Genesis 11:7-8). Genesis 10 records the 70 nations which came about from these groups, which then transferred to the individual cultural and linguistic identities we have today.

Dr. Parker has shown conclusively that when small interbreeding populations are isolated, a wide variation of skin color from very light to very dark can result. In fact, a living testimony to this has been seen in Leigh, England, where a mother had fraternal twin boys, one having blond hair, blue eyes, and light skin while the other having brown eyes, brown hair, and dark skin. The mother's father was Nigerian and her mother was a white Englishmen. The father of the twins came from white English parents as well (Gish, p. 215). Therefore, at the time of Babel when the small, isolated groups were sent out and interbred, the numerous nations we have today came into existence. The isolated gene pools produced a variety of skin colors and physical features, while at the same time group needs, lack of communication, and geographical restrictions brought about the diversity in cultures.

CHAPTER 4
SIX LITERAL CREATION DAYS

"Yom:" A Literal Day

One of the most common ways in which to explain away Scripture so that it fits into the scientific theories is to form your belief system around the old earth theory; that is, a world billions of years old. In order to make this theory fit the Bible, 24 hour days must become vast periods of time. When God says there was morning and evening, the first day, does it really mean many years?

Before we answer this question let us look at why people feel the need to alter what Scripture plainly says. Today one cannot escape the idea of an old earth because it has infiltrated our entire lives with so-called "scientific facts." Radiocarbon dating (combined with evolution) has suggested an age of the earth at 4.5 billion years old. If this number turns out to be false, what will that say about the credibility of the scientific community, let alone our own credibility for believing them? No one likes to admit he is wrong! But the truth is, evolution is dead without vast periods of time. Therefore, rather than admit folly, evolutionists make sure enough time is given to fit their theory, no matter what. In the same manner, the scientific evidence supports the young earth doctrine, but an admission of this would cause ostracization and squelch any opportunities of furthering success to careers. In the past, doctorates have been denied to honest, objective scientists because of their creationist beliefs, producing a stigma within the scientific community.

By far the most perplexing problem of an old earth, as mentioned in Chapter 1, is the rejection of Christ as our Redeemer from eternal death and suffering. Evolution teaches that the fossil record is a result of the death and disease of the many animals which existed before humans. If death existed before man sinned, then death is not a direct result of sin and Christ's death is not the cure for sin; rather, death is a purposeless, natural process that everyone must go through. Therefore, any attempt to make the 24 hour days of Genesis long periods of time, is an effort to destroy Christ. Many people do not think that deeply, but it is important for one to realize the illogical inconsistency of this hypocritical belief.

In this chapter we will focus more on the Hebrew usage in answering the "day length" question. Chapters ten, eleven, and twelve will go into more scientific proofs of a young earth. First consider the Hebrew word for day, "*yom.*" *Yom* has three different meanings in Scripture: a solar day, daylight, or an indefinite period of time. Never does it mean a set period of time over 24 hours. This word occurs 2,291 times in the Old Testament and almost always means a literal 24 hour solar day. In 359 cases (outside of Genesis 1) *yom* appears where it is modified by another number (and the 5th *yom*), none of which means anything but a literal 24 hour day. The plural, *yamine*, occurs 845 times, again always meaning 24 hours. In addition, 38 times this word is modified by "evening and/or morning" with every case meaning 24 hours (Morris,Young, p. 29). The Hebrew language does have words which mean an indefinite period of time, but these words are not used in the Creation account, thus implying a literal interpretation of the word "day."

Many people marvel at how God could create such an overwhelming universe in so short a time. (I have wondered why He took so long). I believe the answer to that question lies in Exodus 20:8-11 where we read, "Remember the Sabbath day, to keep it holy. Six days shalt thou labor, and do all thy work: But the seventh day is the Sabbath of the Lord thy God: in it thou shalt not do any work . . . *For in six days the Lord made heaven and earth, the sea, and all that is in them, and rested the seventh day;* wherefore the Lord blessed the Sabbath day, and hallowed it." Clearly, the reason God took so long to create the universe was to set an example for us and give a pattern for our seven day week. Because God created in six days and rested on the seventh, we too are to work six days and rest on the seventh.

Even honest evolutionists admit *yom* is to be interpreted as 24 hours. Replying to a letter written by David Watson asking various scholars the meaning of *yom* in Genesis, James Barr writes, "Probably, so far as I know, there is no professor of Hebrew or Old Testament at any world-class university who does not believe that the writer(s) of Genesis 1-11 intended to convey to their readers the ideas that (a) creation took place in a series of six days which were the same as the days of 24 hours we now experience. . ." (Morris, Young, p. 31).

Why, then, has the literal interpretation of days in Genesis been argued? Dr. Davis Young, a Christian geology professor at Calvin College, offers an answer: "It cannot be denied, in spite of frequent interpretations of Genesis 1 that departed from the rigidly literal, that the almost universal view of the Christian world until the eighteenth century was that the earth was only a few thousand years old. Not until the development of modern scientific investigation of the earth itself would this view be called into question within the church" (Young, Christianity, p. 25). How true this statement is! Scripture clearly indicates a 24 hour day, but modern scientists have shaped our opinions by their secular philosophies. Paul sums up this opinion-oriented philosophy of life very well when he said, "For since the creation of the world God's invisible qualities-- his eternal power and divine nature--have been clearly seen, being understood from what has been made, so that men are without excuse" (Romans 1:20). Supporting scientific rethinking of Scripture, Dr. Young himself is an old earth advocate and believes, "evangelical scholars will have to face the implications of the mass geologic data indicating that the earth is extremely old, indicating that death has been on earth long before man, and indicating that there has not been a global flood" (Young, Scripture, p. 295). He goes on in saying, "Genesis is divinely inspired, ancient near eastern literature written within a specific historical context that entailed well-defined thought patterns, literary forms, symbols, and images" (Young, Scripture, p. 303). Certainly, Dr. Young will be "without excuse." This prophetic fulfilling belief (see comments on II Peter 3:3-6 in chapter 10) is widespread today, and as Christians we must fight against this hypocrisy with heart, mind and soul. Again we see that when science and the Bible don't seem to agree, science doesn't suffer but the Bible does. When will we start interpreting science in view of Scripture rather than Scripture in view of science?

Some Christians may still want to be theistic evolutionist (those who believe each day may have been vast periods of time). In so doing, one still cannot escape illogical thinking. If each day was a million years long, how did insects pollinate flowers which were created on day three. If the sun was not created until day four, how did those plants created the day before survive millions of years without photosynthesis. Also, Adam lived through day six and day seven yet was only 930 years old. Clearly God created the universe in six, 24 hour days!

Happy ___?___th Birthday Planet Earth

There are a number of problems in determining the actual age of the earth, but we are not left completely without explanation. That nobody agrees on the earth's actual age sends up warning signs. The following are a few of the difficulties involved in this determination expressed by Dr. Henry Morris (Morris, Genesis, p. 43):

> 1) The uncertainty of accurate copying and transmission of the numbers originally recorded, since the Massoretic, Septuagint, and Samaritan texts all disagree in this respect;
>
> 2) The uncertainty as to whether the length of the ancient calendar year was the same as the length of our present year;
>
> 3) The possibility of missing generations in the genealogies of the Old Testament;
>
> 4) The confusing and sometimes apparently contradictory lists of the durations of the administrations of the various judges and kings of Israel and Judah;
>
> 5) The even more unsatisfactory state of the comparable secular chronologies of Egypt and Babylonia;
>
> 6) The still less satisfactory results derived from radiocarbon and other physical methods of dating.

The Bible is clearly the best, most reliable tool to establish any continuity in the estimation of the earth's age. To understand the Biblical framework in using this approach, Dr. Morris's suggestions follow (Morris, Genesis, p. 43):

1) Genesis 1 gives the time from the creation of the universe to the creation of man;

2) Genesis 5 contains chronological data from the time of the first man to the great Flood;

3) Genesis 11 summarizes the chronology from the Flood to Abraham, the founder of the Hebrew nation;

4) The historical books of the Old Testament (especially Genesis, Exodus, Numbers, Joshua, Judges, I and II Samuel, I and II Kings, I and II Chronicles) contain chronological data of the nation of Israel from the time of Abraham to the captivity;

5) The chronology of the captivity and restoration is obtained from the prophetic books (especially Isaiah, Jeremiah, and Daniel) and the post-captivity historical books (Ezra and Nehemiah).

Archbishop James Ussher (1581-1656) has given us what is probably the best interpretation of the above Biblical data. His calculations come up with a date of creation being 4004 BC. There are other interpretations which vary slightly from Ussher's, which take into account possible gaps or other historical records, but usually keep within a 10,000 year estimate rather than a 6,000 year old earth as Ussher believes. Henry Morris thinks that the Bible will not allow for any date in excess of 10,000 (true date probably closer to 6,000) years because no more than five thousand years could ever conceivably be inserted in the genealogies to account for any possible gaps. Some such accounts for the dates of creation are as follows (add about 2000 years to get total age): Jewish, 3760; Septuagint (Greek translation), 5270; Josephus, 5555; Kepler, 3993; Melanchthon, 3964; Luther, 3961; Lightfoot, 3960; Hales, 5402; Playfair, 4008; and Lipman, 3916 (Morris, Genesis, p. 45). Therefore, as a whole, history supports the Ussher account or, at least, in the general time period.

The above dates certainly give understanding how all of history could be recorded in Scripture, especially since up to the time of Abraham only three people were needed to record that history. To explain, due to the longevity of life, Adam lived simultaneously with Methuselah, Methuselah lived simultaneously with Noah, and Noah lived at the same time as Abraham.

One such evidence comes from Dr. Renfrew, an archaeology professor at the University of South Hampton; he writes, "Until the discovery of radiocarbon dating, therefore, there was really only one reliable way of dating events in European prehistory.... This was by the early records of the great civilizations which extended in some cases as far back as 3000 B. C.... The

Egyptian king lists go back to the First Dynasty of Egypt, a little before 3000 BC. Before that, there were no written records anywhere" (Renfrew, p. 21). Archaeologically speaking, the Bible, though much more, is a very reliable historical record. Donald J. Wiseman testifies that "the geography of Bible lands and visible remains of antiquity were gradually recorded until today more than 25,000 sites within this region and dating to Old Testament times, in their broadest sense, have been located. . . . . " (Henry, pp. 301-302). Furthermore, it has been noted that no archaeological find has ever been made that contradicts what we read in the Bible (Geisler, p. 322).

    We see that in order to get any date outside of the creationist belief one must turn to the uniformitarian philosophy of the present geological system which, by true scientific standards, is based upon assumptions and biases that cannot be tested nor proven in the present. The surest way to examine the past, therefore, is by historical records, of which the Bible can be placed as the most valid. Support for a young earth based on Usher's chronology will be discussed in subsequent chapters.

CHAPTER 5
RESULTS OF A GLOBAL FLOOD

A View of Catastrophic Events Today

The earth is a complex system run by scientific laws, many of which we do not understand. Various theories attempt to explain why and how things became what they are today. In general, science has rejected the views of catastrophism and have leaned heavily towards gradualism, the idea of slow and gradual processes by which the earth and all it contains has been formed. Concerning the scientific attitude of gradualism, J. H. Shea comments,

> This dogma is obviously a product of the history of geology. Unfortunately, we have overreacted to that history and have adopted an excessively gradualist view of earth history, refusing in many cases to consider catastrophic events (such as the Spokane flood or the impact of giant meteorites) even when the evidence clearly suggests that sudden, violent, cataclysmic events have occurred. This attitude is changing, however, and we need to free ourselves completely from the artificial constraints of a fallacious dogma that would preclude any possibility of natural catastrophes having occurred even if the postulated catastrophes are perfectly rational and supported by strong evidence (Shea, p. 702).

Gradualism and uniformitarianism (past is the key to the present) are at the heart of evolutionary theory. Without mass time and uniformity animals couldn't evolve and dating methods can't work, which is precisely why this topic is so important. Let us look at the power of catastrophic events and the consequences they have for evolution. So many events not only show how quickly strata is deposited but also what a devastating effect they had on the earth. As we read, we need to keep in mind what devastation Noah's Flood incurred and how it completely altered the earth as we know it, in comparison with these "small" disasters of today.

The catastrophe most significant is Noah's Flood, the most widely rejected of all theories because of its religious connotations. However, a global flood theory and the aftermaths, in many ways, are the missing piece(s) to the laborious scientific puzzle which holds destructive answers to so many scientific uncertainties. How old is the earth? Is radioisotope and carbon-14 dating accurate? How was the Grand Canyon formed? Why are there no transitional forms in the fossil record? These are just a few of the mysteries solved when Noah's Flood is accepted as history.

When we remember Noah's Flood we must not conjure up the image of a peaceful, rainy day with Noah, his family, and the animals hanging their heads out the window of the Ark with smiles on their faces. Rather, Noah's Flood needs to bring up images of hundreds, maybe thousands of volcanoes erupting and earthquakes shaking simultaneously all around the earth. Many have probably experienced the effects of a flood on a local scale. A few years ago in Iowa, much of the state had what was called, "severe flooding." The damage done by only a few overflowing rivers was heartbreaking. I saw the destruction which came from a small amount of water compared to a global flood. Consequently, I further realized what an earth-altering catastrophe Noah's Flood really was.

To gain respect for the Godly power exhibited through nature, we first need to examine various types of recent catastrophes to give us a better understanding of past changes (as in Noah's Flood). Recalling a few cosmic catastrophes, I will show their possible effects. For example, the Tunguska explosion of 1908 occurred in Siberia and, though some disagree about its source, most believe it to be a comet that had exploded. How all this information was gathered I do not know, but its devastation is described by M. W. Brazo: "Above central Siberia on June 30, 1908, at approximately 7:17 AM local time, a small comet entered the atmosphere from behind the sun and moved in a southeast to northwest direction. The comet was composed of about 30,000 tons of water, methane, and ammonia ice with traces of silicates and iron oxides. Penetrating the atmosphere at approximately 60 km/sec (130,000 mph), the object created an intense shock wave which wrapped tightly around its nose. As it descended that sunny morning, its nucleus exploded (possibly 3 times) approximately 8 km above the earth's surface. A huge black cloud immediately appeared following the explosion which released 10^{23} ergs of energy. A heat wave with a temperature of approximately 16.6 million degrees Celsius at the focus was generated that had a tree-scorching effect for a radius of 15 km. The heat wave was followed by air shock waves, which disfigured or toppled 80 million trees occupying approximately 8000 km of Siberian taiga (a radius of 30 km), and initiated a seismic wave of Richter magnitude 5, but, to our astonishment, left no crater. the dust from the tail of the comet moved away from the sun and provided anomalously bright night sky in Europe and parts of Western Russia. No trace of the comet itself was found except for tiny magnetite and silicate globules. The principle consequence was fear and awe among the inhabitants of the region and the physical damage from the explosion. Fortunately, no human life was lost, though more than a thousand reindeer were destroyed" (Brazo, 91-92). Some textbooks testify that horses were knocked off their feet over 400 miles away and the blast was heard 600 miles away. One man described it as seeing the sky split in two while another witness said his shirt was almost burned off his body when he was thrown down and knocked unconscious from the explosion. Though this supposed comet did not leave a crater, other times asteroids have made it past the earth's atmosphere and have collided with the surface, leaving gaping holes as a remnant of its force. A few other examples of the signatures left by these cosmic wonders follow:

LOCATION	CRATER DIAMETER (km)	IMPACT ENERGY (ERGS)
Sudbury/Ontario, Canada	140 km	2.1×10^{30}
Vredefort/South Africa	140 km	2.1×10^{30}
Popigai/Taymyr	100 km	6.7×10^{29}
Puchezh-Katunki/Russian SFSR, USSR	-80 km	3.1×10^{29}
Manicouagan/Quebec, Canada	70 km	2.0×10^{29}
Siljan/Sweden	52 km	7.2×10^{28}
Kara/Yamal-Nenets, USSR	50 km	6.3×10^{28}
Charlevoix/Quebec, Canada	46 km	4.7×10^{28}
Araguainha Dome/Brazil	40 km	3.0×10^{28}

These represent only the top nine given in this source, though others may not be recorded that exceed this magnitude (Grieve, p. 212-229). Possible geological consequences of such events could consist of huge tidal waves; over-pressure in the atmosphere as a result of the blast, releasing large amounts of dust and debris into the stratosphere and causing global cooling, perhaps an Ice Age; changing the earth's rotation; magnetic field reversals; depleting the ozone, resulting in an increase of ultraviolet bombardment; and finally the extinction of various animals (Napier, 455-459). Different opinions exist regarding Scriptural references to these past and future events. Even so, the earth shows the scars of impact, suggesting the earth's environment has been somewhat altered. Later we will discuss how this fits into Scripture. Another example of a catastrophic event is the world's largest *recorded* explosive volcano, which erupted (1815) in Indonesia, the Tambora, Sumbawa eruption. "This magnificent display of power may have produced from 30 to 150 cubic kilometers of ash and rock, killing 10,000 people and starving another 80,000 because of famine. Experts also believe this eruption may have affected the global climate" (Decker, p. 222). The world's largest recorded lava flow occurred (1783) in the Laki eruption of Iceland. Laki spewed out 12 cubic kilometers of lava, which filled two river valleys and covered over 500 square kilometers of land. As a result of the fluorine poisoning produced by the volcanic gases, most of the livestock died and a related famine took the lives of over 10,000 people.

Even more spectacular is the eruption of Krakatoa, an island volcano which blew in the Sundra Strait on August 26 and 27, 1883. The explosion of Krakatoa, heard over 4,800 kilometers away, caused a tsunami (tidal wave) which killed 36,000 people (Symons).

However, other evidence shows these incidents have been small compared to what geological strata suggests. There are "huge deposits of pyroclastic flows that cover thousands of square kilometers and are tens to hundreds of meters thick existing in Japan, New Zealand, Central America, the western United States, and many other volcanic regions of the world. Some of these deposits give every indication that they were poured out in a single enormous eruption that would dwarf Krakatoa. The volume in these deposits is on the order of 100 to 1000 cubic kilometers compared to the 18 cubic kilometers of Krakatoa .... Krakatoa is probably only a small sample of what nature can deliver in the way of a volcanic cataclysm" (Decker, p. 116). In 1960, a tidal wave caused by an earthquake created waves that moved over 400 mph and covered 10,000 miles in fewer than 24 hours (Sippert p. 77).

Probably the most significant volcanic activity of our time was the May 18th eruption of Mt. St. Helens in Washington state.

Figure 11: Over 100 ft. of layered strata laid down in a few hours at Mt. St. Helens.

This volcano challenges gradualism theories at their foundation. Mt. St. Helens is estimated to be equal to 400 million tons of TNT, or the equivalent of 20,000 atomic bombs like those dropped on Hiroshima. Over one-half cubic mile of debris leveled 150 square miles of forest in under six minutes. Even more fascinating was the 600 feet of quickly deposited strata, showing fine lamination details which, according to many geologists before the eruption, formed slowly by seasonal accumulations. The appearance of this strata is the same as that of the Tapeats Sandstone in the Grand Canyon. For years traditional belief held that the Grand Canyon was formed slowly over millions of years by a stream gradually eroding away the sediments; however, a mud flow caused by a subsequent eruption of Mt. St. Helens in March of 1982 eroded in one day a canyon out of solid rock 1/40 the depth of the Grand Canyon. Similarly, geologists always have assumed that the scab lands in Eastern Washington were a result of slow and gradual stream erosion taking place over millions of years. However, the United States Geological Survey (USGS) has now discovered this theory to be incorrect and the truth now seems that the great "Spokane Flood" formed these scab lands from a broken ice dam on the Columbia River, which let the waters from glacial Lake Missoula sweep through the area, carving out more than 15,000 square miles of steep, cliffed canyons in hard lava rock (Parker, p 173). This event brought many to realize that catastrophic agents can form canyons very rapidly and that streams do not cause these canyons. Rather, the streams are there because of the canyons. Furthering this theory, a LANDSAT photograph of the Grand Canyon shows that it passes through an elevated plateau, suggesting the Colorado River could not have formed the canyon because rivers flow around hills, not over them. As a result, many geologists now are leaning toward the theory of catastrophic events, such as those at Mt. St. Helens, to explain the cause of the Grand Canyon (Austin, Helens). Could something like Noah's Flood bring about such a thing?

Yet other "quick" facts that deny long time periods are needed to accomplish what we see today, include the opals that are now made in months (*Creation*, 1995), the flag and tent left in 1911 by Antarctic explorer, Amundsen, that is now under 40 feet of ice and snow *(Salt Lake Tribune*, 1995); coal made in 28 days (*Organic Geochemistry*, 1984); or the squadron of airplanes that landed on Greenlands east coast on July 15, 1942, and are now under 250 feet of ice (*Life*, 1996).

These are a few of the hundreds of examples which show how changes occur quickly, laying down strata rapidly, not gradually as uniformitarian geologists presume. If such catastrophes altered the climate and volcanoes deposited hundreds of feet of strata rapidly, gradualism and uniformitarianism cannot be trusted; that is to say, evolution can't be trusted.

Catastrophism and the Formation of Coal

Mt. St. Helen's eruption prompts examining our conventional theory of coal formation. Children have been persistently taught in school that coal formation requires millions of years because the theory that swamp peat, the substance from which coal is presumed to form, accumulates slowly. One reason for such a theory is that coal consists of woody plant material and other vegetation, all thought to be found in swamps. To illustrate, imagine a swamp in your backyard. After a few years, some of the plants and woody material die and fall to the surface, where they rot. Meanwhile more plants grow as others die, piling up little by little on the surface of the swamp, until finally enough material accumulates to form a coal bed. Today, coal beds nearly 40 feet thick represent an estimated 300 to 400 feet of vegetative material. Some coal seams are so extensive they run from Pennsylvania through Ohio, Indiana, Illinois, and Iowa to Oklahoma. Accumulations of this size suggest a massive flood or catastrophe. This kind of build-up defeats the uniformitarian theory. Reputable scientists assert: "Though a peat-bog may serve to demonstrate how vegetal matter accumulates in considerable quantities it is in no way comparable in extent to the great bodies of vegetation which must have given rise to our important coal seams. . . There is sufficient peat in the temperate regions of the world today to form large amounts of coal, if it were concentrated into coal seams, but no single bog or marsh known would supply sufficient peat to make a large coal seam" (Moore, p. 146). Evidence strongly supports that the plant material in coal was washed into one place by water, as coal seams are almost always found in stratified deposits. Even given enough time this theory is problematic because, when coal is viewed under a microscope we see that it consists of shiny layers which are tree bark. A drained swamp along the coast of Nova Scotia shows peat with a texture much like coffee grounds because of the many roots which penetrate the peat in all directions. In coal, however, there is no evidence of root penetration or coffee ground texture. Clearly something is wrong with the conventional theory. Also some coal found does not appear to be of vegetative origin (Fange, p.45). This coal clearly fits into the Biblical perspective which tells us that some type of petroleum (form of coal) existed before the Flood, for Noah coated the Ark with bitumen, a product of petroleum (Gold too, existed before the Flood - - Genesis 2:11-12). Despite this variance, the conventional theory of millions of years for coal formation still falls short; nor can it be an acceptable explanation for the vast majority of coal which is of vegetation origin. Also problematic for such a theory is the reported presence of a human skull, an iron pot, an iron thimble, a spoon, and a gold chain found embedded in coal (CRSQ, 1991). Even more amazing, on April 10, 1967, the newspapers reported a human bone and a copper arrowhead found in a vein of silver more than 400 feet below the ground in Gulman, Colorado (Sippert, p.37).

After a four year study of a Kentucky coal bed, Dr. Steve Austin (Institute for Creation Research) postulated the floating mat model for the origin of coal. Dr. Austin theorizes that coal can form if a floating mass of land slid over a pre-deposited layer of peat. Peat buried by this mass would produce enough heat and pressure to form coal. Dr. Austin came up with this model in 1979 during his Ph.D. dissertation defense at Penn State University. To his amazement, ten months later Mount St. Helens erupted, sweeping millions of logs into Spirit Lake below, creating a floating mat of logs similar to what he had proposed earlier. Not long after the logs were deposited on the lake, the wind caused them to rub together and all the bark settled to the lake bottom, where there is now nearly three feet of peat deposited. If another catastrophe suddenly buried this peat, coal would soon form (Austin, Helens). A fascinating addition to coal is that the heat for its formation need not be constant if there is a catalyst present. Volcanic ash acts as a catalyst for heat in coal formation.

The right conditions (similar to those of Mt. St. Helens) form coal in less than an hour under laboratory conditions (likewise, oil can now be made in under 30 minutes- not millions of years). If history shows vast evidence of other catastrophic events on earth and the Biblical story of Noah is accurate, a gigantic floating mat of trees and vegetation would meet expectations. Flooding, eruptions, or moving of continents may have covered deposits of peat which rapidly formed coal, a process of plate tectonics.

Catastrophism and the Ice Age

We often hear that the Ice Age, or the Pleistocene Epoch, occurred about two million years ago and lasted as recently as the past 8,000 to 11,000 years ago (creationists believe about 4,000 years ago). Most scientists agree that by the time of the Ice Age man had achieved a solid foot on evolutionary ground, which went back about 15 or 20 million years when our first ape-like ancestor began changing. Fortunately, this theory, although not always looked at as that, does not fit into a Scriptural time period or image of man. Does science give any evidence which supports an Ice Age? If the Ice-Age was but a few centuries, evolution again is left "out in the cold" because there is not enough time given for human evolution.

First, a wide-spread misconception is that the Ice Age caused glaciers over the entire earth. At its height, no more than one-third of the earth would have been ice covered. Currently, only about 10% of the earth is covered with ice, a huge amount. If it would all somehow melt, it would raise the ocean levels by as much as 300 feet (Parker, Dinosaurs). Many scientist believe (finally) that the origin of the Ice Age could have been caused by enormous catastrophes and support the theory that volcanic eruptions and comets may have been the means which initiated the glaciation of the Pleistocene era (Bray, p. 251-254). One example of such atmospheric cooling is the eruption of Laki in Iceland and of Asama in Japan, both in 1783, "which combined to make that year and the two that followed, three of the coldest on record in the northern hemisphere. They caused 'dry fogs' over most of Eurasia and North America. In France, the "fogs" were so dense that the sun could not be seen until it had risen 17 degrees above the horizon" (Williams, p.362). Other scientists have suggested that the Ice Age could occur quickly and end just as abruptly because of an extraterrestrial catastrophe such as the above. Within one year after the initial catastrophe, a subsequent ecological catastrophe would occur. If enough high albedo particles (mass of over 10^{14}) were incorporated into the upper atmosphere, we could expect to see substantial cooling effects at ground level. The warm waters of the ocean would lose excess heat through evaporation, which would become rain and snow. A colder climate would accumulate snow and ice up to 100 feet per year in the polar regions, instigating the Ice Age. Once the ice began to melt, local cooling and reflection would be greatly reduced and the ice would disappear quickly, perhaps in fewer than a thousand years (Hoyle, Comets).

Genesis tells us that the waters of Noah's Flood came from two sources: the windows of heaven opened and the fountains of the great deep burst open. Creationists believe the great deep bursting open would cause tremendous upheaval to the ecological system. Earthquakes and volcanoes would simultaneously occur globally. With the volcanic eruptions warming the already warm oceans, perhaps as much as 15 degrees Fahrenheit, expectations are that heat becomes snow and rain through rapid evaporation. The atmosphere would be filled with the discharged volcanic ash within a short time after the Flood. As the snow and ice accumulated, Noah and his family would experience an Ice Age. Dr. Von Fange and other creationists believe such an ice age would have lasted roughly 500 years before a meltdown occurred. During this time, the vast quantities of water being tied up in glaciers would expose various land bridges, allowing for repopulation of both human beings and animals all over the world (Fange, p 159-161).

Yet other creationists suspect the Ice Age may have been caused by the tilting of the earth on its axis. Presently we have witnessed temperature drops of over 100 degrees in a matter of minutes, but with a catastrophe such as Noah's Flood a temperature drop from 70 degrees above to 200 degrees below zero would have been considered normal. Adding to this variance a possible shift of

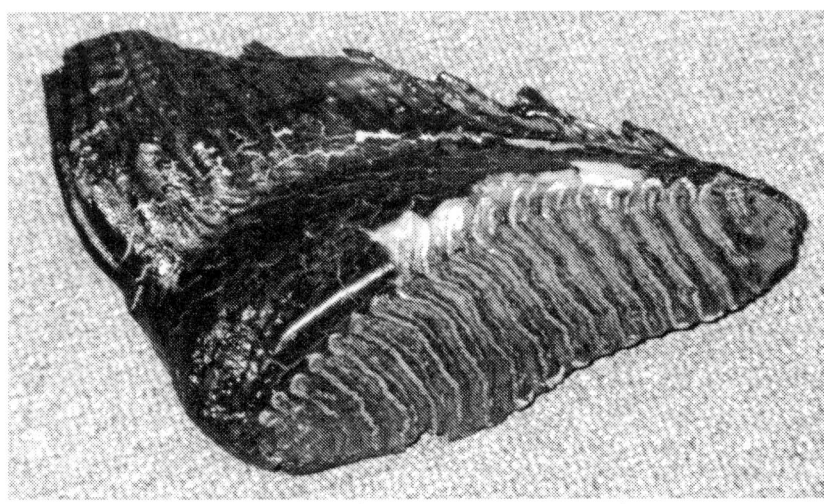

Figure 12: A perfectly preserved mammoth tooth found in Alaska.

the earth's axis to its present 23.5 degrees, the mammoths and other animals would stand no chance of survival. The timing of the Ice Age and other related theories are examined in other chapters.

Even more recently, scientists have discovered that iron could play a large part in the Ice-Age. Since the earth is made up of large amounts of iron, the waters covering the earth during Noah's Flood would have been high in iron content. In 1993 and again in 1995, a 250 square-mile patch of ocean near the Galapagos Islands was seeded with iron sulfate. Within hours the crystal clear waters with visibility up to 200 feet became murky green waters with visibility from four to six feet. Why? The iron caused a rapid growth in phytoplankton which in turn greatly reduced the carbon dioxide content at the surface of the water. About a week later the zooplankton moved in and feasted on the phytoplankton returning the waters back to normal. This showed how during Noah's Flood, iron rich waters could have caused the phytoplankton to flourish and thus reduce the carbon dioxide in the atmosphere, enough to affect the climate globally and aid in the Ice-Age (a reduction in carbon dioxide causes colder climates -*Acts and Facts*, December 1997).

Science certainly supports the Ice-Age as truth but still debates the timing. Near the end of 1992, while drilling for water in Jackson Hole, Wyoming, drillers hit ice, not water (*Ann Arbor News*, 11/2/92 p. A15). Could this be a remnant of an Ice-Age not long past? Evidence consists of hundreds of examples of warm and cold dwelling plants and animals living together at the same time, an enigma for many scientists, but supportive evidence for creationists. For example, tropical fruit trees in the New Siberian Islands have been embedded in solid ice (CRSQ, 1966. p. 63). Of course, we must include Hapgood's fascinating mammoth quickly frozen: "frozen mammoths increase in numbers the farther north one goes. They are most numerous in these islands, accompanied by many other kinds of animals, including the saber-tooth. Today, where only a willow growing an inch tall is found, one sees 90 feet tall fruit trees preserved in the permafrost with roots and seeds, green leaves, and ripe fruit. . .. Many mammoth bodies were preserved so perfectly in the frozen ground as to be edible today. Hundreds of thousands of animals were quick frozen and buried in the permafrost" (Hapgood, 1970, p. 250-260). These mammoths reached a height of 13 feet and weighed 30-60 tons. It has been estimated that 5,000,000 or more animals perished in Siberia alone. In one mine over 20,000 pairs of mammoth tusks were found, some weighing more than 200 pounds. Some mammoths have been found standing upright, leaving a clear memorial to the foolishness of man's wisdom and the power engaged with God's anger, not to mention the sudden catastrophes of His judgment.

In addition, we have much evidence to show terrific volcanic activity associated with the Ice Age, as ancient writings testify: "And then I looked and saw the treasuries of the snow and ice and the angels who guard their terrible store-places. . . And the men then led me to the northern region, and showed me there a very terrible place. . . savage darkness and impenetrable gloom; and there is no light there, but a gloomy fire is always burning, and a fiery river goes forth. And all that place has fire on all sides, and on all sides cold and ice, thus it burns and freezes" (Enoch V.1, X.1) (Platt, 1980, p. 83-84). Similarly, in Oregon, Washington and Idaho, tremendous lava deposits cover an area of about 150,000 square miles and as thick as 8,000 feet, yet ice caves are found therein (Patten, 1966, p. 120-124). Von Fange also writes, "Early settlers discovered the strange phenomenon of ice caves sandwiched between layers of lava. One vast ice cave has been explored for 7,000 feet without locating its end" (Von Fange, p. 155). The evidence keeps mounting in support of a recent Ice Age which involved catastrophic events. Does the Bible give any support?

The book of Job refers to what could perhaps be the Ice Age: "But my brothers are as undependable as intermittent streams, as the streams that overflow when darkened by thawing ice and swollen with melting snow" (Job 6:15-16); or when Job describes the works of God: "From whose womb comes the ice? Who gives birth to the frost from the heavens when the waters become hard as stone, when the surface of the deep is frozen?" (Job 38:29-30). Even the Psalmist records, "He hurls down his hail like pebbles. Who can withstand His icy blast? He sends His word and melts them; He stirs up His breezes, and the waters flow" (Psalm 147:17-18).

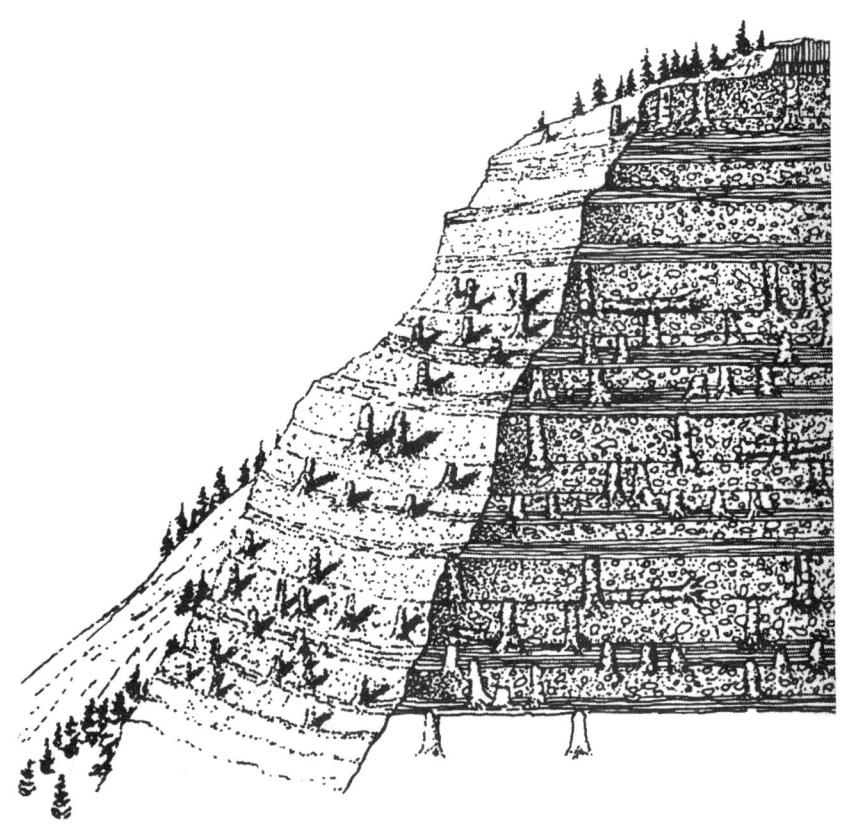

Figure 13: Cut-away view of specimen ridge at Yellowstone.

Catastrophism and Fossil Forests

Yellowstone Park's Specimen Ridge yields a series of fossilized forests, evolutionists claim. A sign standing outside explaining this phenomenon reads, "Across the valley rise the slopes of Specimen Ridge, but the forest you see there today is only the latest chapter in a remarkable story. Buried within the volcanic rocks that compose the mountain are twenty-seven distinct layers of fossil forest that flourished 50 million years ago, . . .Sporadic volcanic eruptions occurring over a period of about 20 thousand years buried many successive forests under blankets of ash and volcanic debris. . . . Many stumps still stand upright in the same sites where they grew millions of years ago."   Again, in order to explain this phenomenon we look back to Mount St. Helens. Over a million logs were floating on Spirit Lake beneath the volcano's summit. This floating mat of logs has greatly decreased in size the past 17 years because, as the logs become water logged they begin to float upright as the weighted end sinks beneath the surface. Eventually, the logs become completely saturated

52

with water and sink to the bottom, but remaining in their upright positions they are buried by sediments in different strata layers, depending upon when the log sank. Logs buried a couple months ago are rather solidly embedded, while those buried only a day or two could be tipped over easily. To verify that these logs were actually being deposited upright at different levels, Steve Austin went scuba diving in Spirit lake, and indeed that was taking place. To produce more concrete evidence, a sonar reading taken of the lake's bottom revealed an estimated 20,000 to 40,000 logs upright there.

Could the theory that the trees of Specimen Ridge grew where they stand today, which is read by thousands upon thousands of people each year, be incorrect? If one would drain Spirit Lake today, it could very well give the appearance of Specimen Ridge at Yellowstone Park. Noah's Flood could certainly produce something of what we see at Mount St. Helens and Yellowstone Park.

One evidence to suggest Specimen Ridge is a result of Noah's Flood

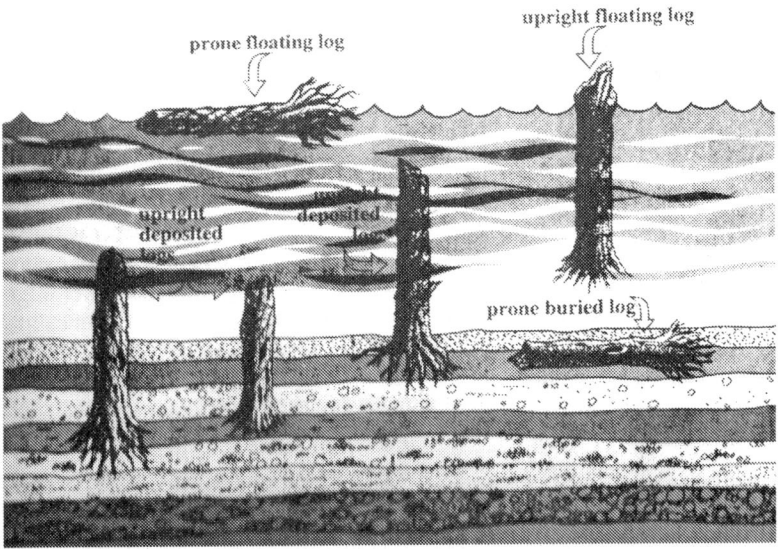

Figure 14: Water-logged logs sink at different times, being buried in different strata.

comes from research done by Steve Austin. Austin took ring samples of various trees in different strata and found that the rings correspond in the various levels. For example, a wide, wide, narrow ring pattern would suggest three years of wet, wet and dry. Therefore, one would expect to see different patterns among trees of supposed different time periods, but Specimen Ridge rather shows similar patterns.

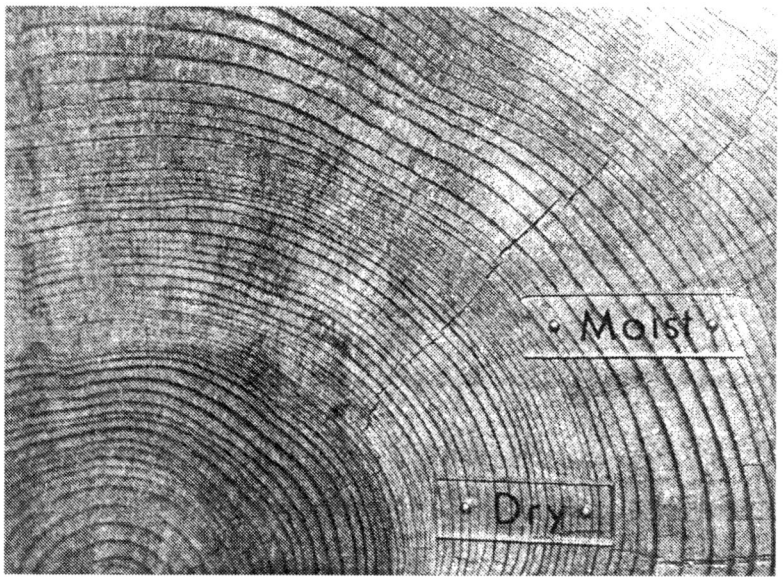

Figure 15: Generally, wide tree rings show wet years and narrow rings show dry years.

Catastrophism and Carbon Dating

Catastrophism affects carbon dating, perhaps another reason for its delayed acceptance in the scientific community. We will discuss the various

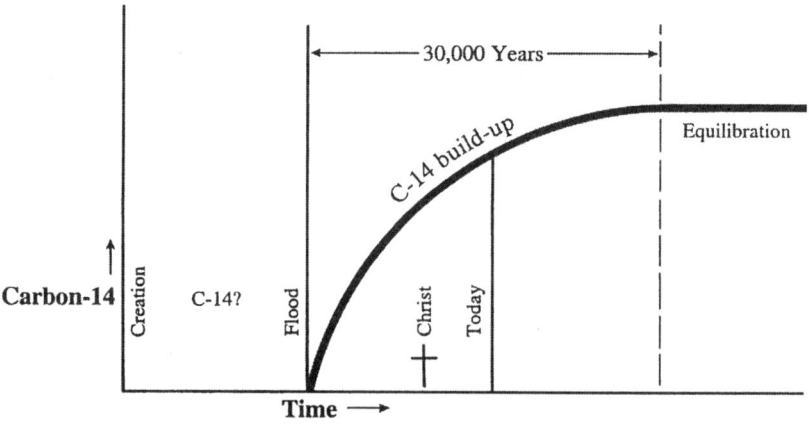

Increase in Carbon-14 Concentration

Figure 16: It was assumed we had reached the C-14 Equilibrium, but new evidence shows this to be incorrect and, therefore, our dating methods flawed.

dating methods and their assumptions in later chapters, but now we will examine one aspect of C-14 dating, the assumption that the amount of C14/C12 ratios of the atmosphere have been somewhat uniform throughout the life of planet earth. Presently, about 18 pounds of C-14 are produced each year and we lose about 15 pounds each year-- a three pound gain. About 62 metric tons of C-14 exist today and the maximum possible is 75 metric tons, the amount at which an equilibrium would come into effect because the total percent coming into the atmosphere would equal the total percent leaving the atmosphere. C-14 dating relies heavily upon this calibration of carbon in the atmosphere, both now and in the distant past. Calibration *cannot* be observed and, therefore, can only be a theory, not fact. The main point is that a large percent of what enters the atmosphere leaves the atmosphere. The result is that the C-14 content is still increasing because the equilibrium has not stabilized. For many years it was believed this equilibrium, which would take around 30,000 years to form under the present conditions, had already been reached since the earth is assumed to be so old; however, scientists now admit that this equilibrium has not yet been reached. Therefore, the assumed calibration of the amount of carbon in the past needs to be changed. But how can we tell how much carbon was in the air 5,000 years ago if we can not observe it?

    Certain catastrophes could release and trap carbon, producing flawed calibration. If the Bible is correct about Noah's Flood, no living plants or trees, essential for carbon, would have survived. Before the Flood of Noah, much greater amounts of carbon existed because of abundant vegetation, as is reflected in the fossil record. Consequently, Noah's Flood would have altered the amount of C-14 in the post-Flood atmosphere by burying tons upon tons of organic, carbon material. The Flood would have also certainly deposited the huge limestone deposits, (calcium carbonates) all over the earth. Carbon, buried and destroyed, would no longer be available for intake by living things and would greatly disrupt the ratio of carbon in the atmosphere, thereby greatly disrupting the present calibration theory of carbon in the atmosphere since the beginning of Creation. Conclusion: carbon dating cannot be accurate using the present calibrations which are based on uniformity.

    Some creationists are of the opinion that carbon dating may be accurate back to the time of the Flood; although, this view again is based upon somewhat uniform post-Flood conditions. Other creationists propose the Flood was only the beginning of a number of successive catastrophes: Sodom and Gomorrah, the Ice-Age, and the division of the earth in the days of Peleg. The Bible does indicate some terrible post- Flood events. The following are a few examples:

> "The earth trembled and quaked, the foundations of the heavens shook; they trembled because he was angry. Smoke rose from his nostrils; consuming fire came from his mouth, burning coals blazed out of it" (2 Samuel 22:8-9); "I will weep and wail for the mountains and take up a lament concerning the desert pastures. They are desolate and untraveled, and the lowing of cattle is not heard. The birds of the air have fled and the animals are gone. I will make Jerusalem a heap of ruins, a haunt of jackals; and I will lay waste the towns of Judah so no one can live there What man is wise enough to understand this? Who has been

instructed by the LORD and can explain it? Why has the land been ruined and laid waste like a desert that no one can cross?" (Jeremiah 9:10-12); "I looked at the earth, and it was formless and empty; and at the heavens, and their light was gone. I looked at the mountains, and they were quaking; all the hills were swaying. I looked, and there were no people; every bird in the sky had flown away. I looked, and the fruitful land was a desert; all its towns lay in ruins before the LORD, before his fierce anger. This is what the LORD says: 'The whole land will be ruined, though I will not destroy it completely. Therefore the earth will mourn and the heavens above grow dark, because I have spoken and will not relent'" (Jeremiah 4:23-28); "Because of this the land mourns, and all who live in it waste away; the beasts of the field and the birds of the air and the fish of the sea are dying" (Hosea 4:3); "Has not the food been cut off before our very eyes-- joy and gladness from the house of our God? The seeds are shriveled beneath the clods. The storehouses are in ruins, the granaries have been broken down, for the grain has dried up. How the cattle moan! The herds mill about because they have no pasture; even the flocks of sheep are suffering. To you, O LORD, I call, for fire has devoured the open pastures and flames have burned up all the trees of the field. Even the wild animals pant for you; the streams of water have dried up and fire has devoured the open pastures" (Joel: 1:16-20).

Even ancient writings indicate similar traumas as Ovid points out in Plato's Timaeus:

"The earth bursts into flame, the highest parts first, and splits into deep cracks, and its moisture is all dried up. The meadows are burned to white ashes; the trees are consumed, green leaves and all, and the ripe grain furnishes fuel for its own destruction. Great cities perish with their walls, and the vast conflagration reduces whole nations to ashes. The woods are ablaze with the mountains. . . Then also Libya became a desert, for the heat dried up her moisture. . . The golden sands of Tagus melt in the intense heat. . . The Nile fled in terror to the ends of the earth . . . the seven mouths lie empty, filled with dust; seven broad channels, all without a stream. . . Great cracks yawn everywhere. . .Even the sea shrinks up, and what was but now a great watery expanse is a dry plain of sand" (Ovid, 1955, p. 28-40).

At this point, it should be mentioned that archaeology records much the same thing. In his book entitled, From Noah to Abram: the turbulent years, Von Fange quotes Norwich: "We know that the driest part of the Sahara was once a place where many people and much wildlife thrived. This region included southeast Libya, southern Egypt, and northern Sudan. It was a land of lakes and rivers full of fish. Meadows, forests, and fertile valleys offered abundant pasture for elephant, giraffe, and hippopotamus. We are speaking of areas where today even the camel turns away in despair" (Norwich, 1968, p. 103). In addition, there has been much archaeological evidence showing that human beings lived in these present desolate regions and devised complex irrigation systems, too (Clark, p 126). As for the melted sand mentioned by Plato, the Gobi desert has areas of glass-like sand formed by intense heat and from an unknown source (Von Fange, p. 308).

The above evidence and records suggest that various catastrophes indeed occurred after the Flood and, therefore, could have altered the C-14 content of the atmosphere considerably. No human present to measure the increase or decrease of C-14, nullifies the calibration needed for a trustworthy dating method.

Catastrophism and Fossilization

The uniformitarianism theory does not fit well with the fossil record, because Noah's Flood submerged both fossils and uniformitarianism. Actually, Noah's Flood and its effects provide a foundation for creation bias. If Christians

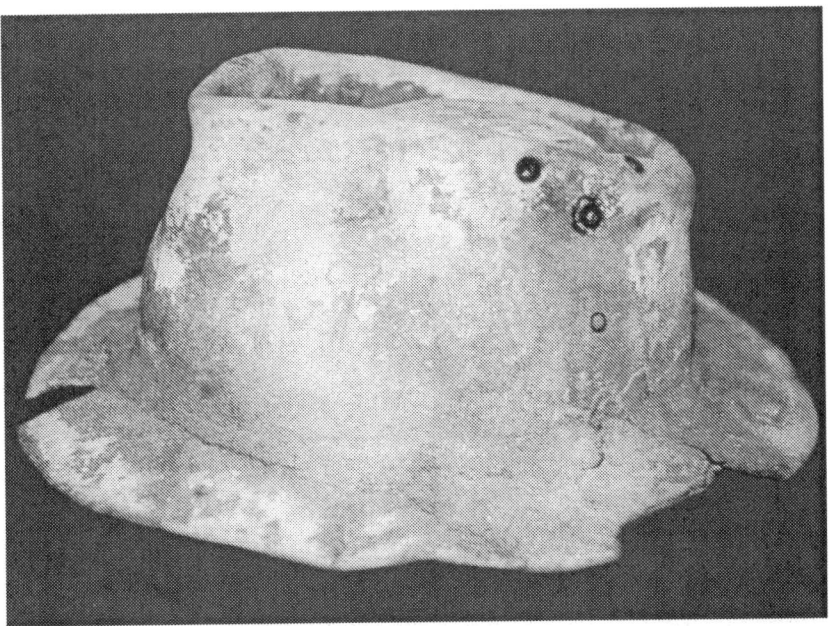

Figure 17: A felt hat that fossilized into a hard hat.

can accept just this one catastrophe then the evidence for a Divine creation is overwhelming, but if we reject the historicity of the global Flood, the evidence for creation leaves many unanswered questions. The Bible clearly says that Noah's Flood was global and altered the earth's surface, including climate, atmosphere, animals, and the human life span. The Flood was sent to destroy mankind, plants, animals, and the entire earth (Genesis 6:7, 17; 7:22; 9:11); it covered the highest mountain, (Genesis 7:19-20); it lasted over a year, (Genesis 7:11; 8:13); and it was recognized as fact by later Biblical writers, (Job 12:15; II Peter 2:5; 3:6; Hebrews 11:7; Isaiah 54:9 and Psalm 29:10). If the Flood was a mere local drowning, this passage and others cannot be true because Noah's Flood would never be sent again. Yet today, huge local floods are witnessed almost every year. The fossil record is just one of the many evidences which support the theory of a global Flood in the past.

Two misconceptions about the formation of fossils are that fossils take millions of years to fossilize and animals need only die to turn into a fossil. To examine the first fallacy -- the necessity of long time periods -- we need only look back in the past 50 years or so to find examples of things fossilizing in a very short time under the right conditions. In Tasmania an old felt miners cap was discovered as a "hard hat" because it had been covered with water for more than 50 years and had been fossilized by calcium carbonates. This fossil now is on display in a mining museum on the west coast of Tasmania (*Creation ex nihilo*, 1995). In South Jetty at Westport, Washington, a clock was found in 1975 embedded in rock (*Creation,* August 1997).

Second, does every animal that dies fossilize? No, most animals that die do not fossilize. Well-known is that very few fossils are forming today because the fossilization process needs rapid burial in aqueous sediments. William J. Miller, a geology professor at UCLA notes, "comparatively few remains of organisms now inhabiting the earth are being deposited under conditions favorable for their preservation as fossils" (William, p. 12). A dead fox requires certain conditions for fossilization. Somehow this dead creature would have to evade scavengers and avoid oxygen to resist the normal decay processes caused by bacteria. The only way to avoid these obstacles is to be buried quickly and solidly, perhaps within 30 seconds or less. Evidence that quick burials indeed occur is seen from fossils where a fish is eating another fish, which is sticking half way out its mouth *(Creation* back cover, May 1997). In another case, a fish is still in the process of giving birth. This speaks of catastrophe, not slow death. If an animal comes in contact with the oxygen in the air for even a short period (one minute) chances are it will NOT fossilize. For this reason it is rare to see any fossilized evidence of the millions of bison which were killed in America's move westward. We will discuss the fossil record itself in more detail in later chapters.

Another interesting feature is the mass quantities of sedimentary rock found all over the earth in which most fossils are found. Sedimentary rock consists of sediments such as sands, gravels, silts, and clay, all of which were eroded by water, carried by water, and deposited by water; finally, pressure and chemical reactions within cause fossil formation.

Rapid burial is very important for the Creationist because it gives solid evidence that the fossil record, almost in its entirety, was laid in a short time because of Noah's Flood. Therefore, the fossil record cannot be used as an evolutionary time scale to date sedimentary rocks. For example, to examine an index fossil (a fossil believed to be laid down during a specific time period and used to date rocks) such as a trilobite requires dating the rock in which this fossil was found, say the Cambrian era. Naturally; sediments above would be from the Ordovician, Silurian, Devonian and Mississippian time periods and with only certain animals among these layers. The Flood model gives a good explanation why evolution is inconsistent and also why the majority of fossils are laid down in this way. In a flood, trilobites and clams would not be able to escape so they would be buried first, while fish could swim and prevent early burial. Meanwhile the land animals, fleeing the rising waters the longest, would be buried last.

Polystrate fossils, an evolutionary enigma, are buried in more than one time period. For example, this fossil may extend into both the Paleozoic and Mesozoic layering. Near Newcastle in Australia, fossilized trees extend through more than 20 feet of coal strata. In some cases, trees are even found upside down, showing that they could not be the remains of the last trees which grew in a swamp, as evolutionists try to claim (Wilson, p. 39). This type of thing cannot be explained by slow and gradual processes; rather only by rapid catastrophic burial. It also explains why there are no transitional forms anywhere in the fossil record. Although evolutionists from time to time claim that an intermediate has been found, this claim has ALWAYS been proven wrong. If animals did evolve, one would expect to find a half-bird, half-dinosaur, but none are ever found. If the Flood occurred, we would expect to find individual species of animals, fully formed and indeed, we do.

Honest evolutionists such as Ronald West admits this problem: "Contrary to what most scientists write, the fossil record does not support the Darwinian theory of evolution because this theory (there are several) . . . interprets the fossil record. By doing so we are guilty of circular reasoning if we then say the fossil record supports this theory" (West, p. 217). Although now, the popular view held by other evolutionists is something called punctuated equilibrium; that is, biological and geological changes occur rapidly, too quick to be shown in the fossil record. Some creationists suggest this is a "last ditch" effort to admit failure of evidence in the fossil record, but Gould and Eldredge, the two men behind this theory, give it full support. Robert E. Ricklefs, a biology professor of the University of Pennsylvania, states, "The punctuated equilibrium model has been widely accepted, not because it has a compelling theoretical basis but because it appears to resolve dilemma. Apart from the obvious sampling problems inherent to the observations that stimulated the model, and apart from its intrinsic circularity

Figure 18: Polystrate tree extending through two narrow coal seems and shale.

(one could argue that speculation can occur only when phyletic change is rapid, not vice versa), the model is more ad hoc explanation than theory, and it rests on shaky ground" (Ricklefs, p. 59).

The Bible clearly teaches that death did not come before sin, rather death was a result of sin, for "Just as sin entered the world through one man, and death through sin, and in this way death came to all men, because all sinned--" (Romans 5:12). We also are taught that "every living thing perished" in the Flood (Gen 7:23). Hence, the fossils certainly do not tell of slow and gradual processes but quick judgment on antediluvians when, "By these waters also the world of that time was deluged and destroyed" (II Peter 3:6).

CHAPTER 6
EVOLUTION BY- LAWS

Second Law of Thermodynamics

A fascinating phenomena about evolution is that it is the only widespread practice in science that goes against so many known scientific laws. The first and second laws of thermodynamics are the two most basic laws in the area of physical science, as Harvard physicist P. W. Bridgman readily admits: "The two laws of thermodynamics are, I suppose, accepted by physicists as perhaps the most secure generalizations from experience that we have" (Bridgman, p. 549).

The first law states than energy is always conserved, that is, energy is never created or destroyed in the present, rather it is changed from one form into another. The second law states that this energy becomes less available for use as time goes on. In other words, everything is getting worse. The watch on your wrist is working towards a day when it will stop, our bodies are aging and will do so until death, the rocks are decaying, the electromagnetic field of the earth is declining, the sun is burning up, etc. This universal move toward destruction is called entropy. Matter remains constant in quantity but deteriorates in quality. Concerning this move toward the less complex, Harold Blum of Princeton writes, "The probability function generally used in thermodynamics is entropy. . . . .Thus orderliness is associated with low entropy; randomness with high entropy. . . . The second law of thermodynamics says that, left to itself, any isolated system will go toward greater entropy, which also means toward greater randomness and greater likelihood" (Blum, p. 595).

To touch on the origin of the first law, by which no energy can be created, creationists have the answer. "For in six days the LORD made the heavens and the earth, the sea, and all that is in them, but He rested on the seventh day. Therefore the LORD blessed the Sabbath day and made it holy" (Exodus 20:11). The first six days of creation involved just creating; but when those days ended, the second law of thermodynamics began. One must accept either eternal God, or eternal matter. Eternal God is the only plausible explanation for science and reasoning. In addition, we read from Hebrews that "His work has been finished since the creation of the world" (Hebrews 4:3). Colossians states, "For by Him all things were created: things in heaven and on earth, visible and invisible. . . all things were created by Him and for Him. He is before all things, and in Him all things hold together" (Colossians 1:16-17; see also Nehemiah 9:6; II Peter 3:7). Currently the creation is over and Jesus now serves not only as our Redeemer but as the Sustainer of the universe as well: "The Son is the radiance of God's glory and the exact representation of His being, *sustaining all things* by His powerful word. After He had provided purification for sins, He sat down at the right hand of the Majesty in heaven" (Hebrews 1:3).

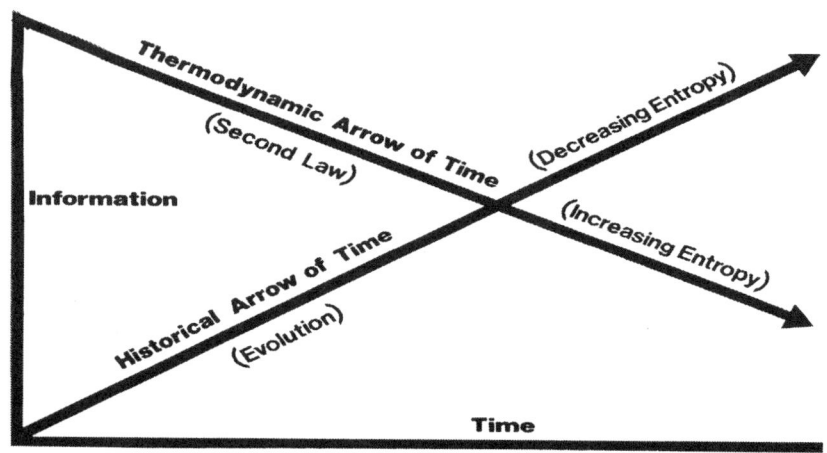

Figure 19: Evolution goes against a well known law of science- the second law of thermodynamics.

The Bible explains the second law: "We know that the whole creation has been groaning as in the pains of childbirth right up to the present time" (Romans 8:22), and "you will eat your food until you return to the ground, since from it you were taken; for dust you are and to dust you will return" (Gen 3:19). See also Isaiah 51:6; Matthew 24:35; I Peter 1:24; Psalm 102:25-26. Of course, this decaying process was brought about by the curse upon Adam shortly after creation, where we read, "Because you listened to your wife and ate from the tree about which I commanded you, 'You must not eat of it,' cursed is the ground because of you; through painful toil you will eat of it all the days of your life'" (Genesis 3:17). Biblically speaking, we would expect everything to decay, but to shed light on this gloom Christ has delivered us so that, "In keeping with his promise we are looking forward to a new heaven and a new earth, the home of righteousness" (II Peter 3:13).

Evolution's problem compounds since the whole theory depends solely upon the simple becoming complex. Julian Huxley defined evolution as, "a directional and essentially irreversible process occurring in time, which in its course gives rise to an increase of variety and an increasingly high level of organization in its products" (Huxley, p. 278). How can a world that is, by law, becoming more and more disorganized be increasing in complexity? Evolutionists have two possible explanations, neither of which really answers the question. First, they cannot be sure that the second law is true. This conjecture is odd because every other area of science never questions the second law. In addition, the second law is not impulsive but has been scientifically tested in the present and in EVERY case it has been found that entropy is increasing. The second possible solution for the evolutionist is to say that this second law only applies to closed or isolated systems; for example, a baby growing into an adult or animals growing into large populations. Again, this theory fails in view of scientific experiments presently taking place. The second law takes place in isolated systems, but, it has only been tested in open systems, which are the only ones that exist in nature. EVERY test of the second law in these open systems shows increasing entropy at an alarming rate (Clark, p. 86-87). Whether by slow and gradual processes or by punctuated equilibrium, the second law of thermodynamics is a thorn in the side of evolutionists.

We view entropy in the variety of species. When left alone, varieties return to their original kind. For example, take a number of hybrid chickens and let them run around the farm yard. It won't be long and these "hybrids" become inferior stock. The same applies to hybrid corn and other seeds. A farmer should not keep seed from his crop of hybrid corn because it will only produce a crop of less yield than the year before. Dog breeders especially know not to let their prize dogs run around the neighborhood. How could evolution produce a superior species when, according to evolutionary theory, these species have been left to random, chance processes.

Ontogeny Recapitulates Phylogeny

Earlier we discussed how some evolutionary followers still use what is described as ontogeny recapitulating phylogeny. In plain English, that is the belief that a fetus in the mother's womb goes through a rapid evolutionary change of being a protozoan, fish, primate, and all the way to a human being.

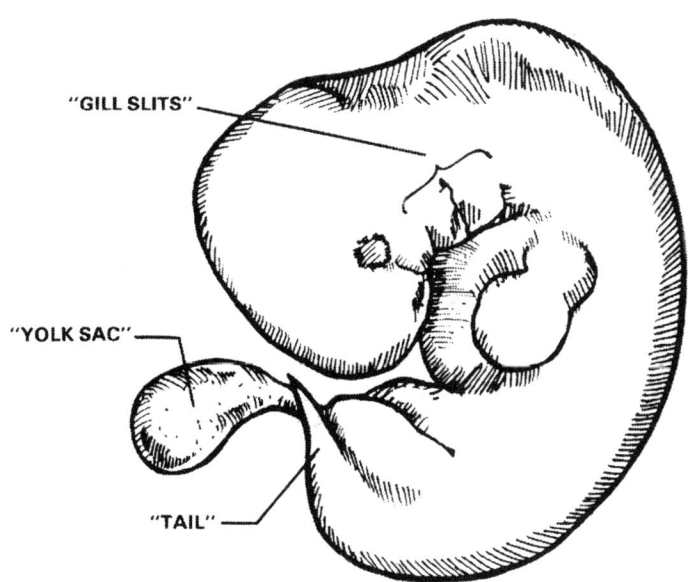

Figure 20: A fetus has the physical appearance of gill slits and a tail, but inwardly is completely different.

This heretical belief was proven false over 50 years ago, yet it is still being combated today. Recently it has been rejected again by the leading evolutionist, Stephen Gould who writes, "the theory of recapitulation . . . should be defunct today" (Gould, p. 144). Despite this apparent opposition, this theory is treated as fact among many doctors and scientists alike. Recently one woman came up to me after a lecture. She mentioned a doctor had told a friend of hers that the mark on her child's neck was from when it had gills. I also took a graduate class in June of 1995 where I was taught that a baby "evolves" in the mother's womb. So, even though there are those who reject this theory, an equal number and more accept it.

Children with Down's Syndrome, otherwise known as "Mongoloid idiocy," were previously believed to have been "thrown back" into the Mongolian stage of evolutionary history. Also, for years it was said that the fertilized egg represented a look-alike amoebae before evolution, based on physical appearance. Likewise, when the fetus has what is a so-called "tail" it looks more like a monkey than a man. The problem with this reasoning is that one only examines the outside of a body when coming to this conclusion. If this is science, then an egg and a marble could be ancestral relatives, even though on the inside they are completely different. The same goes for the tail on an unborn child, which is often called useless. This "tail," otherwise known as the coccyx, is actually where muscles attach in order to keep upright posture. It also serves to cushion falls, hence, your "tail bone". The reason this part of the spine sticks out in a one month old embryo is that the muscles and limbs of the human body do not develop until they are stimulated by the spine. Once the spine develops sufficiently, the muscles grow around the coccyx inside the body. Some children have been born with a fatty leftover of this development (but not the coccyx itself) and are labeled as having tails. While a tail and this fatty leftover are similar in shape, they are not in content. A real tail is made up of muscles, bones, and nerves; the "tail" is merely skin and fat; and can be cut off without doing any harm. Gary Parker explains the origin of these tails: "During development, it rises up in ridges and rolls shut. It starts to 'zipper' shut in the middle first, then it zippers toward either end. Once in a while it doesn't go far enough, and that produces a serious defect called spina bifida. Sometimes it rolls a little too far. Then the baby will be born not with a tail, but with a fatty tumor" (Parker, p.65-67).

In addition to the "tail," a fetus has what is called a "yolk sac," which in many ways looks like that of a chicken. However, this is quite different from a chicken yolk on the inside. While a chicken yolk provides food for the developing young, a human yolk sac stores the first blood cells, without which would cause certain death.

Similarly, the "gill slits" are again very useful and improperly named. Gary Parker again states, "The throat (or pharyngeal) grooves and pouches, falsely called 'gill slits' are not mistakes in human development. They develop into absolutely essential parts of human anatomy. The middle ear canals come from the second pouches, and the parathyroid and thymus glands come from the third and fourth. Without a thymus, we would lose half our immune systems. Without the parathyroid we would be unable to regulate calcium balance and could not even survive" (Parker, p.64).

Today, because of the evolutionary belief, abortions are being justified all over the world. For this reason as well, it has been said that the most dangerous place in the world is a mother's womb. How troubling but true that statement is. If more people could realize that these abnormalities are simple mutations having no connection to evolutionary thought and that a baby is, in fact, a human being, what a difference that could make. Our bodies are full of these genetic mistakes and as Dr. Parker has said, the only reason we call ourselves normal is by common consent. So there you have it, the ontogeny recapitulating phylogeny is perjury and doesn't hold up in the courts of evolution, but that doesn't mean people obey the laws set by the court.

Law of Biogenesis

This chapter is of utmost importance because, if one cannot create life in the laboratory then there is no need to argue the fossil record. If life is NOT a product of chance, evolution is a moot point and I believe this chapter proves that. The Law of Biogenesis states that life cannot come from non-life, yet evolution has life beginning millions of years ago by, as one theory explains it, having lightning striking some primordial soup which provides an energy source for life from inorganic materials. Sounds simple doesn't it. Dr. Michael Girouard MD humorously admits that, "you only have to have the right materials under the right conditions to get the right products of the right kinds from the right amount to get the right reaction to the right location in the right sequence with the right information to build a right structure to do a right function that makes life" (Girouard). He goes on to explain that this was the easy part, now you have to have all eleven processes in the same order all the time." To illustrate this, one only needs to think of a book and all of its letters. The information stored in this book isn't in the ink or even in the letters, but rather in the order of the letters. Likewise, it isn't the chemicals which make life but rather the order that they are in. Sir Frederick Hoyle, after searching out the answer to life with unlimited funds said this, "The chance that higher life forms might have emerged in this way is comparable with the chance that a tornado sweeping through a junk yard might assemble a Boeing 747 from the materials therein" (Hoyle on evolution, p. 105).

Even if life could form (which would be the first miracle) as evolution suggests, it would take a another miracle to change it into a human being. One evidence to support this ape to man transition is that we are 98.4 % genetically identical to a chimpanzee. But, we are still 1.6% different which, genetically speaking, is astronomically different. Dr. Barney Maddox, the leading genetic genome researcher, said concerning these genetic differences, "Now the genetic difference between human and his nearest relative, the chimpanzee, is at least 1.6%. That doesn't sound like much, but calculated out, that is a gap of at least 48 million nucleotides, and a change of only 3 nucleotides is fatal to an animal; there is no possibility of change" (Maddox). Dr. Maddox also states that "science has now quantitated that a genetic mutation of as little as .0000001% of an animal's genome is relentlessly fatal" (Maddox).

Perhaps it is because of the above evidence that NO life has EVER been made in the laboratory. Stanley Miller has done an experiment to try to create a single amino acid. The building blocks of life are amino acids, sugars, and bases. The amino acids form the protein which assists towards life. Similarly, DNA needs bases and sugars for its existence. The experiment constitutes only an amino acid, a substance distant from the necessary components of life. The results of this experiment have been put in textbooks all over the world, despite the fact that it was a flop (though students aren't told that). One high school text book states, "The idea that an organic soup could originate from a primitive atmosphere was tested in the laboratory by Stanley Miller in 1953. This demonstrated that complex organic molecules could have been produced by inorganic ones" (Girouard). These "complex organic molecules" talked about are amino acids, which really are not all that complex, plus the acids produced in this experiment were the wrong type (which the textbooks don't mention). The very next page of this same textbook states, "These primitive cells could have flourished," giving the impression that Miller had created an actual cell, but an amino acid is far from any type of cell. In this experiment, Dr. Miller used methane, ammonia, water vapor and hydrogen because he said these were the initial elements in the first atmosphere billions of years ago. How did he know? Because these were the gases that he thought were needed for life; therefore, he had a prior answer to his question before he started, to ensure success - mere circular reasoning. Sometimes creationists are accused of using the Bible as the starting point for everything. That is where we base our assumptions; however, evolutionists base their assumptions on the fact that evolution has occurred. What a difference! The Miller experiment (despite the fact we must admit eternal God or eternal matter) assumes that the materials suggested existed, but how were they preserved when ultraviolet rays from the sun destroy methane and kill any living organism? The only reason we can live today is that the 21% of oxygen in the atmosphere and ozone protect us from the UV rays. Why doesn't Dr. Miller propose oxygen in his primitive ozone? Because oxygen stops the chemical reactions needed to form the bases, amino acids and sugars. Furthermore, all the above mentioned chemicals would be burned up because of the oxygen. In other words, you need oxygen to create your product but once it exists, the oxygen destroys the thing it creates. Knowing this, Dr. Miller chose not to use oxygen in his experiment, something Carl Sagan even admits is a big problem (Sagan, p 231). One reason that oxygen cannot be objectively left out is because scientists have found it in rocks which, according to evolutionary theory, have been dated over 3.4 billion years old, suggesting oxygen was always in the atmosphere. This being the case, the oxygen would never allow amino acids to form, hence life could not form. But letting Miller have this "minor" detail, he then went on to conduct his experiment by heating up the hydrogen, water vapor, ammonia, and methane in a flask. As the materials were heated, they rose through a tube into an electrical chamber (to simulate lightning). From here the gases went on to be cooled and the end product was trapped in a separate chamber, while the rest of the materials kept circulating through the entire process again. The important thing to remember here is that the end product was not allowed to get back to its original flask. Why? Because if it did, the heat source there would kill the product. Like the oxygen, heat is needed to form the product but it also destroys it (Girouard).

The world is filled with other such interdependent systems, as Michael Denton points out in describing one human cell: "There is much more to the cell than the 'mere' origin of the protein synthetic apparatus. In fact, the protein synthetic mechanism cannot function in isolation, but only in conjunction with other complex subsystems of the cell" (Denton, p. 268). Dr. Denton goes on to show how DNA provides information to the protein synthetic mechanism (PSM), but the PSM at the same time gives protein to the DNA; neither one could exist without the other. Likewise, the PSM gives protein phosphate compounds to the energy system, while the energy system gives the PSM energy to begin with. Finally, the PSM gives energy to the cell membrane, which holds the PSM together. Everything is dependent on one another and one cannot form without the whole part being formed at one time. Only God's creation can provide an

Figure 21: Miller experiment by which amino acids were formed under special circumstances not found in nature.

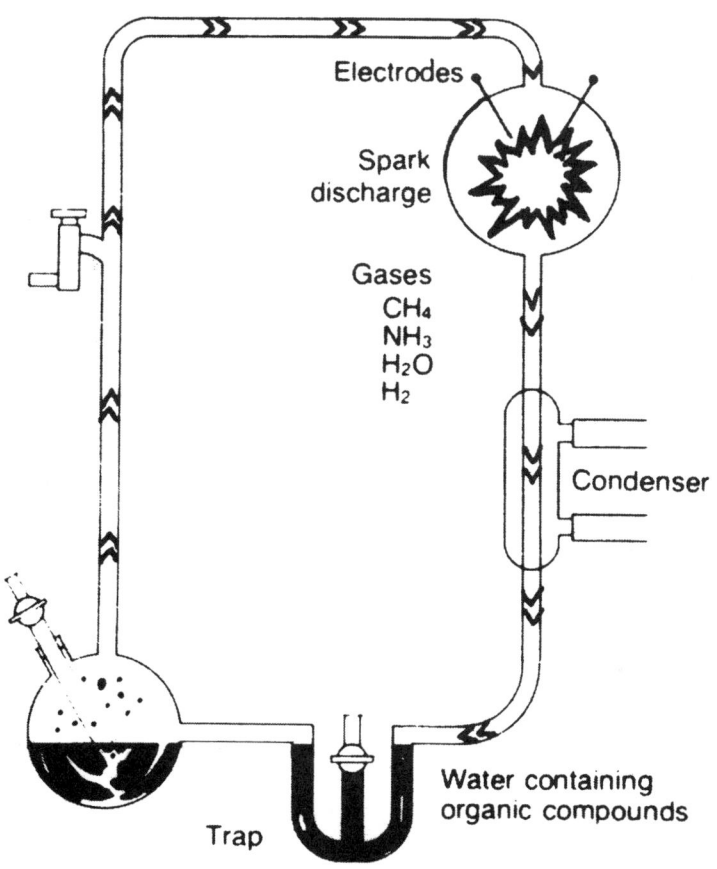

answer to this otherwise impossible question.

Furthering the problem of amino acids is that they come identified as left handed and right handed. In order to produce life, 100% of them must be left handed, but in nature there is a 50% mixture of left and right handed amino acids. Natural evolution can not produce the needed 100% left handed amino acids. Putting this in perspective: the chance of getting struck by lightning is 1 in 600,000; the chance of winning the lottery is 1 in 30 million; the chance of getting 400 amino acids all left handed in a sequence is 1 in 10^{78000}, which is far beyond mathematical impossibility. Also, the chances of getting ONE ecoli bacteria (in the intestinal track to aid in digestion) would be 1 in 10 hundred billion (Girouard). If you would add up all the electrons (the smallest measurable substance) it would take to FILL the entire universe there would only be 10^{130} electrons.

This gives you some idea of the ridiculous numbers involved in forming one amino acid or cell. Even if this could be done, still no life exists; therefore, any logical person should be able to realize that the Law of Biogenesis is that life cannot come from non-life. God alone can create life! If this is not true, and life can be formed by chemicals in a laboratory, then God lied, because Genesis 2:7 clearly tells us, "the LORD God formed the man from the dust of the ground and breathed into his nostrils the breath of life, and the man became a living being." As a creationist, I know God can be trusted and He never lies. Jesus alone is my Redeemer and Giver of Life: "For the bread of God is He who comes down from heaven and gives life to the world" (John 6:33).

CHAPTER 7
FOSSIL RECORD
No Transitional Forms

What once was thought to be the best evidence for evolution is now being reconsidered, since virtually NO evidence surfaced. If evolution is true, there should be a vast record of fossils showing these various animals evolving into higher, more complex creatures. There should be worms (invertebrates) turning into fish (vertebrates), fish developing legs as they turn into amphibians, amphibians developing into reptiles, and the legs of reptiles turning into wings like birds, etc. With so many fossils today, there should be a number of these transitions, but in fact, every creature appears fully formed in the fossil record. A snail is always a snail and a bird is always a bird. Dr. David M. Raup, curator of geology at the Field Museum of Natural History in Chicago, has stated, "Well, we are now about 120 years after Darwin and the knowledge of the fossil record has been greatly expanded. We now have a quarter of a million fossil species but the situation hasn't changed much. The record of evolution is still surprisingly jerky and, ironically, we have even fewer examples of evolutionary transitions than we had in Darwin's time. By this I mean that some of the classic cases of Darwinian change in the fossil record, such as the evolution of the horse in North America, have had to be discarded or modified as a result of more detailed information" (Raup, p. 25). The amazing thing is that Darwin himself felt the fossil record was lacking; he had simply hoped in the future more supporting evidence would arise, but in fact the opposite has taken place.

When one goes into museums he sees wonderful pictures of intermediate forms painted on the walls and glass cases, but all of this is artistic license showing what the evolutionary theory supposes should be in the fossil record. Never mind the fact that there has been no such thing found, someday they hope it will be discovered. What faith is exercised in the scientific community today. No longer is science really the observation of facts and experiments, rather it has become a contest to see who can come up with the best explanation for the continuing existence of evolutionary thought.

We have already established what should be expected to be seen in the fossil record if evolution is true. Next we examine creation expectations. One should see fully developed animals of all kinds, with most of their fossils being deposited at or near the same time. This chapter explains the reality of creation as shown in the fossil record.

Index fossils are those which are used to date the rocks. For example, if a person found a trilobite in the front yard, the yard would be dated around 500 million years old only because this fossil, according to evolutionary theory, did not live until then. Evolution dates the fossils and the fossils are what date sedimentary rocks. That isn't science. Incidentally, a trilobite is suppose to be one of the first examples of evolution from the Precambrian to the Cambrian era and, therefore, should be a rather simple structure (Gish Fossil Record). Just the opposite is true. The trilobite's eyes are very complex, enabling it to have clear underwater vision; for evolution, a mystery, for creation, evidence.

Some fossils extend vertically into a number of different strata layers. Therefore, in order to be consistent with theory, one must admit these trees have lived millions of years, which is impossible. This enigma is called a polystrate fossil. Obviously, a tree could not remain in growth for millions of years, let alone be preserved in coal, where many of them have been found. Also as mentioned earlier, in order for something to fossilize it must be buried quickly, something evolution doesn't provide for. However, creation provides an answer to how even fossil jelly fish have been found. These types of fossils speak of catastrophic events and deny the slow and gradual processes assumed by evolution.

In many other cases, we see that animals once thought to be extinct for millions of years suddenly show up alive today, unchanged in form. In 1939 a coelacanth fish was caught off the coast of South Africa. This animal was supposed to have become extinct 70 million years ago (Gish, Dinosaur, p 84). Likewise in Sydney, Australia, David Noble ran across a small forest of ancient trees of the Jurassic era which were thought to have been extinct for 150 million years (Associated Press, 1995). New and old species are being discovered all the time, both in water and on land. We can't keep track of the things on land, and with 2/3 of the world covered with water it makes you wonder how much more waits to be discovered. (See section on dinosaurs for more fascinating discoveries).

Many times we uncover fossils said to be extremely old (because of the strata layer in which they were found) yet they look exactly like what we have today. In the December 9, 1966, edition of *Science* magazine, Dr. Glen Jefferson wrote of the world's oldest bat, which was dated over 50 million years old but looked 100% like the bats of today. It seems as if someone forgot to tell this bat to change. There was no trace of any transitional form, exactly what a creationist would expect. Furthermore, how would something like a bat, or any other animal as far as that goes, evolve? A bat's sonar is vital to its finding food, personal identification, and flight. Without this sonar the bat would fly into walls and would starve because it couldn't locate any food. It is a marvelous design of its Creator, as we see from the bat's ability to distinguish its sonar from thousands of other individuals flying around with it. I find it too hard to believe any mammal could develop slowly into such an amazing animal. In the same fashion, an ant believed to be tens of millions of years old has been found preserved in amber. Again, it looks exactly like the ants of today. Other examples include centipedes, daddy long legs, and many more, all appearing fully formed as God had created them.

Grand Canyon

Much of this is a summary of an article written by David Menton in the April 24th edition of *Christian News*, 1995. Dr. Menton clearly shows how the Grand Canyon is actual evidence against evolution and uniformitarianism.

The Grand Canyon is about 270 miles long, 11 miles across and over a mile deep in some places. Along its cliffs and rocky edges are exposed 21 distinct layers, almost entirely made up of sedimentary rock (laid down by water). Both the Great Wall of China and the Grand Canyon can be seen from the moon. Near the bottom of the canyon lies the Precambrian strata where, according to evolutionary theory, should lie the microscopic organisms by which evolution first began. But the objects found are something called "stomatolites." It is not known for sure if stomatolites are even a product of a living organisms, though they look similar to something formed by one-celled photosynthetic organisms called cyanobacteria, which are still found in our oceans today.

The next layers include the Tapeats Sandstone, Bright Angel Shale and Muav Limestone (Cambrian strata) ranging from 600 million to 400 million years old. Fossils of trilobites, oysters, corals, clams, worms, and brachiopods all appear suddenly in these strata, all fully formed with no hint of any transitional forms. How could these evolve from a single-celled organism without leaving any evidence of the upward move? Ripple marks from waves and many worm burrows showing a "U" pattern in movement are fossilized in the Tapeats. These "U" shapes are known by many geologists as "escape burrows" indicating the worms may have been trying to escape the coming waters (Snelling, Canyon).

Next up the canyon wall comes the Redwall Limestone and the Supai group (300 million to 200 million years old). As other layers of the canyon, the Supai layers show fine lamination of sedimentary sand particles, indicative of fast moving water, just like what we see at Mount St. Helens. In this area we find continued marine invertebrates, including the relatively simple bryozoans, crinoids and foraminiferans, all of which are represented in the oceans today. The interesting part about the foraminiferans is that evolutionists say this was one of the first organisms to have evolved a nucleus. But why, as Dr. Menton asks, "are these 'primitive' single-cell organisms first encountered halfway up our 'ladder of life'" (Menton, p. 3).

Also, starting in this Supai layer and going all the way up into the next Hermit and Coconino layers lie numerous footprints of over 20 different species of amphibian and reptile tracks (but never a single bone). In fact, no one has ever found a fossilized bone in the Grand Canyon. However, several miles away from the canyon in higher strata, bones of tetrapods (four-legs) have been found which may match these tracks. Menton states, "the occurrence of foot prints in strata well below the layers in which fossilized bones are first found is not unique to the Grand Canyon. Geologists concede that this is a worldwide phenomenon! How then can we consider the fossils in the geologic column to be a reliable record of evolutionary succession? Are we to believe that foot prints evolved 150 million years before feet? Those who accept the Biblical account of Noah's Flood might prefer to think that the common occurrence of foot prints in strata below those bearing the bodies themselves reveals something about how long these tetrapods could tread water before drowning!" (Menton, p 3). Also noteworthy, as in many layers, the Hermit shale lying directly above the Supai has a knife edge separation with no erosion and, therefore, must have been laid quickly.

Another interesting fact about the footprints in these layers is that they almost always are headed uphill in a northerly direction. Park rangers at the canyon explain this phenomenon by saying that the lizards walk up the hills but to get down they often slide. Dr. Menton's comment on this is, "certainly one could make a more plausible argument for reptiles running uphill to escape the advancing waters of Noah's Flood than one could for 'lazy lizards'" (Menton, p. 3). Also supporting this hypothesis is that many footprints end and start up again a few feet later, suggesting a possibility that the animal was thrown ahead by water where it began walking again. In addition, the front feet dig in more so, which is the exact thing seen in laboratories when this theory is tested (Snelling, Canyon).

Finally, we reach the top layers of the canyon, the Toroweap and Kaibab. No footprints are found in either layer, but some fish teeth and fossilized sponges are seen in the Kaibab. Again, fish should make it longer than most other animals in the Flood. As for the sponges, this is embarrassing for evolutionists because, though they remain on top, they are presumed to be the first multicellular organisms to ever evolve.

David Menton closes his article in writing, "there is no evidence of evolutionary progress in the fossils of the geologic column! I was surprised to learn that evolutionists are already aware of this fact, although you would never guess it from the evolutionary indoctrination presented in public schools and popular media. Harvard evolutionist Stephen J. Gould appears to have no illusions about the evidence for evolutionary succession in the geologic column when he says: 'I regard the failure to find a clear vector of progress in life's history as the most puzzling fact of the fossil record' (*Natural History* Vol. 93, p. 23) A hike to the bottom of the Grand Canyon is a sure cure for evolutionism" (Menton, p.3).

Archaeopteryx

There are a number of so called, "transitional forms" found in the fossil record which are now realized to be fully developed and functioning animals. One of the most talked about fossils is archaeopteryx, which was once believed to be the transitional form from reptile to bird. It seemed to have reptilian characteristics such as teeth and claws on its wings, yet was bird-like with fully formed feathers, perching feet, a bird-like skull, and a furcula (wishbone) unique only to birds. Evolutionists naturally jumped to the conclusion that this was half bird and half reptile, not taking note of the fact that today we have birds such as the ostrich and the young hoatzin which both have claws on their wings. No

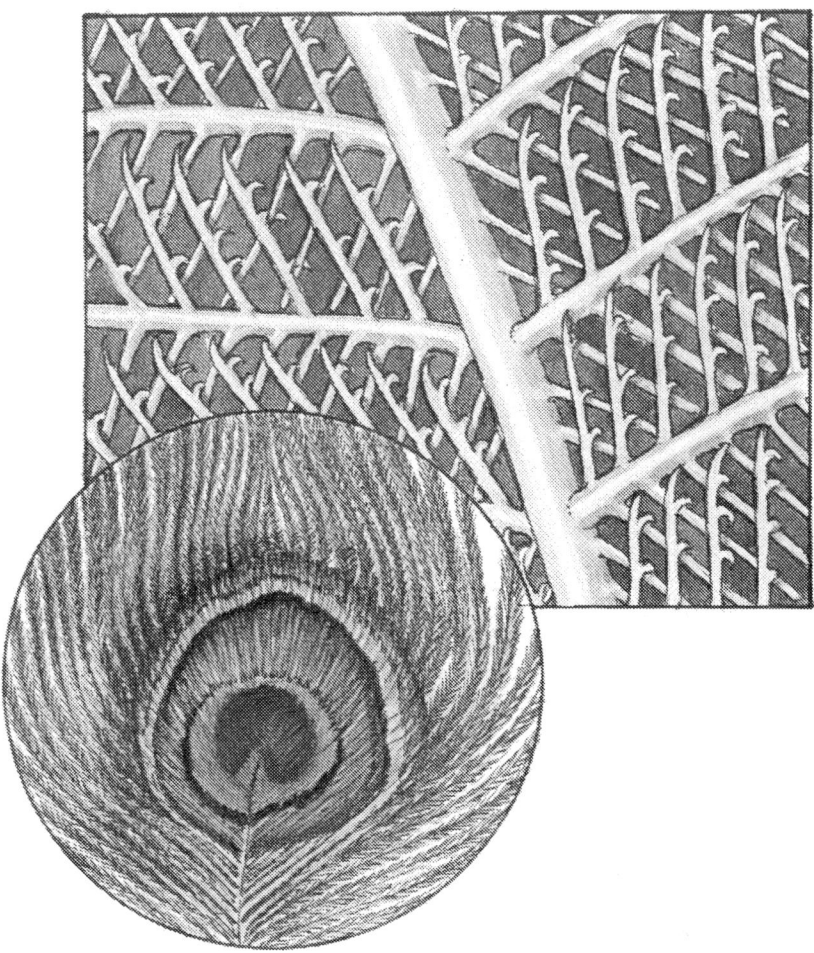

Figure 22: Enlarged feather shows intricate design showing feathers could not come from frayed scales.

modern birds possess teeth but others in the fossil record do (as do some mammals, reptiles and fish). Just like some humans have teeth and others don't, some birds have teeth and others don't. Probably one of the biggest embarrassments for the evolutionist is that another fully formed bird called *protoavis* was found in an earlier strata layer dating 75 million years older, and therefore *Archaeopteryx* cannot be evolving into a bird (Ostrom, p. 212). Most evolutionists now agree with this as well, and recognize *Archaeopteryx* as just a bird. Dr. Swinton of the British Museum of Natural History stated, "The [evolutionary] origin of birds is largely a matter of deduction. There is no fossil evidence of the stages through which the remarkable change from reptile to bird was achieved" (Swinton, p. 1).

To give an explanation of how the theory of evolution explains the unseen transformation from a reptile to bird, one must try to keep a serious face.

First of all, it is believed that the scales of the reptile eventually became frayed and turned into feathers. Problem--feathers are actually quite complex, involving hooks and eyelets that act as zippers to hold the feathers together. The feathers are "zipped together" by hundreds of barbs and barbules (which branch off from the barbs) which cannot be seen by the naked eye. In fact, each feather of an eagle has over 250,000 tiny hooks to keep it strongly held together. When we consider the fact that the average song bird has between 1,100 and 4,600 feathers, we have a lot of hooks (Gish Dinosaurs, p. 67). If we watch a bird preen itself, it is likely that it is running its beak through its feathers to rehook this mesh like zipper.

Second, once this reptile had developed its wings, so to speak, it had to learn how to fly. One theory states that in a desperate attempt to catch insects the reptile ran after them, throwing its two arm/wings together in front of it to trap the insect in its feathers. Sometimes the reptile would actually jump after them, hence flight was developing. Even though this doesn't explain how the reptile could get the insect from its wing to its mouth in order to eat it, it still is a better theory (as far as fairy tales go) than some of the others. For example, some say the claws could have been used to climb up in trees and then jump out of them in order to learn how to fly. The problem with this is that the creature had only one shot at learning or else it died. Remember, no bird like this has ever been seen, alive or in the fossil record. These theories are not only frivolous, but don't answer many other questions, such as why the bird had feathers on its tail if it wasn't used for anything, and why did this reptile have chicken feet? Furthermore, evolution says that these animals evolved by a number of happy accidents (beneficial mutation, which does not occur), all leading to greater complexity. But what happens when a reptile is evolving into a bird and only 25% of its wings have developed. It can't fly yet, nor can it run because it has these useless attachments where its legs used to be. Such a disadvantaged creature would surely be killed in the "survival of the fittest" world of the animal kingdom.

The latest "reptile to bird link" was described in a May, 1997 issue of *Nature*, which described a supposed carnivorous creature named, *Unenlagia comahuensis.* Only about 20 pieces from a leg, rib and shoulder were found in Argentina. They believe it stood about four feet tall and are basing its "link" status on a shoulder girdle that is tilted out, which could *perhaps* have allowed for the flapping of wings. Not much evidence to stand on.

In 1993 *Mononykus* was a favored link for a while as well. *Time* magazine even put this creature on their cover complete with feathers, even though no evidence of feathers was found (April, 1993). Although not portrayed by *Time*, Dr. Novas admitted this could not be a missing link as it was 55 million years younger than *Archaeopteryx*, a complete bird. However, he claimed that this must be what the missing link would resemble. Again we see the desire and hope of a missing link overshadowing true science even when no missing links have been found!

In a desperate attempt to find an answer to these questions, another theory called punctuated equilibrium has come about. This theory states that changes happen so quickly (speaking on a geological time scale) that mutations are unseen in the fossil record. In other words, evolution is like fishing, with long periods of boredom (in my opinion) and short periods of change and excitement. One example of the propaganda pushing this theory can be seen in a book called, *The Wonderful Egg*, in which a dinosaur egg hatches into a beautiful bird with feathers and song capabilities. The problem with this theory is how could anything reproduce by itself, not to mention the biological impossibility of one species changing into another.

As mentioned earlier, if creation is true the fossil record should show "billions of dead things, buried in rock layers, laid down by water, all over the earth" (Parker, Dinosaurs). In chapter three we discussed how catastrophic flooding has laid down a mind boggling amount of sedimentary, fossil filled rocks.

I would now like to take the time to point out what we call mass graveyards. Agate Springs, in Northwest Nebraska, is the site of one such graveyard on the top of a hill covering about 10 acres. First discovered in 1876, this hill contained the bones of an estimated 9,000 complete animals, including rhinoceroses, camels, giant wild boars, and many other types. What could bring together herbivores, carnivores, mammals, birds, plant remains, sea shells, and fish of all sizes to this lonely hilltop? Could it be Noah's Flood? Alfred Rehwinkel believes this is the only answer: "A great flood of water is the only reasonable explanation for this strange phenomenon. . . One can see the terrified and panic-stricken beasts stampeding to higher ground and to the hilltops before the onrushing Flood. The lion took no heed of the lamb, nor the wolf of the hare; all were bent on saving their own lives. . . But one by one these mouths were stopped as the waters of the Flood overtook them, until at last even the tallest and strongest succumbed. . .The earth opened its mouth and swallowed them. . .and there the Almighty has preserved them for a memorial and a warning that generations of men yet to follow may behold and learn that the Lord, our God, is a jealous God, visiting the iniquity of the fathers upon the children unto the third and fourth generation of them that hate Him" (Rehwinkel, pp. 183-187).

Why Human Bones and Dinosaur Bones are not Found Together

There seem to be a number of disagreements among creationists and evolutionists regarding man living with dinosaurs. Abundant evidence suggests that the two were coexistent; however, we do not get to hear of this evidence for a number of reasons. Those cases in which we do hear, the evolutionary assumption of an old earth and the problematic radioisotope dating skew the results to fit the evolutionary bias.

Von Fange argues three main issues of why dinosaurs and humans are not found together: 1) Ecological differences between man and dinosaur, 2) fear of losing your career, and 3) the circular reasoning of the dating methods (Von Fange, pp. 46-47). Regarding the ecological differences, we certainly wouldn't say that tigers and deer never lived together at the same time just because they live in different climatic areas of the earth. Therefore, perhaps because of geographical differences as well, man and dinosaur are not found together. I believe this is a poor argument, although nonetheless possible. I believe man indeed lived with dinosaurs, and there is vast evidence to suggest that they did live in the same geographical area, as we will discuss further in the next chapter.

Another major factor of man/dinosaur separation is the fear of losing your career. I will add to this the fact that evolution is a belief held together by faith as well. To explain, if a devout evolutionist would find a dinosaur bone lying directly on top of a man, he would almost certainly explain the evidence away (as we will discuss in point number three) or discard it completely, because he would become a laughing stock among his colleagues, not to mention that he may be shunned just for entertaining this thought. This seems harsh, but it is the same thing Christians do in arguing their faith. If a Christian had a dog and woke up the next morning with a dat (half dog, half cat) he probably wouldn't want to share this information for fear of hurting Christianity, being kicked out of the church, or losing his friends and family. We are all biased; it is just a matter of which bias is the best bias of which to be biased. In the next chapter we will see a real life example of such defending of the faith from both sides.

Probably the most far-reaching issue, however, is the deceitful twisting of evidence in order to make the outcome fit the presupposition. All fossils are dated by the rocks in which they are found, and the rocks are then dated by the same fossils. This dating process means that if dinosaur bones and cow bones were found together, they would automatically be dated millions of years apart just because of the assumption of evolution. Tom Kemp, an evolutionist, admits this process is a dubious practice when he states, "A circular argument arises: Interpret the fossil record in the terms of a particular theory of evolution, inspect the interpretation, and note that it confirms the theory. Well, it would, wouldn't it?" (Kemp, p. 67). In addition, Niles Eldridge writes, "This poses something of a problem: If we date the rocks by the fossils, how can we then turn around and talk about patterns of evolutionary change through time in the fossil record?" (Eldridge, p. 52). But let's say that we did find dinosaur and cow bones right next to each other, how could you say they were two different ages of rocks? Simple- if it looks as if the majority of the area is very old, the cow bones are called intrusive, meaning they fell in a hole which led down to the dinosaur bones. If the majority of the area or other bones seem to be young, then the dinosaur bones are said to be redeposited with the cow bones. This means that a flood or some other earth moving process carried these bones to this location; the dinosaur didn't really die there. With this reasoning, we know we won't find humans and dinosaurs in coexistence, no matter how many human bones we would find riding the dinosaurs.

CHAPTER 8
DINOSAURS

Are Dinosaurs Really Extinct?

In 1977, the crew of a Japanese fishing boat named Zuiyo Maru was fishing near New Zealand. When they pulled up their nets from a depth of 900 feet, they were amazed to see a creature about 32 feet long and weighing around 4,000 pounds. Even more impressive than the size was the fact that it looked almost exactly like a plesiosaur. The fishermen did not know for sure what it was, but it had been dead for only a short while before

Figure 23: An unknown creature captured in fishing nets in 1977. Note the scales that run along its back.

they caught it in their nets, so it had a terrible stench and was oozing all over. Fearing it would spoil their previous catch of fish, as well as the fact that the smell was making them ill, they took pictures, bone and flesh samples and threw it back overboard with attached buoys, in hopes of later finding it. Needless to say, the scientists who later saw the pictures were not pleased that they left this behind, and they sent out a number of other vessels to try to find this creature again. One scientist said, "It seems that these animals [*Plesiosaurs*] are not extinct after all. It is impossible for only one to have survived. There must be a group" (Gish Dinosaur, p. 86). This remarkable story, as well as others we will discuss, does leave open the question of dinosaur extinction. All over the world there have been reports of strange, giant animals, many of their descriptions matching that of a *Plesiosaurus* or a *Mosasaurus*. However, I suspect that these great creatures are indeed dead, but as earlier mentioned, we cannot even keep track of the animals alive on land, let alone in the water (which covers 70% of the earth), so I wouldn't be totally surprised if one is discovered.

In 1976, a Navy ship accidentally snagged a 15 foot long creature with seven rows of teeth, now known as the Megamouth Shark. Previously, no one new such an animal existed. Now as recent as 1990, a live Megamouth was caught in a swordfish net north of San Diego.

In July of 1915, a German U-boat captain recorded seeing an estimated 60 foot long, crocodile shaped creature with webbed feet and a long tail tapering to a point. He was able to witness this after a torpedoed World War I British Steamer sank under water and exploded. Shortly after, this animal shot into the air 60 to 100 feet struggling and throwing its body all around. It wasn't long before it went under water, never to be seen again (Gish Dinosaur, pp. 85- 86).

The famous Greek historian Herodotus records seeing a live creature, which when described sounds just like *Rhamphorhynchus*. He also later found fresh bones of the same animal in Egypt (Parker, Dinosaurs).

Another encounter of man and dinosaur occurred on May 13th, 1572, when an Italian peasant heard a hissing sound coming from the bushes. He killed the animal and took it to a biology professor who dissected and recorded everything about this creature. Now, with further fossil evidence, we see that what this man saw was the dinosaur called *Tanastophia*.

The natives in the Northern Congo claim that there is a great creature they call Mokele Mbembe that roams somewhere in the seven and one-half million acres of swamp and dense jungle. This area is so remote and difficult to walk through, even the pygmies seldom venture there. When shown pictures of various dinosaurs, they identified Mokele Mbembe as looking most like an *Apatasaurus*.

Again, on April 26th, 1890, an article was found in the newspaper, *Tombstone Epitaph*, which told of two cowboys in the desert outside of Tombstone, Arizona. These men saw a huge flying creature with tremendous wings, a long slim body, and claws on both feet and wings. After shooting it they found that it had a wing membrane like that of a bat, a head similar to an alligator about 8 feet long, protruding eyes, and a mouth full of teeth. This incredible story fits the description of the *Quetzalcoatlus*, a member of the *Pteranodon* family, of which a fossil was found in Texas in 1972 (Gish dinosaurs, pp. 16-17).

Are dinosaurs extinct? Who knows, maybe time will tell.

Did Dinosaurs and Man Live at the Same Time?

Two things we need to examine in answering this question are Biblical and fossil evidences. I often ask people if dinosaurs are mentioned in the Bible and usually get both yes and no answers. They are both right. The word "dinosaur" does not appear in the Bible, but dinosaurs are talked about. The

Figure 24: Evidence suggests that horned dinosaurs may have blown fire like Leviathan in Job 41.

word dinosaur isn't in Scripture because the word never existed until 230 years after the Bible was translated into English (1611). Not until 1841 did Sir Richard Owen call the recently found fossils, dinosaurs, meaning "terrible lizards."

However, the word, dragon is mentioned in the Bible. Genesis tells us God created great "sea creatures," which in the original Hebrew (*tannin*) translates as "dragon" (Genesis 1:21). In fact, this same Hebrew word is used almost a dozen times in other parts of Scripture where it is translated as "dragon." This would explain the hundreds of legends about dragons all over the world. In fact, many historians believe that legends are actually history, although at times embellished. Henry Morris believes legends are no more than the passing down of oral records and traditions from one generation to the next (Morris, Record, p. 69). Consider the Tower of Babel. When everyone was separated, these stories of actual events, now considered to be fairy tales, went with them. Two legends which literally overrun the world are that of a great Flood killing all but one family and the stories of dragons, many of them fire breathing.

Archaeological digs have discovered that Nebuchadnezzar had a dragon called Sirrush carved into the Ishtar Gate of Babylon.

Maybe you have heard of St. George and the dragon. This story takes place somewhere around AD 250 to 300, at which time a ferocious dragon lived in a nearby lake. The breath of the dragon was said to have poisoned the entire countryside. In order to content this unwanted neighbor, the local people had to feed it two sheep daily. Eventually they ran out of sheep, so the dragon began feeding on the people until there weren't many of them left either. One day, an angry mob tied the king's daughter to a post and waited for the dragon. It just so happened that St. George came along and saw this woman tied up, so he released her and faced the dragon himself. In his bravery, he killed the dragon with his lance and gave all credit of this success to Christ. As a result, all the townspeople were baptized as Christians. We do know as fact that St. George was a real person who was martyred on April 23, 303, because of his faith. In 1350, he was made a patron saint of England and was highly respected by the Crusaders (Gish Dinosaurs, p. 80-81). Perhaps this legend was true after all.

As mentioned, many legends and fairy tales (Puff, the magic dragon) have dragons blowing fire. This must be part of the embellished part of a legend, right? Maybe not. We read from the Holy Bible, "Can you pull in the leviathan with a fishhook. . . or pierce his jaw with a hook? . . . Can you make a pet of him like a bird or put him on a leash . . . Can you fill his hide with harpoons or his head with fishing spears? If you lay a hand on him, you will remember the struggle and never do it again! Any hope of subduing him is false; the mere sight of him is overpowering. . .. I will not fail to speak of his limbs, his strength and his graceful form. Who can strip off his outer coat? . . . Who dares open the doors of his mouth, ringed about with his fearsome teeth? His back has rows of shields tightly sealed together; each is so close to the next that no air can pass between. . .. His snorting throws out flashes of light; his eyes are like the rays of dawn. Firebrands stream from his mouth; sparks of fire shoot out. Smoke pours from his nostrils . . . His breath sets coals ablaze, and flames dart from his mouth" (Job 41:1-21). Is the Bible filled with legends as well? Certainly not! The Bible says it, so I believe it; that should be the motto of every Christian on earth today. But so many times when what Scripture says doesn't fit our minuscule human wisdom and reasoning, we automatically throw it out, explain it away, or call it figurative. NO! NO! NO! We can never interpret the Bible from the words of man, who wasn't there and who doesn't know everything. Let every man hear the Word of God as He spoke to Job, "Where were you when I laid the earth's foundation? Tell me, if you understand" (Job 38:4). The Bible says it, I believe it.

Even though we shouldn't need scientific evidence to substantiate such a thing, the evidence is there. Alive today is an amazing creature called the bombardier beetle. Though only about 1/2 inch long, this animal really packs a punch (pop may be a better word) because without a moment's notice, the beetle can shoot out its hind end a nauseous gas over 212 degrees Fahrenheit. Remarkably, it never misses its target. The force of this "explosion" is strong enough that a pop can be heard when the beetle fires. How does it do it? Inside the beetle's body are stored chemicals, one of which is hydrogen peroxide, and when these chemicals are mixed together and come in contact with oxygen in the air - - kaboom!

An interesting fact about some dinosaurs in the fossil record, such as the *parasaurolophus* and the *pteranodon*, is that they have these unusual hollow, bony structures on the backs of their heads. There is much speculation regarding their use but, in general, scientists don't know the purpose of those bony structures. Probably the most popular theory is that it was a type of horn in order to make noise (Begley, p. 50). However, as some scientists have suggested, these hollow structures could have been used as storage chambers for chemicals similar to those in the bombardier beetle. When these chemicals came into contact with the higher oxygen content of the early atmosphere (LA Times, 1995) . . . kaboom! Further evidence is displayed in the fact that these hollow chambers actually lead directly down to the nostrils, where if you recall, "Smoke goes out of his [Leviathan] nostrils" (Job 41:20). We have chemicals today that, by themselves, combust when introduced to oxygen; therefore a creature like Leviathan in Job is possible.

One last example from Scripture comes from an earlier chapter of Job, where we read of a creature named Behemoth who has a tail like a Cedar tree. If you read Bible commentaries you will know that these "human footnotes" say that the animal talked about here is an elephant or a hippo. Have you seen the tail of either one of these modern day animals? Their tails are more like toothpicks, not trees. Some then try to say it is an alligator, but the problem then

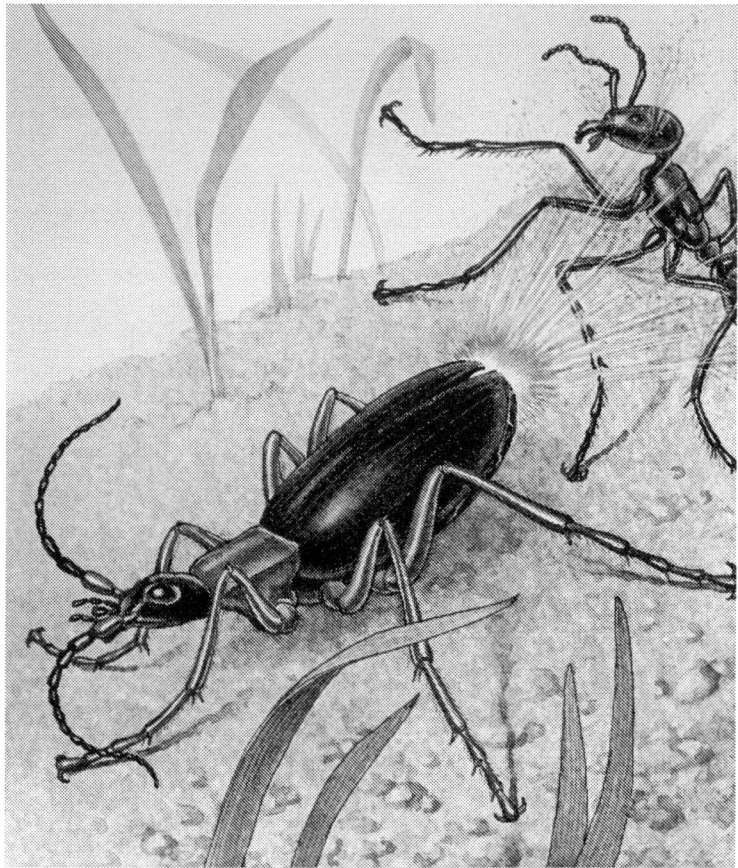

Figure 25: The bombardier beetle can shoot out its back end a noxious gas over 212 degrees Fahrenheit.

is that Job says Behemoth eats grass like an ox. Why do we always have to explain Scripture in the context of today's world? There are a number of animals now extinct that this animal could very likely be; two of them are the *Diplodocus* and *Brachiosaurus*. Yes, dinosaurs are in the Bible, to God be the glory!

We now know what Scripture states; what about the fossil record? Before going into this subject, we must recall from earlier chapters that according to evolution and the scientific practices thereof, man and dinosaurs never lived together, even when their bones are found together. They are either overlooked, thrown out, called intrusive or redeposited, and dates from dating methods are occasionally not "selected" to be used. So in this section we can only provide evidence which has been found, but explained away by the faith of evolution. However, before condemning the evolutionists, understand that creationists do the same thing. While lecturing I have come across a number of people who have gone so far as to deny the existence of dinosaurs because they felt they were not Biblical and, therefore, they had to defend their faith. Likewise, I have visited with expert paleontologists who deny the existence of possible human footprints with dinosaurs. I have seen these human-like footprints and dinosaur bones, and there is no question about the existence of either, but both sides feel the need to defend their faith. Remember, evolution is not science; it's a religion. It is this author's opinion, and many others, that this is concrete and valid evidence which supports the Biblical account of creation exactly - - man and dinosaurs were created on day five and six of creation (day five were swimming and flying dinosaurs, while day six were land dinosaurs).

EVOLUTION IS RELIGION

Figure 26: The creation evolution debate is not science, it's a battle of faith. (reprinted by permission of *Answers in Genesis*, PO Box 6330, Florence, Kentucky, 41022, from the Book <u>The Lie: Evolution</u> by Ken Ham).

Over 100 years ago, two dinosaur bones were found, displaying cuts at regular intervals that appeared to be from a flint knife. In discussing this find, the author notes that if these bones were from a mammal, nobody would have questioned that humans made these marks (VI, 1889 23:209). Capellini also described cut bones, tools and skulls found in a Pliocene bed (5-7 Million) looking very modern. As a result, the discovery was thrown out and ruled impossible (VI: 1886, 20:89).

The May, 1997, issue of *Creation* magazine also showed pictures of Inca or pre-Inca artifacts with engraved images of what clearly appear to be a *T. Rex* and *Triceratops*. These stones are a smooth andesite (volcanic) rock with desert sand deeply encrusted over even some of the engraved areas, suggesting it is an authentic artifact. Further, it even has a film of oxidization over it.

In the San Rafael Swell in Utah is a carving of something looking like a pterosaur (flying reptile) that was found carved on the rocks. Interestingly enough, the University of Ohio found a fossil *Pteranodon* not far from this site (*Creation* 1997).

Figure 27: Stone art that appears to be a dinosaur.

Even more surprising for evolutionists is the fact that recently, actual dinosaur bones have been found in Alaska (not fossilized). There are literally tons of them found falling out of the ice. If dinosaurs went extinct 65 million years ago, these bones have been frozen at least that long, which is an unlikely event even under evolutionary thinking (*Creation*, Aug, 1997, p. 49). On the same lines, Mary Schweitzer of Montana State University has isolated a heme molecule in hemoglobin (carries oxygen in red blood cells) from a *T. Rex* bone. If this is confirmed, molecular biologists readily admit such a thing could not survive for millions of years and, therefore, would disrupt evolutionary theories of dinosaur extinction; at least it should, but probably will not (*Science News*, Nov, 1995 p. 314). Even after the latest studies it is appearing as if it is indeed hemoglobin. Upon asking the renown Jack Horner about this possibility he suggested that Mary not try to prove that it was hemoglobin in the dinosaur bones but rather try to prove that it wasn't. Mary states, "So far, we haven't been able to" (M. Schweitzer, 1997).

Many human-like footprints have been found contemporary with dinosaur tracks, but this evidence has fallen prey to much criticism largely because of past memories. In the 1930's many tracks were removed from their

Figure 28: A dinosaur track reportedly found near human footprints.

locations and sold. While dinosaur tracks were in demand, human tracks were not. Unfortunately, some people capitalized on making their own tracks; some of which have been passed on to people today. Most of these tracks have been identified, but skepticism remains. These tracks have been removed from their original location, which automatically compromises their usefulness to science. However, many freshly uncovered tracks remain, while others are being revealed by natural erosion.

In 1987, a human-like footprint known as the Clark print was found in a lower limestone layer and appeared to be crossing the trail of dinosaur tracks. The Clark print was apparently examined by the Dallas Crime Lab Forensic Department, who claimed that it was a real human footprint (Helfinstine, pp.26-27, 94).

Although controversial, another trail of possible human and dinosaur footprints, with many overlapping each other, has been identified as the Taylor trail. Dr. Roth writes, "This amount of evidence leads to the conclusion that the Taylor Trail is a sequence of superimposed human-like footprints over *tridactyl* dinosaur prints up to the last identifiable prints in the trail where the two tracks are side by side" (Helfinstine, p 94). Unfortunately, one of the best tracks was destroyed before casting or much study could be done on it. Who or why would anyone want to destroy evidence of man and dinosaur coexisting?

The Burdick track, another human-like footprint found in the same strata as the saber-toothed tiger and dinosaurs has been sectioned, showing pressure patterns and therefore, some say, authenticity. It should be noted, however, that these pressure patterns are very fine, due to the makeup of the rock in which they are preserved. However, further evidence of its validity comes from calcite crystallization beneath the track, which forms due to pressure. Despite this, some respected creation researchers still question whether or not the Burdick track is indeed genuine (as does this author). At this point there is no way to be sure.

There hasn't yet been a good explanation for these tracks, which appear to be human and contemporary with dinosaurs. I questioned park officials at Dinosaur Valley State Park. Their answer was that a dinosaur stepped down and failed to follow through with his forward motion (And this answer came after two earlier denials from other officials who said the tracks never existed). Years ago, nearly a dozen human like tracks were directly above some *brontosaur* tracks. These tracks were even marked so that those who asked about them could be directed to their position. Now, of course, the park officials claim no knowledge of their existence, even though they still remain there (though much eroded now).

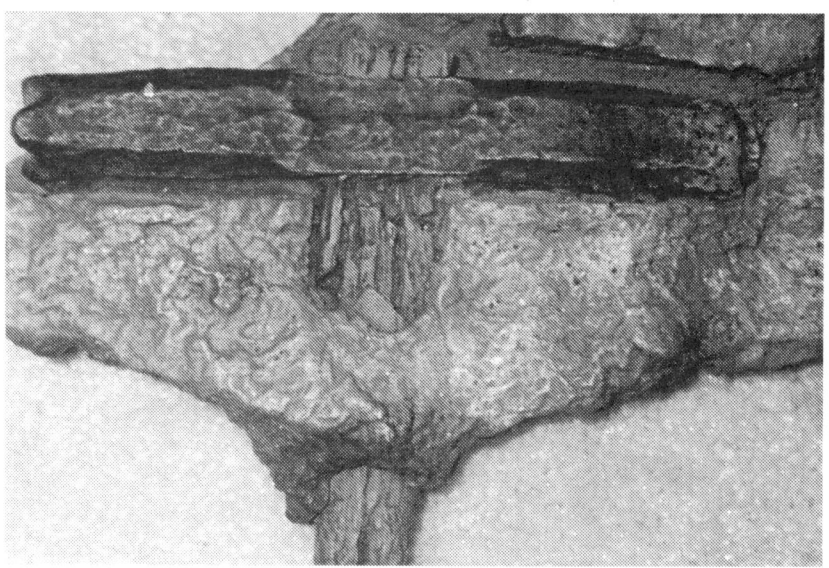

Figure 29: A hammer found in Cretaceous rock

Why so much controversy? In the April, 1974, edition of *National Geographic*, Mary Leakey had found human footprints in East Africa dating 3.6

million years old, according to the uniformitarian methods. It did not take much convincing to show these prints to be human. Why then are the tracks along the Paluxy River in question when many of them have retained their features so much more clearly than those of Mary Leakey. Answered simply, the Paluxy tracks do not fit with evolutionary history. Hundreds of tracks are available for viewing if one knows where to look. Near Glenrose, Texas, the Creation Evidences Museum is able to direct visitors to right locations. Also, John Morris's book, Tracking those Incredible Dinosaurs, outlines detailed maps. This book has now been pulled from publication at the request of Dr. Morris, due to the concern of objective science. Though Dr. Morris has seen human-like footprints along the Paluxy River, he questions the validity of the dinosaur and human tracks found contemporary. It is to hard to prove authentic, and one opens himself up to much debate in arguing this evidence.

The London Artifact, otherwise known as "The Hammer" is an actual man made iron hammer with a wood handle found in Cretaceous rock (144 million years old and at the time of dinosaurs) near London, Texas. Not only did this artifact attest to the coexistence of man and dinosaur, but also to the intelligence of man. When Batelle Lab (same respectable organization that tested the moon rocks) did a Scanning Electron Microprobe elemental analysis (SEM) on this artifact, it was found to be 96.6% iron, 0.74% sulfur and 2.6% chlorine, with no trace of nickel or carbon. This metal does not rust and is homogenous in molecular pattern, giving an equal strength throughout the hammer head. Those who work with metals will know that this is extraordinary. We cannot make metal like this today, especially since we cannot combine chlorine and metallic iron except on a microscopic level; the entire hammer is mixed with chlorine. The amazing capability of man found in this hammer should be no surprise to the Bible student, because all the way back in chapter four of Genesis we see that "Tubal Cain forged all kinds of tools out of bronze and iron" (Genesis 4:22).

As one can see, much evidence is out there showing that man and dinosaur once roamed the earth together, but the faith driven belief system of evolution won't accept the evidence; rather they turn their faces away in pride and ignore not only the scientific evidence but God Himself, and "although they knew God, they neither glorified him as God nor gave thanks to him, but their thinking became futile and their foolish hearts were darkened. Although they claimed to be wise, they became fools" (Romans 1:21-22). Do not fear, however, for "God chose the foolish things of the world to shame the wise; God chose the weak things of the world to shame the strong" (I Corinthians 1:27).

Dinosaurs or Birds?

Millions of people recently paid money to be indoctrinated by the movies Jurassic Park and The Lost World. Many children have come up to me before and after lectures giving me all kinds of information about the infamous Raptor as seen in the movie. However, what these children (and most of the time the parents as well) do not realize is that this movie is not science. For example, you may recall the dinosaur having a skin-like membrane open up shortly before spitting out a blinding mucous. Never has there been any evidence in science that any creature could do such a thing. Unless in rare cases, skin is not preserved in fossilization, and we have never been able to tell what color or what type of skin and cartilage attachments dinosaurs had. Media and artistic license has given us the impression that scientists are just short of God, fitting the pieces of the past into a nice, neatly finished puzzle. In fact, so much speculation is involved that if average people knew how much of the puzzle was put together from only a few pieces, they would shake their heads in disgust. Here are a couple of the larger assumptions. If a child asks what is the heaviest dinosaur, the answer would probably be *Ultrasaurus*, a close relative to the Brachiosaur (maybe the same thing). It is estimated that this animal weighed from 45 to 55 tons (A blue whale can weigh up to 200 tons). But even more fascinating is that the pictures and facts of this creature all stem from only ONE CRUSHED VERTEBRATE. That is all that has ever been found. Likewise, the longest dinosaur, *Supersaurus*, comes from ONE scapula. And the well known *Seismosaurus*, three vertebrate and a leg (London Museum of Natural History). How do they find so many pieces of the puzzle from so few? The bones they do find are very large and, therefore, they use scaling ratios for size. Then, because the bone looks to be in the sauropod family and similar to a *Brachiosaur*, they make him look like *Brachiosaurus*. Ken Ham notes that out of the hundreds of dinosaur kinds, some evolutionists believe that there may actually only be less than 50; the others are simply different sizes of the same thing (Ham, What Happened to the Dinosaurs). Not all dinosaurs revolve around so many assumptions, but as you will see from the examples below, behavior patterns and evolution may be based on even more assumptions than listed here.

There is a "hidden" message at the end of the movie Jurassic Park. When the helicopter is flying away from the island, a flock of birds are seen and the main scientist shows a little satisfactory smile. The reason for this is because one of the current theories, and perhaps one of the most widely accepted, is that dinosaurs never went extinct, they evolved into birds. It was no coincidence that the raptor of Jurassic Park walked and sounded like a bird either.

Jack Horner, Curator of the Museum of the Rockies in Montana and one of the people Jurassic Park was modeled after, had done major work with the duckbilled dinosaurs, especially *Maiasaura* (meaning good mother). Horner has found nests with 15 fossilized babies of all ages, a fossilized embryo, over 300 whole or partial eggs, over 60 whole or partial skeletons of all ages, and nine nests with egg shell fragments. The reason *Maiasaura* got its name is that the nests were only spaced about the distance of one adult away. This supposedly shows they "nested in flocks" similar to birds. Since many of the eggs had been broken, it suggests that the babies stayed in the nest rather than just hatching and leaving, which again is cited as showing bird characteristics.

Another example of dinosaur to bird assumptions goes back to the 1920's, when there was a major search for dinosaurs near Mongolia in a Cretaceous area. The search paid off with 101 *protoceratops*, only four theropods (meat eaters), and numerous eggs. Naturally, since there were so many eggs and so many *protoceratops* they assumed *protoceratops* laid eggs. Later, it was discovered that one of these meat eaters was on a nest of eggs and, therefore, assumed that it was eating the eggs. Since *protoceratops* must have laid these eggs, they named this dinosaur *Oviraptor*, meaning egg eater. Later still, however, a find of eggs with embryos showed baby *Oviraptors* inside and, therefore, this creature wasn't trying to eat the eggs, rather to incubate them. This made sense because of the fact that the *Oviraptors* are supposedly closely related to birds. It was stated that the egg shells were birdlike in structure, similar to ostrich eggs. Also, they found two very young raptor skulls with teeth like those of birds in the same time era. These baby teeth are said to be replaced by knifelike teeth when older.

Recently as well, *Tyrannosaurus Rex* has received a new posture with a backbone parallel to the ground. While once a tail dragging, ferocious predator, *T. Rex* has now been demoted to a wimpy, bent over, scavenger with big teeth. One reason for this change is that the footprints of *T-Rex* show no evidence of a dragging tail. Secondly, as *Newsweek* noted, "The new pose emphasizes the close relationship between the Mesozoic dinosaurs and modern birds" (Begley, p.58). This same article also called this new positioning a "stalking pose," even though many scientists believe that *T-Rex* was a scavenger. Some have stated that the small arms of this dinosaur wouldn't be strong enough to hold on to its prey, let alone defend itself. However, new evidence based upon the only complete arm ever found, suggests that these small arms could lift the equivalent of a half dozen people (BSN, p. 15). Despite this new evidence, however, I suspect that *T-Rex* may still have been a scavenger and maybe even a plant eater. Originally, both man and animals were created as vegetarians (Genesis 1:29-30) and the teeth of *T-Rex* may support this belief. Fossil teeth of this monster are around six inches long but they are only embedded about an inch into the jawbone (Parker, Dinosaurs). This doesn't give much support to tear away at meat, let alone to hang onto prey while it is struggling about. For years we have had the misconception that an animal with big, sharp teeth must eat meat. But there are plenty of animals alive today, such as the fruit bat (with wingspans of four feet) and the koala bear, which have sharp canines yet do not eat meat.

Archaeopteryx, which has previously been discussed, has nothing in common with dinosaurs, yet because evolutionists need a connection between reptile and bird, they make themselves see what they want to see.

The point of all this is that science keeps changing because of previous assumptions being proven wrong with subsequent evidences. Over and over the evolutionary ideas seem to swing back toward what creationists have been saying all along (but usually in a different time frame). I don't believe creationists have all the scientific answers, but in many cases we remain one step ahead in trying to determine the past by basing our assumptions on the Bible, which is truth. Sometimes the Bible doesn't tell us all we would like to know, but it certainly points us in the right direction. But how can our children tell the difference between assumption and science? By being trained in Scripture! Evolution is one big assumption, but yet is taught as fact. While we wait for more evidence to surface in opposition to evolution, (and it does) our children fall further and further from the inerrancy of Scripture.

What Really Happened to the Dinosaurs?

There are many theories as to what may have caused the possible extinction of dinosaurs, with most of them simply consisting of the best fairy tale that can be made up. Some scientists have actually proposed "scientifically" that a plant caused the dinosaurs to become constipated to the point of death. Others have said that caterpillars ate all the leaves on the trees. My personal favorite is that the temperature became so warm that the males became sterile and couldn't reproduce (this has been called the "tight shorts" phenomena). There are literally hundreds of theories flying around, but, thankfully most don't receive much attention.

One theory that is the most widely accepted may actually fit into the destruction associated with Noah's Flood but, of course, this is also different from the time frame evolution proposes. It is believed that at the Cretaceous/Tertiary boundary on the evolutionary time scale (65 million years ago), a great comet named Chicxulub (meaning devil's tail, but who knows, maybe devil's tale), with a diameter of over 6 miles, hit the earth and created a crater 185 miles in diameter. The crater is completely covered and cannot be seen even from the air, but core samples and gravitational anomalies have identified the site. The claim is that when this comet hit, it released large amounts of carbon dioxide and sulfuric acid into the atmosphere causing, a green house effect. This result didn't have much effect until the dust, which blocked out the sun for a period of time, had settled. The interesting thing is there is evidence that soot and fire burned an estimated 25% of the biomass. Mammals, able to withstand temperature changes better, survived, while the dinosaurs died out.

The consensus is that this led to the final end of dinosaurs, but there is debate as to whether or not the dinosaurs were already in decline, making this perhaps the final blow. I would say most favor the fact that they were in decline, because of vast evidence that near the end of the Cretaceous there was vast environmental degradation, perhaps due to the curse found in Genesis or Noah's Flood.

For the sake of room and not getting too scientific, I feel the need to mention only one major problem with this theory. Recently, a comet hitting Jupiter received a lot of media attention. Well, we haven't heard much more about this shaking news, perhaps because it has now been seen that it didn't produce the expected effects. As always with science today, there are a vast number of assumptions made that now seem to be false, and the impact of this comet (if in fact it did occur) would not have produced near the "earth shattering" predictions made. This problem alone pretty well defeats this theory.

Obviously this theory is filled with problems and it isn't quite as simple as I have made it, but the interesting thing is that the evidence presented by evolutionists in defense of their theory fits what creationists believe occurred;

namely, environmental degradation. The Bible gives many indications of global changes and perhaps fire and brimstone, in some cases, describes meteorites slamming to the ground. We simply cannot say for sure. But we do know that the curse, the Flood, and something at the time of Peleg, altered the earth entirely. Even some evolutionists believe evidence fits a flood of great size, they just won't call it the Flood of Noah. Richard Carington writes, "Of the many kinds of animals inhabiting the earth at the time, vast numbers were swept completely away. Not only individuals but whole races were destroyed, an extermination overtook the animals of land, sea and air with equal indifference, when the holocaust was over the whole aspect of life on earth had changed" (Carington, p. 155). John Horner, another evolutionist writes, "Judging from the concentration of bones in various pits, there were over 30 million fossil fragments in that area, at a conservative estimate we have discovered to the tune of 10,000 dinosaurs. *There was a flood*, this was not an ordinary spring flood from one of the streams in the area but a catastrophic inundation. That's our best explanation, it seems to make sense and on the basis of it, we believe that this was a living breathing group of dinosaurs destroyed in one catastrophic moment" (Horner, p. 131 emphasis added). This too would explain why millions of fish have been found fossilized with eyes bulging and fins upright in a state of horror as they were buried beneath tons of sediments (Miller, p. 221); and why an 80 foot whale was deposited and fossilized on its tail (C & EN, Oct. 11, 1976). These are evidences which are not explained by the comet theory.

While other evidence of a Flood (not a comet) has been seen in earlier chapters, we have not yet talked about the atmosphere. This alone may have had a lot to do with the extinction of many animals. In this chapter we will not go into great detail about the pre-Flood atmosphere (We will cover this in the chapter "The 'Very Good' Pre-Flood World") but will mention only the differences involved.

There is evidence that may support a pre-Flood atmosphere (before the protective canopy collapsed) having higher air pressure, higher oxygen, higher carbon dioxide, less solar radiation, subtropical climate year round all over the earth, and a higher electromagnetic field, all of which would contribute to longer life span as the Bible indicates. When the Flood comes, however, the firmament which God had placed in the sky collapsed, thereby altering all of the above mentioned. The dinosaurs may not have been able to properly adjust to the harsher climate with less vegetation and food. However, dealing with the past leaves us with mere speculations in the present and, therefore, this requires much more research.

Some scientists believe that dinosaurs such as *Seismosaurus* and *T- Rex* would not be able to live in today's atmosphere because their rib cage was far too small to support a lung large enough to get oxygen to the deep inner cells of such a large body (Anderson). The same problem is presented with the extremely long necks of other dinosaurs as well. How could they get blood to carry oxygen all the way up to the brain with only one heart pumping? Again, scientists have all kinds of answers from multi-valved hearts and multi-hearts, to keeping their head down most of the time. All of these theories present problems; however, the Flood model and its canopy clears things right up. With a little more oxygen combined with more air pressure, the body would be able to assimilate the needed oxygen much easier and more efficiently.

Other creationists believe that dinosaurs may simply have been hunted to extinction. The Bible suggests that the hunting was abused. "Any Israelite or any alien living among you who hunts any animal or bird that may be eaten must drain out the blood and cover it with earth" (Leviticus 17:13). There were certainly those capable, as Gen. 10:9 speaks of Nimrod as "a mighty hunter before the LORD." We have in some museums great buffalo, much larger than those seen today, with arrowheads in their skull. Even the woolly mammoth was hunted and killed on numerous occasions (Parker, Dinosaur). In fact, evolutionists used to think that mammoths went extinct 40,000 years ago, but when flint spear points were found in mammoth bones they had to rethink their theory and alter it a bit (Bowser, 1983). Also, the Anasazi Indians, who lived in the southwest U.S. around 150 BC to 1200 AD, drew pictures of mammoths on the rocks that are still seen today (Campbell, p.117). While entertaining this theory, we must remember that the average size of the dinosaur in the fossil record was that of chicken to lamb; however, there would have been those too large to kill, as Job 41 pointed out earlier. Keep in mind, however, that Job was written after the Flood and, therefore, dinosaurs made it on the Ark as "two of every kind" of animal were taken. This will be discussed further in the chapter on Noah's Ark.

Our answer, of course, cannot be found (ever) because we were not there to observe what happened, but the Bible gives abundant support of a changed climate and atmosphere, as later chapters explain. These changes would provide adequate cause for the extinction of dinosaurs. The evidence used to support evolutionary theories again seems to show what Scripture has said all along, yet the evolutionists still will not concede to the time frame given in Scripture, nor will they admit the events, such as the Flood. This is not to say that all evolutionary assumptions themselves always fit the Bible, but rather that much evidence used to support these theories supports the Bible. We close with how Ken Ham answers the question of "What happened to the dinosaurs?" They died!

CHAPTER 9
FOSSILS: "HUMANLY" SPEAKING

Examining the Evidence

According to evolutionary theory, man has evolved from an ape ancestry anywhere from 5 to 30 million years ago, depending on various "experts." Never has an intermediate form ever been found; man always appears suddenly and fully formed in the fossil record. Almost all are interested in their origin, and perhaps this is why anytime anything is found the press jumps all over it. We have heard of such creatures as Neanderthal man, Nebraska man, Lucy and more. But is this evidence that man has come from ape? Let us examine this evidence and you decide.

First, to give some background of human evolution we need to look at Sir Wilford Clark, a British anthropologists who studied primates and the tree shrew. Noticing similarities, he theorized that they must be related and publicly claimed that humans not only go back to ape, but even further back to the tree shrew. Today, this idea has been popularized in the scholarly world, although we hear very little about it outside of the scientific communities. After the first primates developed from the tree shrew, they turned into monkeys, then to apes, then to people (*Homo sapien*). Primates are classified by having: 1) grasping hands, 2) a poor sense of smell but keen sight and hearing, and 3) a somewhat large brain (three times larger than an ape). Therefore, humans are called primates along with the monkeys and lemurs.

Regarding the absence of transitional forms, A. J. Kelso writes, "The transition from insectivore to primate is not documented by fossils. The basis of knowledge about the transition is by inference from living forms" (Kelso, p. 142). Dr. Camel, in the July 22, 1966, edition of *Science* magazine, also declared that there was no relationship between the tree shrew and primates. In fact, Dr. R.D. Martin studied the maternal behavior of both the shrew and primate. He believed that if they were related there should be similarities, but he found none. The primate mother spends lots of time with her young, while the shrew only spends about 10 minutes of every 48 hours with hers, and that is just to feed it. His conclusion: The general consensus reflects no evidence of the two being related.

Next, the lemur-like creatures are said to have evolved into monkeys. There are two types of monkeys: Old World (narrow nosed) and New World (broad nosed). Both are generally considered to have separate origins. But as a creationist would expect, both turn up abruptly in the fossil record. Kelso writes regarding the New World monkeys, "The details of the evolutionary background of the New World monkeys, the platyrrinae, would doubtless be informative and interesting, but unfortunately we know very little about them" (Kelso, p 150). Also concerning the Old World monkeys, Kelso states, "Clearly the fossil documentation of the emergence of the Old World monkeys could provide key insights into the general evolutionary picture of the primates but, in fact, this record simply does not exist" (Kelso, p151). It looks like another dead end in tracing back the evolutionary line of either monkey.

Next come the apes from the monkeys. Apes such as the gibbon spend much of their time in trees swinging from the branches, which is why they have such long arms and short legs. When on the ground they are habitually upright (the only ape which is) but seldom go to the ground because of the uncomfortable position. However, all apes are quadrupeds, walking on all fours. Of course humans are bipedal. The chimpanzee, gorilla and other apes can walk upright but do so for only short distances and are habitually knuckle walkers, just as they appear in the fossil record.

From ape, supposedly came man. Somehow millions of years ago, either from one common ancestor or from separate individuals of isolated groups, man developed into what he is today. All the animals in this human line are said to be hominids. This line goes from *Hominidae* (20 million years ago); to *Ramapithecus* (10-17 million years ago, but now removed as possible missing link); to *Australopithecus* (1-4 million); to *Homo erectus*, involving Java and Peking Man (.5-1.5 million); to *Homo sapien*, involving Neanderthal, Cro-magnon and modern man (100,000 years). This being the case, there should be hundreds of intermediates where ape begins walking upright, the brain enlarges and the face structure changes. Where are they? From here on out we will examine this line of Hominidae.

Physically, the jaw of ape and man are quite different; unfortunately, when fragments of bones are found, there is a lot of room for interpretations according to what one would like to see. An ape jaw is in a "U" shape, with large incisors and a gap between them and the canine teeth. The pallet of man is in a parabola shape, which can easily be brought together to form a "U" if only fragmentary. In the 1960's, *Ramapithecus* was claimed to be an upright walker based upon only fragments of a jaw. (Wow!) A picture that stood in the Chicago Museum of Man only about 25 years ago showed *Ramapithecus* as a hairy ape-like creature, but of course, upright and having many man-like characteristics. Later, in the 70's, *Ramapithecus* was again reconstructed by Peter Andrews and Alan Walker based upon more complete findings and showed more ape-like features. Based on the cranial skeleton and face, Walker notes it is an orangutan and not in the line of modern man.

In 1924, Raymond Dart found a baby *Australopithecus* skull in South Africa. The skull was typical of ape but the teeth were more man-like and, therefore, Dart reasoned it to be an intermediate. At first even most evolutionists rejected this theory, but as time went on it generally became accepted. Later, in 1959, Louis and Mary Leakey found another *Australopithecus* skull in East Africa. It was grossly ape-like with big brows, hardly any forehead and a big crest on top of the head.

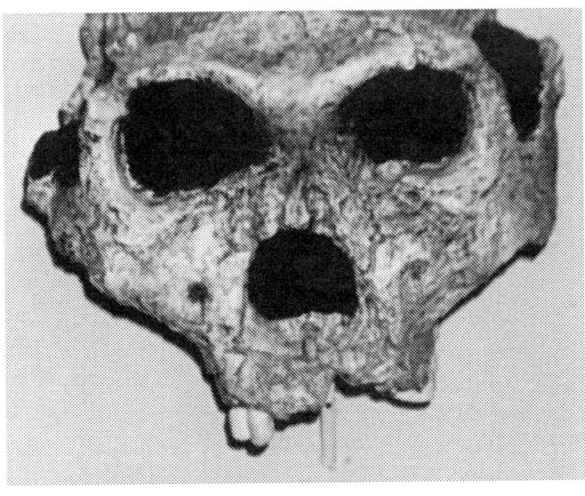

Figure 30: Australopithecus skull.

In 1974, Donald Johansen discovered 40% of a skeleton called "Lucy" (named so because it seemed to be a woman) in Ethiopia and named it *Australopithecus oferensus*. Dr. Johansen became famous practically overnight by claiming Lucy walked upright but was ape-like from the neck up. The reconstructed skull of Lucy was again grossly ape-like, and the consensus of textbooks and *National Geographic* was that she was man's ancestor. However, reputable people disagree. In fact, once Lucy was discovered Johansen would not let anybody look at the bones for years (meanwhile he became famous). After nearly a decade, he finally released the bones and upon examination most scholars concluded Johansen was wrong. Even the long famous Leakeys deny Lucy to be an intermediate. Lord Zuckerman, an evolutionist and head of the Department of Anatomy at the University of Burmingham, studied these remains for over a decade with highly trained staff and technical equipment. The consensus among them was that Lucy was not an intermediate. Also, Charles Oxnard, professor of anatomy and biology at the University of Australia, after examining these bones with the most sophisticated computer analysis, removed Lucy from the list of man's ancestors (Buckna, p. 7). Now, depending upon the artist, we can find pictures of this creature looking like an ape or an extremely hairy woman. In 1995, a biology textbook from Prentice Hall states, "At the present time, scientists cannot agree on how many species of *Australopithecus* there were or whether or not they were ancestors of human beings." In August of 1995, *Australopithecus anamensis* was found in Kenya but it apparently lived at the same time with another prehuman species four million years ago, causing *Worldbook Science Year, 1997* to admit that there are "conflicting interpretations."

Over a century ago a man named Eugene Dubois got the idea that man originated in the East Indies (Indonesia), so he joined the Dutch Army and requested to be placed in the East Indies. For the next two years he spent much time searching but found nothing. Later, in 1890, he was reassigned to Java and within a year he found his "missing link," a skull cap appearing very ape-like with no forehead, flat top and large eyebrow ridges. One year later and 50 feet away he also found a femur (thigh bone). Naturally, he assigned both finds to the same creature, even though the femur was very human-like, and called this "upright intermediate" Java Man (*Homo erectus*). Dubois, obviously because of career reasons, also forgot to mention to the public that with this find he also found two fully human skulls at nearby Wadjak in approximately the same strata layer. Had he made this known, Java man would not have been accepted, so it wasn't until 1920 that he announced the Wadjak skulls (Buckna, p. 6). The interesting thing is that even Dubois himself later admitted this couldn't be an intermediate, and 15 years before his death he called it a giant gibbon (ape).

Peking Man is one of my favorites. In 1922 a single tooth was found near Peking China in a limestone cliff. Upon searching further they later found fragments of jaws, teeth and parts of skulls from over 40 different man and ape individuals (the bones were mysteriously lost however, between 1941 and 1945). Also, other evidence showed humans had been mining limestone at the same site (*Scientific American* p.86-94). But the evolutionists took note of the fact that the skulls had been bashed in from behind in order to eat the brains and, therefore, these intermediates were called cannibals and classified as *Homo erectus*, just as Java Man was. It was said that the hunter was hunted (Gish, Man). Later a Frenchman named Marcellin Boule examined the tools and bone fragments and found the tools to be too complex for these creatures and, therefore, asked the question, "who was the hunter?" In answering his own question, he stated that *Homo sapien* (man) was the hunter. He said besides, you can't have man eating his ancestor, it just wouldn't work. Boule agreed with Dubois and the fact that *Homo erectus* was not an intermediate. Still later, Louis Leakey found *Australopithecus* and *Homo erectus* in the same layer in East Africa; therefore, they could not be relatives. In fact, in the layer beneath he found circular huts and fully formed humans. Like Dubois and Boule, Leakey called this creature a giant gibbon. It is now recognized that Peking Man was a Sinanthropus ape, which is now extinct, perhaps because they were eaten to extinction. Hunters may have brought the heads of these creatures back to their site where they bashed the skulls in so they could eat the brains (Taylor, pp. 234-241). So as Ken Ham says, it wasn't ape-like creature using man-made tools, it was man made tools used on ape-like creature. Peking man wasn't man's ancestor, he was man's lunch. As it turns out, even today in many countries the brains of a monkey are considered to be a delicacy.

Almost everybody has heard of Neanderthal man, who was first found in 1860. An almost complete male was discovered in France in 1908 showing him to be hunched over with large eyebrow ridges. For nearly a century it was thought that Neanderthal man was a "long armed, knuckle dragging, beetle browed, bow legged, stupe shouldered, subhuman intermediate" (Gish, Man).

However, Neanderthal man was eventually found fully human, and it is now known that the hunched over posture was caused by arthritis and rickets (*Nature*, 1970). X-rays of the bones show that they all had rickets, a vitamin D deficiency which causes bones to become soft and deformed. Another cause for this can be cold, damp living conditions (think ice-age). Now Neanderthal is considered to be *Homo sapien* (man). One man once said, regarding the museum pictures of Neanderthal, that if you would just give him a haircut, a bath and put him on the subway, nobody would take a second look. Dr. Gish made the comment that if he was like some people, you wouldn't even need to give him a bath (Gish, Man). Also, Neanderthal had a larger brain capacity (1400 cc to 1600 cc) than we have today. One Neanderthal infant found in a Northern Syrian cave showed both a larger brain size and a high level of cultural sophistication (*Weekend Australian*, 1995). Some of this cultural sophistication was seen in a Slovenian Neanderthal who had a flute made of a bear's thighbone (*Science News*, 1996). Also, a German scientist was "speechless" when he found perfectly preserved wood spears and other artifacts showing a highly sophisticated society (*Sydney Morning Herald*, 1997). **How could an alleged 400,000 year old spear be perfectly preserved?** In the Yearbook of Physical Anthropology, 1996, L.A. Yaroch stated, "the uniqueness of Neanderthals appears to have been exaggerated, . . ." They were completely human.

Recently, Neanderthal DNA was found suggesting they were not human. However, the DNA was recovered from an old human bone that was so filled with the bone disease of rickets, that even his legs had bowed. Only 379 base pairs of this mitochondrial DNA out of 16,500 were found (only 2%). These 379 base pairs differed from human mitochondrial DNA in 27 locations, when modern human DNA should only differ in about 8 locations (out of the 379 base pairs) on average. Therefore it was concluded that Neanderthal was not human. This is a rather premature accusation as modern mitochondrial DNA *can* vary with the differences going beyond that of what was seen in the above 27 distinctions out of 379. Simply put, Neanderthal DNA does not make him nonhuman.

Back in 1937, *Life* magazine showed what was to be called "Piltdown Man," found near Piltdown in 1912. The only thing found were fragments of the jaw and skull. The jawbone appeared ape-like, while the skull and teeth looked human, but very old. It was not until 1950 that this was proven to be a hoax. Someone took a modern jaw bone of an ape and a human skull, treated it with chemicals to make it appear old, altered the teeth to make them look human, and planted the bones in a gravel pit. For almost 40 years this fooled the world's leading "experts." Gish stated that it is amazing how many human features were seen in an ape jaw bone and how many ape-like features were said to be seen in a human skull. *This wasn't a case of "if I didn't see it I wouldn't believe it," but rather "if I didn't believe it I wouldn't have seen it."*

Finally, Nebraska Man appeared looking like an intermediate in the December, 1922, *London News*. The picture showed Nebraska Man with a wife and tools. All of this inferred from the one tooth found in which ape-like characteristics were said to be seen. Isn't Science amazing? In 1925 the

American Museum reaffirmed the authenticity of this find by claiming that never before had a tooth been examined with such scientific scrutiny, and yet the results showed it to be that of prehistoric man. William Gregory and Henry Osborn, the leading men in the field of evolutionary studies, both declared these studies valid. Even the famous Scopes "Monkey Trial" in 1925 used this evidence to support evolution. However, two years after the trial, after the world was once again told an intermediate to man was found and evolution was true, additional bones were discovered showing Nebraska Man to be a PIG! There is even a herd of these wild pigs living today in Paraguay (*Science*, p. 379). See what happens when our preconceived ideas get in the way of science? Gish put it well in saying, "Evolutionists made a man out of a pig and a pig made a monkey out of evolutionists" (Gish, Man). But we must take a sober warning from these events. The *Omaha World Herald* wrote concerning Nebraska Man, "It isn't so much the loss of this tooth's fame which we mourn as it is the loss of our faith in the infallibility of science. If there is so little difference between a pig's tooth and a man's that the one may be mistaken for the other for eight years, aren't there infinite chances for error in the identification of the fossilized fragments out of which such an amazingly strange prehistoric fauna has been recreated for us?" (Sippert Evolution, p.133).

Dr. Duane Gish, in his film on the Origin of Man, quoted Lord Zuckerman, an evolutionist who wrote Beyond the Ivory Tower. In this book Zuckerman had two chapters dealing with the search for man's ancestors where he wrote, "If we exclude the possibility of creation, then obviously man must have evolved from an ape-like creature but if he did, there is absolutely no evidence for it in the fossil record" (Gish, Man). I agree with Dr. Gish and many others; it was special creation.

More recently, molecular anthropology has surfaced to trace human history. However, even here our technology is coming up empty as far as answers are concerned. DNA studies seem to be incompatible with the hypotheses of human origin. Takahata states, "Even with DNA sequence data, we have no direct access to the processes of evolution, so objective reconstruction of the vanished past can be achieved only by creative imagination" (Takahata, p. 344). Clearly, evidence is lacking in this debate. Takahata continues with this remarkable statement: "There are not enough fossil records to answer when, where, and how *H. sapiens* emerged" (Takahata, p. 355). *Time* magazine agrees when they stated back in 1994, "Yet despite more than a century of digging, the fossil record remains maddeningly sparse. With so few clues, even a single bone that doesn't fit into the picture can upset everything. Virtually every major discovery has put deep cracks in the conventional wisdom and forced scientists to concoct new theories, amid furious debate."

Genetic Similarities

Many people argue that evolution must be true because man and chimpanzee are 98.4% genetically identical. For the average student this information seems remarkable and, unfortunately, quite convincing. However, the 1.6% difference makes them biologically light years apart. A large number of evolutionists have now rejected blood, DNA, or other chemical similarities as a relevant argument for evolution (Denton, p. 287-288). The December 4, 1995 issue of *U.S. News & World Report* explained, "We are finding that humans have very, very shallow genetic roots which go back very recently to one ancestor. . . that indicates that there was an origin in a specific location on the globe and then it spread out from there. . .researchers suggest that virtually all modern men - 99.9% of them, says one scientist- are closely related genetically and share genes with one male ancestor, dubbed 'Y-chromosome Adam." For further discussion on this see the chapter on Biogenesis, or *Science* vol. 11 no. 7, 1986 pp. 280-283; *Science* vol. 234 no. 4773, 1986, pp. 194-196.

Why are so Few Human Bones Found?

Using current population standards, the population of an earth which is millions of years old should reflect an incredibly large number of people. The current population increase is almost 2% a year. To be generous, lets assume a 1/2% increase. At this rate it would only take from four to five thousand years to get to the population of the earth today. Evolution says that man was around for at least 100,000 years under the Stone Age conditions before history even started. Today the average is about one generation (25 years) of time to grow up and have children. Dividing this 25 years into the 100,000 year proposal for evolution (which is generous, considering that the harsher Stone Age life would bring the generation age down), we come up with 4,000 generations (Humphry, Evidence Part I). If people have been around for millions of years, as is the current theory most accepted, there should be 10^{8600} people (Morris, Earth, p. 70). Where are all the people?

Creationism does not suggest the absurd number of people in our past to be beyond mathematical possibilities like evolution; however, it has been estimated that at the time of the Flood there could have been up to 350 million people living. Therefore, the population argument serves better for evidence of the Flood rather than a young earth, but the 10^{8600} factor should have indeed produced more human bones. The main point being that a catastrophic event such as the Flood would destroy almost all human flesh.

We must remember that things do not fossilize well unless buried quickly. This would include dinosaurs, fish, and all of the fossil record we have today. Therefore, if these things are fossilized without catastrophic events, which many evolutionists try to say, the 4 billion humans should be represented equally in the fossil record as well. However, accepting Noah's Flood would change things a bit. The following reasons are why most humans would not fossilize:

1) People have the ability to escape floods for a time by swimming, climbing trees, etc. Animals do not have as great an escaping ability

and, therefore, humans would be less likely to be buried rapidly exposing them to bacteria, etc.;

2) Land vertebrates (especially mammals), tend to bloat when they die and, therefore, they would float on top after drowning;

3) Land vertebrates are dismembered much easier, allowing for rapid decay;

4) Human bodies especially have a low fossilization capability, and the water would destroy the soft flesh while preserving mostly hard outer shells;

5) The main goal of the Flood was to destroy mankind;

6) With the incredible amount of Flood sediments around the world, even with 350 million people the probability of finding human fossils is low (Morris, Earth, p. 71).

The above mentioned is why 95% of fossils today are marine invertebrates (mostly shellfish); 4.75% are algae and plants; 0.2375% are other invertebrates, including insects; and the remaining 0.0125% are all of the invertebrates (mostly fish). Of this 0.0125%, 95% of these fossils consist of less than one bone. In addition, most of the mammal bones we do have were deposited during the Ice Age. This speaks loudly of a global Flood (Morris, Earth, p.70).

Did Life Originate on Mars?

There has been a lot of discussion regarding the recently announced "Mars Rock," wondering if life has been found on other planets.

First, let me give you a little background on this find. This meteorite is an igneous rock with a mineral make-up similar to that of Mars. The theory is that about 3.6 billion years ago Mars contained liquid water, which seeped into the cracks of this rock bringing carbon dioxide from the atmosphere with it. About a billion years later, life evolved in this rock and micro-organisms became fossilized in the rock. Then, about 16 million years ago a comet or meteorite hit Mars and caused this rock to be thrown into space. After floating in this vacuum for millions of years, it finally entered earth's atmosphere about 13,000 years ago as a fireball in Antarctica, where it was discovered in 1984.

Some problems surrounding this theory are as follows:

1) The chemicals of this meteorite are said to represent life, yet the same chemicals can also be formed from non-living sources. One scientist even admitted that these "fossils" could be the result of mud or contamination from earth.

2) A lab in New Mexico which specializes in meteorites examined the same rock and concluded that the ratio of chemicals in this rock does not indicate life.

3) Are the dates theorized correct? Creation Instruction Association has already pointed out problems with radio-isotope dating; especially with water contamination, which would render these dates inaccurate.

4) Assuming the theory is correct, could organic material resist vaporization for 16 million years in the vacuum of space, let alone re-entry into earth's atmosphere? In the 13,000 years on earth, was there no contamination? Are the fossils (1/1000 the diameter of a human hair) really fossils?

5) Could this be a media effort to gain special funding? NASA scheduled another space probe to Mars in November of 1996. President Clinton was briefed the week before the August 7th announcement of this find and called for additional funding. Meanwhile, as the media is making much of this topic, most scientists are being more skeptical, and many even disagree.

6) Could a meteorite impact really send rocks off the surface of Mars hurling to outer space? Sounds like a long shot. If true, could a rock from earth be ejected out to Mars and then be ejected again back to earth?

7) What if they did find bacterial spores on Mars? *Creation* magazine has pointed out that creationists for years have said that the pressure of light, aided

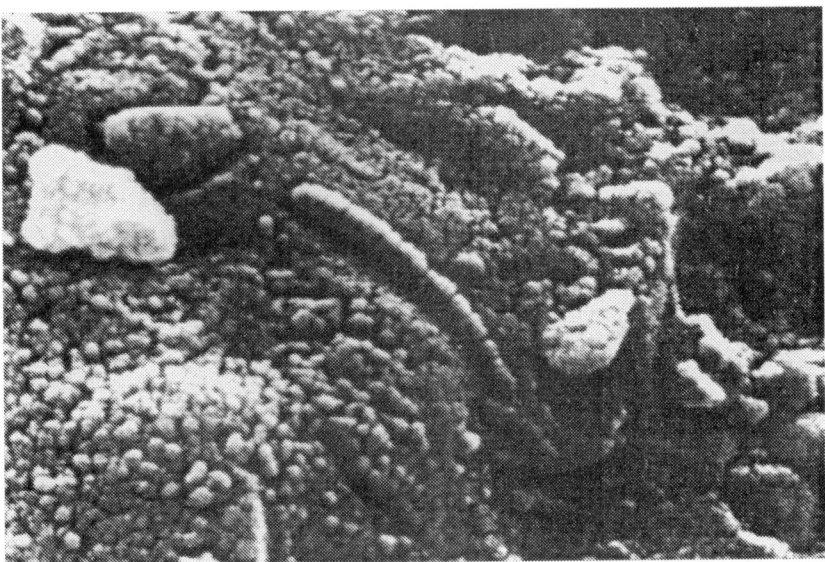

Figure 31: Mars rock with fossil 1/1000 the diameter of a human hair.

by solar flares would send dust particles and spores from earth out into the solar system. Therefore, Mars could already be contaminated by earth.

In May, 1997, an *Air and Space* article read: "Most meteorite experts think last summer's 'discovery' of Martian life was just a load of hype. And those are the ones who are being polite" (Petit, p 36). The article goes on to explain how NASA had suspended the distribution of any more pieces of the "rock" until further research and direction could be made. However, by this time over 47 scientists already had samples from NASA's Johnson Space Center and quickly viewed their samples again. Jeffrey Bada, a cosmochemist at the Scrips Institution of Oceanography then took a hunk of ice from the Allan Hills region of Antarctica (same region as Mars rock was found) and let it melt. Upon examining the remains (water), the same organic molecules that exist in the Mars rock were present here. Not only this, but the same matter was also found in other Antarctic meteorites having no connection with Mars. This led Bada to the conclusion that the Mars rock was not infected with extraterrestrial life, but rather contaminated by the water seeping into this meteorite before its discovery (Petit, p.37).

Derek Sears, a University of Arkansas chemist noted, "I must have had phone calls, e-mails and other communication from 40 to 50 people [in the field], and not one of them showed anything but serious skepticism" (Petit, p 40). Clearly, even the most professional chemists are disagreeing with the NASA report and voicing their skepticism. What is this all leading to?

A few years ago Alan Morrison in his book, <u>The Serpent and the Cross</u> wrote: "The increasing number of UFO sightings has nothing to do with genuine extraterrestrial civilizations, but is part of an ongoing strategy of the 'powers of darkness' (Eph 6:12),...who are engaged in convincing the minds of the gullible that 'something out there is trying to contact us.' To those whose minds are attuned to such contact, demonic beings will actually manifest themselves as benign 'extra terrestrials' who wish to offer help to humanity... We should not be at all surprised if these developments occur in the near future as part of the advancing strategy of the powers of darkness to discredit the Gospel, debunk the Bible, and eradicate the concept of a transcendent Creator God...It is not at all beyond the bounds of possibility that demons posing as 'highly evolved beings' from another world will be involved in the massive deceptions surrounding the revealing of the final manifestation of the Antichrist." Examples of such prophetic statements can be found everywhere. Robert Jastrow is now claiming that the spirits are actually highly evolved beings (which is why we can't contact them). Newspapers too, are jumping on the Mars rock. "*The Daily Mirror*" (7/8/96) responded to the Mars rock by saying, "A tiny fossil will today be held up as proof of life on Mars... The amazing discovery could prove the existence of alien life-forms. It may. . . help to explain where the human race came from. The fact that we are descended from Martians is also a staggering possibility. "*The "Daily Telegraph*" (7/8/96) also wrote, "This discovery will back the suspicion of many scientists... making alien life inevitable."

As Morrison stated, "friends, all this is so obviously the next major stage in the softening-up process. . .to receive the big announcement: 'They're here!'"

C.S. Lewis once noted that if there is life on other planets, God put them there too. However, I see this as a moot and rather unnecessary argument. God clearly tells us that we must all die as a result of sin. He also tells us that one of our main purposes in life is to spread the Good News of the Gospel. If there is life on other planets that have fallen into sin, we need to witness to them. Many people come back saying, "maybe they didn't fall into sin." If this were so, God would be unjust because He will destroy these sinless societies at the end of the world, along with the sinful one we live in. The book of Revelation says that the heavens and earth will be judged and destroyed. In their place will be a new heaven and a new earth (Chapters 6-22). If we can't witness to these alleged aliens, they are not sinful. If they are not sinful, they will be judged unfairly and God is not unjust. Therefore, if they are out there, they are not aliens but demonic beings as seen above.

For years we have been sending radio signals into space in hopes that someone would respond. Not only is this illogical, but it is also inconsistent with evolutionary beliefs. It is illogical because of the vast distance these creatures would be away from us. Even the nearest star which is 25 trillion miles away would take 870,000 years to reach at the speed of the Apollo spacecraft. At 1/10 the speed of light it would still take 43 years; however this speed in itself is illogical. Even space dust would destroy a spaceship at these speeds. Therefore, any so called aliens that have the technology to reach us are not going to have any interest in us and probably would not be peaceful. How will we benefit them? Show them the V8 engine. This attempt to find ET life is also inconsistent because we are simply looking for any type of regular or ordered signal that would indicate intelligence. However, when we see the vast amount of order and design in a simple cell, we interpret it as random processes of chance. With this reasoning, how could we be sure that orderly signals from space, which supposedly prove life, are not just coincidences by chance. This would be illogical unless of course we are talking about Creation and biology etc., then order is simply a happy accident.

I think one can see the problems involved with this rather premature announcement. I would like to conclude with a quote from Ken Ham in his AIG newsletter, showing where our true focus should be: "These scientists...are so excited at the prospect that life came to Earth from a rock. As I hear all of this, I feel like finding every Christian in the world and shaking them out of their apathy and say, 'Come on--let's yell it loud and clear to the media, the scientists, the whole world--let's shout it from the rooftops: Yes! Life did come to Earth from a rock. But you're looking at the wrong rock! This is a lifeless rock. Please look at the real living Rock. This Rock created the universe, and created life on Earth. This Rock has been living forever, and this same rock came to Earth to be a Man so that those who acknowledge Him as the true living Rock of salvation can have life eternal with Him. ... We need to bow down and worship the Rock--not a lifeless, small rock in a glass case but the living Rock, the Lord

Jesus Christ, the One who is the 'resurrection and the life.'" And he said, "The LORD is my Rock, and my Fortress, and my Deliverer; the God of my rock; in Him will I trust: He is my shield; and the Horn of my salvation" (2 Sam. 22:2-3). AMEN!

Now that the Mars probe has landed safely on the planet, NASA scientists are thrilled with pictures coming back. They interpret these pictures as showing evidence of a vast flood plain created by one of the largest floods in history. Again, I find it so ironic that they are proposing a flood of "Biblical proportions" on a planet with no liquid water, yet to propose such a thing on an earth with 70% water is crazy. Unlike Mars, on earth we can explain where the water came from and where it went to. The earth was made for man as "The highest heavens belong to the LORD, but the earth he has given to man" (Psa 115:16).

CHAPTER 10
DATING METHODS

Sedimentary Rocks

The current dating methods are perhaps one of the biggest fallacies that lead to the belief of an old earth. In polling children of Christian schools, I found over 70% of them believed in an earth millions of years old. With evolution infiltrating every aspect of media and life, this is really no surprise. The problems of the dating methods are really not a problem at all, once we understand the assumptions involved in them. Let us say a rock contained a fossilized clam. To discover how old that rock was you could take it to the nearest geology professor at a college or university. The professor would then show you a book called, <u>Invertebrate Paleontology,</u> and would open it to the section on clams. He would page through until he found a picture of a clam that looked just like the one in your rock. Upon seeing this he would give, as a matter of scientific fact, the date of that rock. Neat huh? It was the fossil that dated your rock, but evolution dates the fossil; therefore, evolution is what dated your rock. This is how our children are being lied to. If our children can understand the reason they hear what they do, they won't fall prey to it. Because this clam had not evolved until a certain period of time according to evolutionary theory, it was only alive between certain dates as seen in the fossil record. Since this clam must have been living when this sedimentary rock was formed, the time in which this clam lived is the age of your rock. David B. Kitts, an evolutionist himself, realizes how absurd this circular reasoning is when he states, ". . . the record of evolution, like any other historical record, must be construed within a complex of particular and general preconceptions, not the least of which is the hypothesis that evolution has occurred" (Kitts, p.353-354). Any sedimentary rock with a fossil in it is dated in such a way. Then, all the rocks found near the rock which was dated are given the same date. Therefore, if a fossilized dinosaur has been designated 105 million years old, remember that is because evolutionists assume this is the time period in which it lived. It has nothing to do with the rocks themselves.

Even flint tools found inside a limestone bed have proved embarrassing for evolutionists. The fossils in the limestone dated the tools to be of Miocene age (25 million years old), but obviously *man-made* flint tools can't be that old (Cremo p. 214). This is a perfect example of the many discrepancies found between fossil dating and archaeological evidences.

A common theme throughout this entire chapter (as in others) is the question of which bias is the best bias of which to be biased. If I assume that creation and a young earth are true, the evidence fits my assumption like a glove. However, if I assume evolution and an old earth are true, again the evidence fits like a glove. We all interpret the data according to our presuppositions.

Radioisotope Dating

Radioisotope dating is a **little** more scientific than the above sedimentary rock dating methods. These methods, which include those such as uranium-lead, rubidium-strontium, rubidium-strontium isocron, and potassium-argon, are those which date igneous or metamorphic rocks, meaning these rocks were once in a molten state and solidified into a solid one. Only rocks in the "millions of years old" category can be dated by these methods.

Let's assume finding a piece of lava to date. A geology professor would send it to a lab to grind it into powder, isolate the minerals, measure the amount of elements in the powder and punch the figures into a computer. A number of tests would produce a range of dates varying in millions of years. Now a necessary question is asked: "Where did you find this rock?" "Just below a limestone layer." This reply dates the rock. What happened to all of the other dates varying in age that were received from the number of different tests? They were thrown out because they did not fit the time scale allowed in order to be below a limestone layer. For example, because one date may have been 600 million years old, it was thrown out because that is too old to be in a limestone layer. Other dates of around 100 million years old were thrown out because they were too young to be in a limestone area. As soon as you tell the man dating the rock where it was found, a general idea of the age of the rock is conjured up in his head. Now one only needs to date the rock to verify what you expected. Again, we have circular reasoning, where the dating methods depend entirely upon the theory of evolution. Most labs will not even date rocks unless they know where they were found.

To explain further, let us look at the process in more detail. All of the dating methods are under the same assumption but simply use different elements. One dating method is the uranium-lead method. Uranium is a radioactive element which degenerates gradually into lead (less complex atoms) at a presumably known rate. All methods assume that at the time a molten rock becomes a solid it should date at zero, having no lead in it at all because the newly formed uranium has not had time to decay. For example, a molten piece of lava solidifying dates a rock at zero days old, since it contains all uranium and no lead. Uranium is said to have a half life of 4.5 billion years, meaning that it would take 4.5 billion years for half of the current uranium to decay into lead. For example, a rock with a pound of uranium (exaggerated figure) at the moment of solidification would have no lead, but 4.5 billion years later it would be half a pound of uranium and half a pound of lead. Now I should mention that the uranium does not decay directly into lead, but rather goes through a number of changes from U-238 to Th-234 to Pb-234 to U-234 to Th-230 to Ra-226 to Rn-222 to Po-218 to Pb-214 to Bi-214 to Po-214 to Pb-210 to Bi-210 to Po-210 and finally to Pb 206. The change from U-238 (parent) to Pb-206 (daughter) is the complete process, or half life of 4.5 billion years.

In order to accept these dating methods, a number of assumptions are involved, the first one being a constant decay rate. This means that the rate of decay at a 4.5 billion year half life has never changed in the past; that uranium

238 has never for some reason begun to decay a little faster or slower. Scientifically, we do have evidence to question this, but for now I am going to let the evolutionists have this assumption. I don't believe there has ever been a rock that has seen a complete half life go by, but nonetheless we will, for now, assume the rate is constant.

The second assumption is far more serious and is one in which the creation model dominates. This assumption states that there is no loss

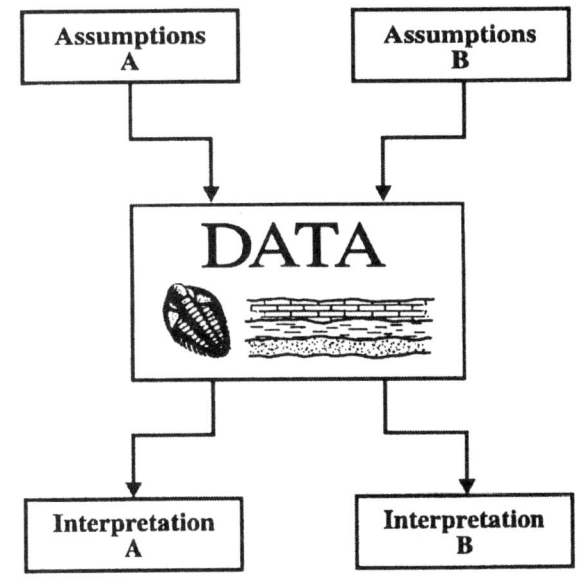

Figure 32: Our bias determines how we interpret data. If my bias is Noah's Flood, the earth is young. If my bias is no flood, the earth is old.

or gain of the parent (uranium-238) or daughter (Pb-206) material, meaning at no time in the history of the rock has any uranium or lead (or any intermediates, some of which are highly-mobile gases) been added to or taken from this rock. Well, when an evolutionist goes to find a rock to be dated, he takes great care to try to find a rock that has not been contaminated. Guess what contaminates rocks? WATER! Yes, water will leach in or leach out these materials at random, thereby causing results to be inaccurate. Remember our lava we had dated where only one date was chosen out of many. The way they justify throwing the other dates out is by claiming that they were contaminated. Creationist hold that very few rocks would have been untouched by the ground breaking, mountain covering deluge of Noah's Flood. Andrew Snelling writes concerning the undetectable contamination of rocks, "...the U/Pb system, including its intermediate daughter products, especially Ra and Rn, has been so open with repeated large scale migrations of the elements that it is impossible to be sure of the precise status/history of any piece of pitchblende selected for dating. Even though geochronologists take every conceivable precaution when selecting pitchblende grains for dating, ...no one could be sure that the U and Pb they are measuring is 'original' and unaffected by the gross element movements observed and measured....In addition, the pitchblende grains don't have uniform compositions so that 'dating' of subsections of any grain would tend to yield widely divergent U/Pb ratios and therefore varying 'ages' within that single grain.

..the evidence clearly indicates that these dates are meaningless" (Snelling, uranium pp. 44-57).

The third assumption involved in this process states that there are known amounts of daughter present at the start. This means that we assume we know for sure that when my lava solidifies it has ZERO lead in it. This should be a fairly easy assumption to put to the test with all the volcanoes that are, and have erupted all over the world. Sunset Crater in northern Arizona is known to have erupted about 900 years ago. We know this from Indian artifacts found in the rocks formed by the eruption as well, as from tree ring dates and the stories left by the Indians who lived near this volcano; all confirm the same time. However, when the dating methods were applied to this volcano, dates ranged from 210,000 to 230,000 years old (Dalrymple, pp. 47-55). The explanation for this erroneous result was that there was too much argon. What kind of explanation is that? Another example comes from the Kaupelehu Flow, Hualalai Volcano, in Hawaii. We know this volcano erupted in 1800-1801 but dating methods (12 dates) show a range from 140 million to 2.96 billion years (Funkhouser, pp. 4601-4607). Again, no suitable explanation is given. Finally, one more example (though there are hundreds more) comes from the Grand Canyon's volcanic flow, which occurred after the canyon was formed because the lava runs down the side of the canyon walls. Some dates of this 'young' lava flow date older than the oldest rocks in the Grand Canyon (Morris, Young Earth, p. 59).

One other problem with this dating method concerns the atmospheric conditions of the pre-Flood world (more detail in later chapters). For our purposes here, one needs only to realize that evidence suggests cosmic radiation in the past was much lower. Assuming this to be correct, the radiation levels in the rocks could have been much lower, thereby making this dating method useless. In fact, scientists have now discovered that their are 14 different radionuclides which have had there decay properties changed by temperature, pressure, electric fields, and magnetic fields, all of which have been different in the past (Sippert, Evolution, p.247).

It seems the dating methods are flawed and that it all depends upon our bias. If we believe in Noah's Flood, the rocks are contaminated, if we don't we still have other assumptions to get past. To sum up radioisotope dating, if you have rocks of a known age, radioisotope dating doesn't work. However, if you have rocks which you have no idea how old they are, radioisotope dating works every time.

Because of evolution and the assumptions (denials may be a better term) involved, I believe we are closer to the end times than we ever have been. I know that sounds like a common sense type of statement, but let me explain. II Peter 3:3-6 states, "You must understand that in the last days scoffers will come, scoffing and following their own evil desires. They will say, 'Where is this coming He promised? Ever since our fathers died, everything goes on as it has since the beginning of creation.' But they deliberately forget that long ago by God's Word the heavens existed and the earth was formed out of water and by water. By these waters also the world of that time was deluged and destroyed."

Note that it says "in the last days" two things are going to take place: 1) scoffers will say everything goes on as it has since the beginning of creation, and 2) people will willingly deny Noah's Flood. The first assumption is that the past is the key to the present, sometimes referred to as uniformitarianism. This theory was not made popular until the mid 19th century, yet we read here that it will be in the last days. Regarding the denial of the Flood, again this is something made popular only in the past 50 years. Why the change in attitude? Evolution! Evolution and the pseudo science that comes with it has fooled the nation into believing the earth is millions of years old. In order to believe in the dating methods described above one must: 1) Deny Noah's Flood and, 2) say that all things go on unchanged since the beginning of creation (4.5 billion year half-life is steady). Indeed, man will go to great lengths to avoid worshipping his Creator. The evidence stares us in the face, yet we deny God's mighty hand in all that He has done. The truth is that Noah's Flood would have deposited most of the fossil bearing record we have today and contaminated the rocks as well. Evolutionists deny this fact, but if the Flood was a global event as the Bible teaches, there is NO evidence for evolution or an old earth.

"God saw all that He had made and it was VERY GOOD" (Genesis 1:31). God created a wonderful world at the beginning but now, "we are looking forward to a new heaven and a new earth, the home of righteousness" (II Peter 3:13). What happened to "very good?" Now we are waiting for "very good" to come about. The answer is found in the third chapter of Genesis, where the earth is cursed in verse 17, animals in verse 14, plants in verse 18, humankind in verses 16, 17, and 19, and now death reigns (Romans 8:19-22). The Bible clearly teaches that things have not gone on as they have since the beginning because, "the wages of sin is death, but the gift of God is eternal life through Jesus Christ our Lord" (Romans 6:23). If this is false, as evolution teaches, and if death is not a result of our sin, then Christ is not our deliverer from our sins or eternal damnation. But I know that evolution is false and the message in Romans 6:23 is true, and Christ is my Redeemer who lives now and forever, AMEN!!!! To God be the Glory!

Carbon 14 Dating

Carbon 14 can only date things of organic matter, meaning it must have been alive and contained carbon, things such as plants, trees, animals, or humans. We are limited to about 60,000 years (with evolutionary timing), so only fairly recent items may be dated by this method.

The general concept behind C-14 dating is quite simple, but first we need to explain how we get C-14. C-14 is made in the upper atmosphere, as nitrogen-14 (N-14) is bombarded by cosmic rays. Through this process the N-14 is changed into C-14. Also in our atmosphere is a great deal of carbon dioxide, which also contains C-12. As you know, the C-12 in carbon dioxide would naturally be cycled through plants and animals because we use it in photosynthesis and breathing. The C-14 acts much like the C-12 by entering our bodies as well. The only difference is that the C-14, after being formed, is radioactive and begins to immediately change back into N-14 (similar to the uranium decaying into lead).

The air we breath has a certain amount of C-12 and a certain amount of C-14, creating what is called a C-14/C-12 ratio. We expect to find an equal ratio everywhere on the earth because of its being mixed so thoroughly. It is like making Kool-Aid; the mixture spreads evenly throughout the entire jug of water. Likewise, the ratio of carbon would be the same in the atmosphere as in our bodies because we continually take the carbon in. However, once we die we stop taking in carbon, and the C-14 which is decaying is not replaced. Therefore, knowing the decay of C-14 to have a half life of 5,700 years, we simply measure how much C-14 is left in the body or plant to see how much has decayed, hence how much time has gone by.

The problem with the above process is that we must assume that we know what the C-14/C-12 ratio was thousands of years ago (millions of years for the evolutionist). Scientists do not claim that it has remained constant, because it is well known that the industrial revolution changed this ratio by producing a large amount of C-12 through the burning of coal, etc. Tree rings show us what the different ratio was before the industrial revolution; and this change is calculated into the formula when the dating is done. However, how can we assume that this has been the only change in the ratio for the past eons of time?

Still another problem is that as C-14 enters the atmosphere, other C-14 decays into N-14 and leaves the atmosphere. Therefore, the more C-14 coming into our system the more it will leave our system as N-14. Dr. Snelling uses this example of this process: Picture a tank designed to hold water but having small holes in it. Once you turn on the water, some water will go into the tank while some water will leave through the small holes. Gradually, the water will build up to a point where the water leaving the tank will equal the amount of water being put into the tank and a balance will be established. The same scenario is going on with the C-14 in the air, as more comes into the atmosphere, more goes out until a balance is established, having equal amounts coming in and leaving simultaneously. At present, about 18 pounds of carbon enter our atmosphere a year and 15 pounds leave (total of 62 metric tons). In order to reach our balance, we need to have about 75 metric tons, which we do not yet have (Humphry, radiocarbon). W. F. Libby, the man who invented this dating method, as well as other scientists, for years assumed that this balance had already been reached, because from the moment the C-14 began to enter our atmosphere (when the faucet was turned on in our analogy) to the moment a balance would be reached should be only 30,000 years (Snelling, Answers, pp. 65-69). Obviously, evolution states the earth is far older than this and, therefore, this balance should have been reached millions of years ago.

Libby was wrong. In his day the amount of C-14 entering the atmosphere was about 12% more than what was leaving the atmosphere and, therefore, this system must be younger than 30,000 years because this balance has not yet been reached. Later, more sophisticated technology used by nuclear chemists, Fairhall and Young, showed that the system may be as much as 50% out of balance (Fairhall, p. 402). Others have measured it to be less at 35% and, therefore, the inconsistencies should send out warning signs as to the accuracy of both the ratio measurements and the dating method itself (Snelling, Answers, pp. 69-70). Tree rings and other outside information indicate that this process is not as simple as once believed and, therefore, we should proceed with extreme caution, especially since there are other assumptions involved as well. (Is the Kool-Aid really equally mixed?)

Many more problems arise with dating methods when we take into consideration what Scripture tells us. The firmament, or cloud canopy which covered the earth before the Flood, would have shielded the atmosphere from cosmic bombardment and the level of C-14 would be drastically lowered. Therefore, if one is trying to date organic material that died as a result of the Flood, it would be dated as extremely old because there would be an absence of C-14. Evolution would claim that the C-14 decayed, while creationists would say there wasn't much C-14 to begin with (coal is a good example). Furthermore, the Flood surely would have buried massive amounts of carbon caught up in the organic systems of that time, leaving the limestone, coal and shale deposits we have today (all are loaded with carbon). This removing of carbon from the atmospheric system would disrupt the balance or C-14/C-12 ratio, not only at the time of the Flood but for perhaps a few centuries after as the earth was replenished. The higher electromagnetic field of the earth before the Flood (see pre-Flood world or Biblical Pangea) would again cause the amount of C-14 to be significantly less. Therefore, any attempt to find uniformity in the C-14/C12 ratio is pointless, making the entire dating method useless, at least in pre-Flood artifacts and probably even post-Flood ones.

Other warning signs come from the inconsistencies in actual datings. The following examples from Dr. Snelling are some things evolutionists probably would not want you to know about:

1) A freshly killed seal dated by C-14 showed it had died 1,300 years ago;

2) Living mollusk shells were dated at up to 2,300 years old;

3) Living snail shells showed they had died 27,000 years ago;

4) Coal from Russia from the 'Pennsylvania,' supposedly 300 million years old, was dated at 1,680 years;

5) Natural gas from Alabama and Mississippi (Cretaceous and Eocene, respectively) should have been 50 million to 135 million years old, yet C-14 gave dates of 30,000 to 34,000 years, respectively (Snelling Answers, pp. 73-74).

Because of results such as those mentioned above, Dr. Lee, though an evolutionist, writes: "The troubles of the radiocarbon dating method are undeniably deep and serious. Despite 35 years of technological refinement and better understanding, the underlying assumptions have been strongly challenged, and warnings are out that radiocarbon may soon find itself in a crisis situation. Continuing use of the method depends on a 'fix-it-as-we-go-' approach, allowing for contamination here, fractionation there, and calibration whenever possible. It should be no surprise, then, that fully half of the dates are rejected. The wonder is, surely, that the remaining half come to be accepted. . . . No matter how 'useful' it is, though, the radiocarbon method is still not capable of yielding accurate and reliable results. There are gross discrepancies, the chronology is uneven and relative, and the accepted dates are actually selected dates" (Lee, pp. 9, 29).

It is refreshing to see others also opening their thoughts to accepting a catastrophic, global disaster to render these methods inaccurate. Dr. Frederick Jueneman, an *evolutionist*, writes: "There has been in recent years the horrible realization that radio-decay rates are not as constant as previously thought, nor are they immune to environmental influences and this could mean that the atomic clocks were reset during some global disaster; an event that brought the Mesozoic [age of dinosaurs] to a close may not be 65 million years old but **rather in the age and memory of man**" (emphasis added -Jueneman, p.21).

Even those working in the field question the results. In describing a conversation John Morris had with a famous archaeologist from the University of Pennsylvania, involved in an excavation in Turkey, Dr. Morris states, "He had discovered an ancient tomb with wooden timbers. I had asked if he had sent timber samples off for dating through the C-14 method. . .he had of course, . . . but claimed he would never believe anything that came back from a carbon-14 lab. Nor was he aware of any archaeologist in the world who would accept such dates. . .He was obliged to carbon-date artifacts to keep his grant money coming in, and so he always did so, but, he did not trust the method or its results" (Morris, Young Earth, p. 65).

One last thing to discuss before leaving this topic is how scientists came up with date of 4.6 billion years (present theory, anyway) for the age of the earth. If the earth was a big molten blob for millions of years, then the above dating methods won't work because they will only give a date from the point something becomes a solid. Rocks date only around 3.8 billion years old, so how did they date the earth at 4.6 billion? By a meteorite! Scientists have used a lead to lead dating method on rocks that fall from outer space, and this age is then transferred to earth. Obviously some questionable assumptions develop with this hypothesis.

Radio Halos

Physicist, Robert Gentry has discovered a remarkable characteristic of radioactive decay in granite that shows the earth to be very young and, indeed, created in a short period of time.

When a radioactive atom decays it, in a sense, bursts and gives off energy which leaves its mark in the material therein. Each element which decays has its own amount of energy and upon "bursting" leaves its own distinguishable mark called a pleochroic halo, or radio halo. As a result, by observing these halos one can determine what element has decayed.

Granite is found worldwide from 8 to 16 miles in thickness and, according to evolutionary theory, was a molten material that cooled to its present, solid state over a period of 300 millions years. However, radio halos found in granite show that the rock was formed (created) almost instantaneously. The radio halos of polonium 218, 210 and 214 were found in granite, but the half life of polonium 218 is 22 days. Even better, the half life of polonium 210 is under three minutes and the half life of polonium 214 is 0.000164 seconds. That is faster than the snap of a finger, which means the granite had to go from a molten (if it ever was to begin with) to a solid in a single moment. This fits well with the Bible, which states, "And God said, let the water under the sky be gathered to one place, and let dry ground appear. And it was so" (Genesis 1:9).

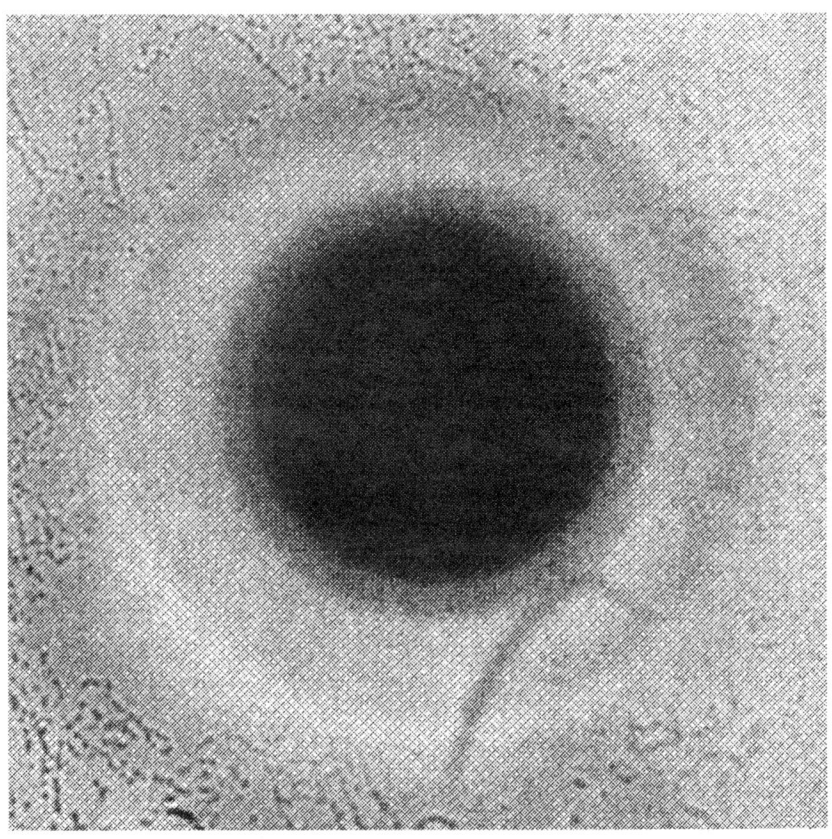

Figure 33: A radiohalo

CHAPTER 11
"UNIVERSAL" PROBLEMS FOR THE OLD EARTH THEORY

Meteoric Dust From Space

The old earth theory is one of the most destructive devices of evolution. It is largely because of this one belief that the Bible has come into question by so many Christians. If the earth and solar system was shown to be young, far more people would take God's Word at face value. The sad thing is the evidence does support the idea that the earth is young, but the propaganda put out by evolutionists does not accurately reflect this evidence. This chapter's focus is to show general evidences, misconceptions and assumptions that we normally do not get to hear about because it doesn't fit evolutionary theory.

Not too many years ago, the NASA space program was preparing to land on the moon. One area of great concern for the astronauts and those working on the program was how to keep the moon craft from sinking into the dust on the moon. Great amounts of time were spent trying to design ways of keeping the "ship afloat."

The reason for such concern was the rate at which meteoric dust entered our atmosphere; hence, five billion years of time should produce about 150 feet of dust on earth. Obviously erosion, rain, and the mixing of sediments would not necessarily be seen or measured. On the moon, however, without erosion, rain, wind etc., it was presumed that it must have accumulated to a great depth. Surprisingly, when man landed on the moon, only about an inch of dust existed, seeming to show that the universe wasn't as old as expected or the rate of dust accumulation was wrong.

For years, creationists have used this as evidence to support a young earth, but evidence has recently surfaced causing us to use caution when arguing this. Dr. Snelling of the Institute for Creation Research has done extensive studies on this topic showing that dust accumulation occurs in varied fluxes (Morris, Young Earth, p.88). The point being that we simply cannot be sure about the actual rate of dust entering our atmosphere, especially assuming at a constant rate. Nonetheless, if the universe is the extravagant age which is suggested, much more than an inch of dust would have accumulated on the moon, with or without fluxes.

Comets

From what we know, comets are made up of bits of ice, snow, and rock. Comets have a relatively short life span because as they orbit they crumble and burn up; especially as they near the sun, where they lose from 5 to 10% of their mass. The suggested age for comets is fewer than 100,000 years old, with many being fewer than 10,000 years old because of shorter orbits. Haley's Comet, according to evolution, has been dated to be about 90,000 years old. The problem we are beginning to see is that they are much too young to be in a solar system that is estimated to be 5 billion years old.

The reasoning then is that new comets must enter into our orbit, or else the earth is young. Note that they observe that comets are young (scientific evidence) but theorize that the world is old (bias) so they come up with an explanation that fits their theory (explanation consistent with bias). This is not science, but religion. Anyway, evolutionists now need a source for these comets, they obviously cannot come from nowhere. Actually, they do come from nowhere, at least in the way I see it. The consensus is that somewhere in outer space, far beyond even Pluto, there rests what evolutionists call the Oort cloud, made up of ice and snow. Every now and then pieces of snow and ice break off from the Oort cloud and are later bumped into our orbit.

The first major problem with this idea is that the Oort cloud is a hypothetical object which has never been seen or recorded, though you don't get this impression from many college professors. Nobody knows how many Oort clouds there could be or even how many comets. Just because the assumption of an old earth is made, the imagination comes up with an explanation to fit the evidence (comets are young).

The second major problem with this theory is that the probability of such a thing occurring is incredibly low. Once a piece of snow and ice somehow broke off the Oort cloud, how would it be bumped into our orbit (Humphry, Evidence)? This is a poor attempt to fit young comets into a supposedly old universe.

Winding of the Galaxy

Our galaxy, the Milky Way, is estimated to be 10 billion years old; however, the evidence argues strongly against this hypothesis. The problem is that galaxies wind themselves up too fast. Scientists have observed and recorded the speed at which galaxies turn and wind up. All galaxies move at different speeds, but all wrap around themselves with the movement being faster near the center, just like on a merry-go-round.

The present spiral of our galaxy shows it to be only about 0.2 billion years old. I don't mean to suggest that it is even this old, but nonetheless that date is far less than 10 billion. The 0.2 billion assumes it began in a basic straight pattern, and I suspect God had created a mature, fully functioning galaxy right from the start. After all, Adam was a fully grown man and the trees were created bearing fruit, why wouldn't the galaxy be set in motion. Therefore, using this assumption (which I feel is justified) the 0.2 billion years would be drastically lowered (Humphry, Evidence).

Atmospheric Conditions

The amount of helium in the atmosphere is a great argument for creationists. As you know, helium is a very light gas which is found in rather large quantities in our atmosphere. It is produced under the earth's surface through the radioactive decay processes. The helium, being a lightweight and a mobile gas, moves through the cracks and pores of the ground up to the surface, where it then goes into our atmosphere. Sensors which have been made to record the amount of helium entering our atmosphere show an astounding 13 million atoms per square inch are released every second.

Helium also escapes our atmosphere into outer space at a presumed rate of 0.3 million atoms per square inch every second as well. By observing the tremendous amount of helium entering and the small amount leaving, we should have a great deal of helium in the air if the earth is 4.6 billion years old. In fact, we should all have some really strange voices by now, but we don't. Why? Because the amount of helium in the atmosphere could have accumulated in no more than two million years (assuming we started with zero). Again, I do not propose this age for the earth because I am sure God created a functioning earth to begin with, but two million is far from 4.6 billion.

Other possible explanations that would bring the two million year date even lower involve Noah's Flood. With the earth's crust being broken up, the helium would escape at a much faster rate. (Morris, Young Earth, pp. 83-84).

As always, evolutionists do not have an adequate explanation; maybe even more so in this case, however. God indeed created a world in six, 24-hour days.

Earth's Magnetic Field

To understand this concept in relation to creation, we must first understand how the earth's magnetic field is created. It is not like a magnetic metal bar we often see in science class, because permanent magnetism like that is destroyed by heat. As we mentioned earlier, the earth's interior temperature is over 12,000 degrees Fahrenheit. Therefore, the earth's magnetic field is due to an electromagnetic field caused by the electrical currents of the earth's interior.

Since 1829, the electromagnetic field of the earth has been measured, and it has been found to have decreased by 7%. This suggests the magnetic field of our earth has a half life of 1400 years (Morris, Young Earth, p.75). If this has not changed, then we had a much stronger magnetic field prior to the Flood and will have a much weaker field in the future. This also means that if we would go back in time only 100,000 years, we would have the electromagnetic field of a neutron star, upon which life could not exist. Once more, this is a "far cry" from 4.6 billion years, not to mention the fact that 100,000 was to the point of destruction. In the same manner, if we go ahead into the future our electromagnetic field will cease to exist, which means life could not exist either.

We will discuss further in the chapter on the pre-Flood world how a stronger electromagnetic field would be a benefit to us, but for now it fits well into the 2nd law of thermodynamics (entropy) because everything is affected by this field. The less it gets, the worse off we are (Dubrov, p.61). Part of the reason for this is that it helps reflect the harmful cosmic rays back into space. Remember, also, that with fewer cosmic rays bombarding N-14, the less C-14 you would have, thereby making the C-14 dating methods yield dates that are too old.

While on this subject, I feel it necessary to discuss reversals in the magnetic field. Much evidence does indeed suggest these reversals took place, and I believe the creation model can ascribe to this as well. Evolution, however, puts the date of the last reversal at 700,000 years ago, although some less accepted views have proposed 20,000 (Morris, Young Earth, p. 80). This does not fit well with creation or science because with long periods involved in reversals, this means long periods of extremely weak fields, which means very harmful living conditions, as mentioned earlier. This, too, is not what evolution needs to move from a simple organism to a better, more complex one.

To describe quickly how these reversals can be explained by creation expectations, we can turn to the secular world. Paul H. Roberts has shown that the electromagnetic field can change in as rapidly as 15 days, the time it took for a molten mass to cool and solidify (*Nature*, 1995). In addition, Michael Aerate has shown how lightning strikes can cause local reversals as well (Aerate, pp. 170-181).

A rather interesting side note is that Dr. Humphrey graphed the magnetic field intensity from creation to the present. Upon finishing the graph, it showed an increase of intensity at the time of Christ and a decline after He left the earth again. (Morris, Young Earth, p. 82). I find this fascinating, considering the energizing power of the Holy Spirit. The Bible tells us that "the earth was formless and empty, darkness was over the surface of the deep, and the Spirit of God was hovering over the waters" (Genesis 1:2). The Hebrew word for "hovering" is *rachaph* and only appears two other times in the Old Testament. In Jeremiah 23:9 it is translated as "tremble" and in Deuteronomy 32:11 it is translated "hovers" in describing a bird flapping its wings. This gives the impression of a back and forth energizing movement (Morris, Record, p.52). It is difficult to say for sure but it would seem that the Spirit of God is the energizer for the world here. Colossians alludes to Christ as being the Creator of the past (Colossians 1:16), the Sustainer in the present (Colossians 1:18), and the Reconciler of the future (Colossians 1:20). This, too, would explain why at the time of Christ an increase in electromagnetic current (the scientific life-Sustainer) was present.

An Orderly Universe

Recently, an international team of scientists published new information regarding galaxy clusters in *Nature* (January 9, 1997). They concluded that "the large-scale structure of the cosmos is an orderly rectangular, three-dimensional latticework of clusters and voids." Apparently, the clusters of matter are spaced fairly evenly about 91 million-light-year intervals apart. Kathy Sawyer of *The Washington Post* admits this is a surprise, because order goes against the leading theories about the big bang, which should produce random spacing of matter. An internet post commented on this find as needing, "new laws of physics" to explain it (*Chronicle Telegram*, Jan. 14, 1997).

In addition to order, material make up is also becoming a problem for evolutionary theories. According to the big bang theory, deuterium, a heavy isotope of hydrogen, was theoretically formed after this explosion. David Tytler of the University of California and his team have recently shown that there is only about 10% of the deuterium present in the universe that was previously expected. Gary Steigman of Ohio State University stated, "It's a potential crisis for cosmology" (*New Scientist*, May, 1996 p. 18).

One reason for support of the big bang theory is that the universe has a "red shift," which supposedly indicates expansion outward from a center point. The red shift is used to measure the speed at which a star is moving away. If the big bang were true, one would expect stars to be moving away at the same speed, but this is not the case (nor do all seem to be moving away). William Tifft of the University of Arizona was the first to announce this discovery and was ignored because of its implications of the present theory of the origin of the universe. However, two UK astronomers, Bill Napier of Oxford, and Bruce Guthrie of Edinburgh, are now backing Tifft, saying the evidence is real. According to Napier, they even tried to prove this theory wrong but failed *(Science*, Feb. 9, 1996, p. 759). Geoffrey Burbide of the University of California says, "Big bang cosmology is probably as widely believed as has been any theory of the universe in the history of Western civilization. It rests, however, on many untested, and in many cases, untestable assumptions. Indeed, big bang cosmology has become a bandwagon of thought that reflects faith as much as objective truth" (*Scientific American*, Feb., 1992, p.96).

The Sun

The sun is 93 million miles away and it is a burning ball of gas. Scientists have measured that about five feet of the sun are burned up every hour. This means if you go back into time 10 hours, the sun was 50 feet larger. If you would go back into time around 1 million years ago, the sun would almost touch the earth. We would have burned up a long time before that. The earth is situated at the perfect distance from the sun; much closer we would burn up and much further away we would freeze. God clearly designed the entire universe with us in mind. This is not random, chance process but intelligent, loving design.

The sun, also a star, serves a distinct purpose, taking care of man. God promised Abraham that he would have descendants numbering the stars in the sky and the sand on the seashore. Up until the last century, only about 3,000 stars were visible to the naked eye; hence, Abraham's promise did not seem to fit logically with astronomy. However, now that God has blessed us with telescopes we see that there are trillions of stars in many galaxies. Indeed, God's promise was scientifically correct. Even before science could say it, the Bible stated in Jeremiah 33:22 that the stars were more numerous than one could count: "countless as the stars of the sky and as measureless as the sand on the seashore."

Even more fascinating is Scripture reveals that heavenly bodies were made differently. I Corinthians 15:41 states, "The sun has one kind of splendor, the moon another and the stars another; and star differs from star in splendor." The NASA space program has recently found this to be true as well, with each heavenly body composed of different elements and characteristics (unfortunate for evolution). Many bodies, such as Venus and Uranus, rotate in opposite directions from the other planets. David Stevenson of Caltech said in a September issue of *Science*, "The most striking outcome of planetary exploration is the diversity of the planets." Another scientist said, "I'm surprised at the versatility of nature. . .you put together the same basic materials and get startlingly different results. No two are alike; it's like a zoo" (*Science*, 1994).

If the big bang theory was correct, should there not be uniformity among the heavenly bodies? God truly is an awesome God creating a variety of splendor both in the heavens and on earth! Genesis 1:14 records reasons for the sun and stars: "For signs and for seasons, and for days, and years." Historically, the sun, moon and stars have been used as a calendar system for time and planting seasons but perhaps, most importantly, as signs for various events (star of Bethlehem). There will come a day, however, when the sun will be no longer (Matthew 24:29).

The heavens were designed for mankind. The entire universe was made for the benefit of human existence. While the sun is located in just the right spot for life to exist, the atmosphere, too, is necessary for holding the correct temperature and protecting us from solar radiation. Without it, the evenings would reach temperatures far below freezing and the radiation would be deadly. If the earth rotated even 1/10 as fast as it currently does, the days and nights would extend to ten times their length, causing scorching heat in the day and freezing temperatures in the evening. The moon is located in just the right position so that the tide does not submerge the earth twice every day. All the other planets and moons have conditions unsuitable for life. For example, even the earth's moon varies in temperatures from 270 degrees above Fahrenheit to 230 degrees Fahrenheit below zero in the evenings as a result of no atmosphere. Our closest planet, Venus, has air 50 times as dense as earth's and has extreme temperatures. NASA described Venus as the "classical view of hell." Human beings on Venus would either boil or be crushed. These are just a small sample of the hundreds of fingerprints left to show God's direct care for his special creatures--human beings. Even Eugene Cernan, an astronaut of the Apollo 10 and 17 missions, said in the Mankato *Free Press* 11-30-92, "The earth is moving with beauty and you get a feeling that you are looking at our earth as God envisioned it when He created it.. . . . I know there is someone bigger than us all behind this because of what I saw and felt." When the cosmonauts first went into space, they claimed to prove there was no God because they didn't see Him. Ironically, vast evidence of God's existence is right outside a spacecraft; step out and one would even see Him in person.

CHAPTER 12
"DOWN TO EARTH" PROBLEMS FOR THE OLD EARTH THEORY

Salt in the Sea

Swimming in the ocean teaches people not to take water into their mouth because of the large amounts of salt. It is from water similar to this that evolutionists propose life came about some 3 to 4 billion years ago. We know that the oceans continue to get saltier all the time because of rivers and other sources carrying in dissolved salts from land and, therefore, it would stand to reason that since the oceans were salty billions of years ago, they would be even more so now. In order to get a somewhat accurate prediction of how much salt should be in the oceans, we need to look at the input and output processes.

Dr. Steve Austin and Russell Humphreys have made a number of salt measurements of the mechanisms by which salt is added to, and taken from the oceans. These sources of salt input/output have been well accepted for years, so this isn't something just accepted by creationists. In reporting their results, Austin and Humphreys gave the absolute minimum for salt input and the absolute maximum for salt output, giving the evolutionary standpoint a great advantage.

The following is a list of salt input sources: 1) rivers bring dissolved sodium; 2) rivers carry dissolved chloride and sulfate; 3) rivers carry salt back to the ocean that came on land due to "sea-spray"; 4) some ocean floor sediments release salt; 5) salt released from glacier ice; 6) salt released from sediments in glaciers; 7) atmospheric and volcanic dust; 8) erosion from the shoreline; 9) steam from volcanoes; 10) ground water seepage; and 11) hot water springs from beneath the ocean floor.

The following is a list of salt output sources: 1) waves produce sea-spray which is carried to land; 2) ion exchange; 3) absorbed water of sea floor; 4) other sea-floor clays absorb salt; and 5) zeolites from volcanic ash absorb salt.

Using the above considerations, the present salt content of the oceans (assuming they started with no salt) show them to be 62 million years old (Morris-Young Earth, pp. 85-86). Again, this is a long way from 3 to 4 billion, especially when using minimum inputs and maximum outputs (regular measurements showed 32 million). Obviously the input/output levels could have changed easily in the past, especially since the Flood could have deposited 2/3 of the present salt, lowering the age considerably (Humphrey, Evidence for Young Earth). But, evolutionists believe in uniformity and no Flood; therefore, I feel justified in arguing this evidence with them. Either way, they lose.

Preservation of Fossils

Near Swindon, Wiltshire, England, unusually, cold, bubbling mud springs are pushing out fossils that are supposedly 165 million years old. Not only can we not explain the source or cause of this mud spring, but the preservation of the ammonite fossils is also surprising for evolutionary scientists. According to Dr. Hollingworth, a paleontologist with the Natural Environment Research Council in Swindon, "many still had shimmering mother-of-pearl shells. . . .There are the shells of bivalves which still have their original ligaments and yet they are millions of years old" (Nuttall, *The Times*, 1996). To an unbiased observer, obviously an ammonite in a state of preservation such as this could not possibly be millions of years old. Both these fossils and the strata they are embedded in must be rather young; perhaps these fossils were entombed by Noah's Flood.

Geophysics Computer

In the June issue of *US News and World Report*, 1997, an article described a new computer program invented by a well respected scientist named John Baumgardner. Baumgardner's computer program (Terra) is marveled at among the secular community and Christian community alike. The article states, "Run Terra one way, and you can watch Noah's Flood take place before your eyes, mathematically calculated by a supercomputer. Run Terra another way, and you get the standard geological story of 4.6 billion years. The results obtained from the code are . . . dependent on the numbers fed into it in the first place" (Burr, *US News*). Again it comes down to presuppositions, not actual science. Science supports an earth about 6,000 years old, as Baumgardner believes, or billions of years, depending on your bias before science is applied.

Soil Erosion

Soil erosion is another example where we can measure the amount of soil being eroded and carried by rivers into the oceans. Evolution says that our continents are about 3.5 billion years old. Dr. Humphreys, a creationist, has estimated an amazing 25 billion tons of continent are carried into the ocean every year (Humphrey, Evidence for Young Earth). Others have proposed up to 27.5 billion tons, but we will use the lower figure. At the very maximum this means that all the continents would be eroded in 15 million years.

Another thing to consider is the uplift of the continents which formed the mountains. The creationists have a little different opinion as to how the mountains actually were formed, which in this case is irrelevant. Other measurements show that the amount of material above sea level is about 383

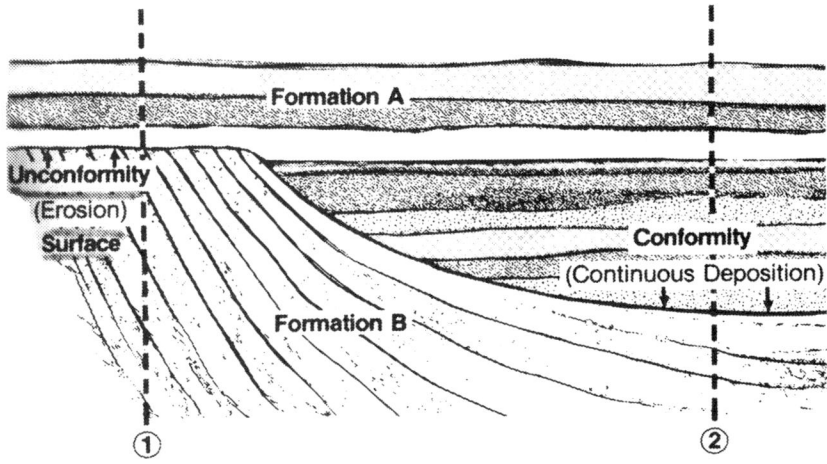

Figure 34: Two deposits being cut out by erosion can produce unconformities.

million tons. It would only take under 14 million years, not 3.5 billion, to have all of this eroded away under the current conditions (Morris, Young Earth, p.89). The erosion rate is simply too fast. This rate speaks against an old earth and the slow, gradual erosion of the Colorado River in the Grand Canyon.

Along the same lines, one can measure the amounts of sediment entry into our oceans. Currently it seems to be coming in at 27.5 billion tons per year. Knowing that only 410 million billion tons are presently in the ocean, we arrive at a date of only 15 million years (Morris, Young Earth, p.90). All the evidence keeps coming back showing a young earth!

Again, I am sure things have not remained the same in the past; in fact, Noah's Flood would have deposited great amounts of material very quickly, but since evolution uses the uniformitarian principle, we will too.

Finally, creationists would predict that the Flood would make large deposits of sediments quickly and also involve large scale erosion rapidly. Evolution, on the other hand, would generally suspect slow erosion, thereby leaving a different geological record. Erosion can be viewed today by conformities and disconformities. Conformity is where rock layers conform with the layers above or below them by following the same general pattern of deposition. Disconformity shows rock layers which are inconsistent in appearance. Noah's Flood provides an explanation for such disconformities by providing a means for rapid erosion through rapidly deposited sediments. If rapid erosion from water runoff removed the sediments between the dotted lines in the figure shown above, the left side would show disconformity while the right side of the canyon may show conformity.

Where are the Soil Layers?

Observing rock formations shows that there is no evidence of soil layers in between the strata. Evolution states that these strata layers are a result of vast periods of time by means of slow and gradual depositions. If this is the case, there should be evidence of soil because soil is a necessity for abundant life, something certainly seen in fossil record. In fact, the vegetation shown in the fossil record is much more plentiful and much larger than what we see today. Without soil, this would be impossible.

Let us take a moment to examine how soil is made. Soil consists primarily of rock which has been broken up by chemical deterioration, root and animal penetration, wind and water weathering, and the freezing/thawing cycle. In addition, to this is the organic materials from decaying plants or animals and other animal wastes. Once formed, even if buried by water, evidence of the materials therein should be seen, if not the layers themselves.

Sometimes "underclays" are said to be evidence of soil layers, but this does not seem to be the case. Underclays are usually found under coal seams and are said to have been leached out by water. The problem with this theory is that underclay does not contain materials that would be able to support abundant life, let alone in a swamp (where evolution believes coal was formed).

We come to the conclusion, then, that the soil layers are missing, probably because they never existed. This is exactly what creationism and a young earth would predict (Morris, Young Earth, pp.97-98).

Stalactites

Stalactites and stalagmites are those beautiful limestone formations in many underground caves. Evolutionists have long claimed that these wonders take millions of years to form as dripping water carries dissolved minerals into the cave, creating icicle shaped structures on the ceiling (stalactite) and floor (stalagmite) of the cave. *Creation* magazine has shown more than one example of how this is false. One mining tunnel was found to have these formations, yet the tunnel was only 150 years old. As a result, slowly but surely people are beginning to open their eyes and recognize this problem. A recent secular magazine thankfully stated, "What geologist used to believe was fact, in terms of dating a cave, now is speculation . . . . From 1924 to 1988, there was a visitor's sign above the entrance to Carlsbad Caverns [New Mexico], that said Carlsbad was at least 260 million years old. In 1988 the sign was changed to read 7-10 million years old. Then, for a little while, the sign read that it was 2 million years old. Now the sign is gone. . . . In short, he says, geologists don't know how long cave development takes. And, while some believe that cave decorations such as S.P.'s beautiful icicle-looking stalactites took years to form, Trout says that through photo-monitoring, he has watched a stalactite grow several inches in a matter of days" (*Arizona Highways*, 1993). That says it all. Even cave dating involves many assumptions.

Archaeology

Archaeology suggests that civilization dates back to about five thousand years when the beginning of written history is found. This fits perfectly with what the Bible suggests. After all, Adam could talk far beyond primal grunts (Genesis 2:20) and could also write to record history (Genesis 5:1). Man was made in God's image and was in charge of the animals (Genesis 1:26); he was made just below the angels (Psalm 8:5); used agriculture from the beginning (Genesis 4:2); he built cities (Genesis 4:17); performed with and made musical instruments (Genesis 4:21); and practiced metallurgy (Genesis 4:22). All of this, not to mention the extreme wisdom that would have been gained from living hundreds of years. Job tells us "Ask the former generations and find out what their fathers learned" (Job 8:8). Surely much wisdom can be gained by seeking out the past and learning from it. Ken Ham once said at a seminar in Albert Lea, MN, that there is no such thing as prehistoric times because as long as man has existed, history has been recorded.

This section will be larger than most in this chapter because it records substantial evidence. Archaeology provides us a glimpse of the past that cannot be seen in mere speculation of uniformitarian processes. Therefore, the best evidence to show us the past is history itself.

The above-mentioned is in sharp contrast to evolution, which states that man evolved around three million years ago from his ape-like ancestors. Through his upward development he gradually moved into the Stone Age, the Bronze Age, the Iron Age, and finally into modern times. Under this assumption, then, archaeological digs should reflect the gradual increase of intelligence in the artifacts uncovered. But the exact opposite is seen.

All over the world evidence has been found of entire civilizations being established immediately, fully functional and highly developed. Also, in most cases evidence suggests that they were destroyed just as quickly, and many times because of some type of catastrophe. In the previous chapter on cave men we discussed why, in some cases, stone tools would have been used, but this is poor evidence for unintelligent man, especially when at the same time you have people building pyramids and other great wonders. In fact, it has been figured that in order to build a pyramid with over two million blocks quarried from over 500 miles away, 100,000 men using modern equipment would need to place 26 blocks every hour for 12 hours a day, seven days a week, for 20 years. Amazingly, these "prehistoric" men did just that.

The fascinating thing about archaeology is that the further back in time one goes, the more complex things become. That is why some are of the opinion that the bigger pyramids were the first ones and they go down hill from there. Even the architecture of ancient Greece is far less complex then those of previous buildings. Even *Readers Digest* said, "New findings have made shambles of the traditional theories of prehistory" (*Readers Digest*,1975). Literally hundreds of books have been written with titles of "mysteries of this" and "mysteries of that," because archaeology has presented serious problems for evolutionary theories of ancient man's incapabilities and understandings. The real evidence suggests that we are going downhill, not uphill, because we do not understand ourselves, how the ancients did the things they did. Let us examine some of these fascinating mysteries.

Near Mount Ararat over 500 furnaces have been found that were used for metallurgy. Near the Danube Basin, extremely sophisticated tools were found that predated Christ. In Egypt, electroplated daggers and batteries have been found. In China, belt buckles made of 5% magnese, 85% aluminum and 10% copper were found. Yes, the ancients knew how to extract aluminum from bauxite, heat it to the over 1000 degrees and apply electrolysis in order to use it in this way. In Peru, objects have been found made from platinum, which requires temperatures up to 1,750 degrees Centigrade. Many of these metals were mined long before mining was thought to take place. In fact, "Bronze Age" mines have been found with over 200 shafts. They also reveal that copper ingots weighing 22 pounds and being 97% to 98% pure. This is a degree of purification that we ourselves have achieved only in modern times. Other swords in China have been shown to have 13 metals within. On the Island of Crete, ancient civilizations were wiped out from two catastrophic events 50 years apart, coinciding with the dates of the Exodus and Joshua's long day. Various temple reconstructions show complex architectural design having natural ventilation and air conditioning. Also among these temples is the artwork of swastikas used by Hitler (which he got from the occult). In recent times, huge ancient statues carved out of rock were moved in order to build a dam, but even with modern technology we needed to cut them up into 20 ton blocks, yet the ancients moved things in excess of this all the time. In fact, a tremendous rock used in architecture has been found that weighs over 2,000 tons (Oakland, Ancient Man). At Sachsahuaman in Peru, stones weighing over 100 tons were used. In fact one is even estimated to weigh more than 20,000 tons and is as tall as a five story building. Today, the largest crane in the world is only capable of lifting about 3,000 tons (Chittick, p. 80). Cold and hot water pipes have been found in ancient Minoan cities where bathrooms had running water and flushing toilets. There were also man-holes for routine inspection of these very modern pipes. Optical lenses and evidence of brain surgery have been found. The Mayans built a temple over 200 feet tall, which remained one of America's highest buildings until the first skyscraper was built in New York City. The Maya also had a calendar calculated out to 365.2420 days, and today, we have a calendar based on 365.2422 days. Though they were a pagan culture, the Mayans support our belief in a young earth. Their calendar begins at zero indicating that creation, or the beginning of time was only 56 years shorter than the Ussher record of 4004 B.C. King Tut's tomb showed crafts of incredible technology and skill. In Bolivia, a city stands 13,000 feet in the Andes which was already in ruins when the Incas were there (Airplane pilots are required to have oxygen at this height). An interesting characteristic of this city is that it seems to be built on a scale fit for giants, and the Bible speaks of giants (Genesis 6). All of this, and one can say that man is getting more intelligent (Oakland, Ancient Man)?

Other examples include some type of electrical device found in a geode, which appears to have acted as a spark plug. Inside this rock was a porcelain or ceramic insulator wrapped around a metallic shaft with threads. Not only does this show intelligence, but that rocks are capable of forming rapidly under the right conditions, since this artifact was discovered inside a geode. An analog computing device was also recovered from a shipwreck in the Aegean Sea from the first century B.C. It consisted of complex differential gears, which were not re-discovered until modern times (Chittick, p. 3,4). It also appears that the ancients may have been able to fly using hot air balloons. The Nazca Desert, just south of Lima, Peru, is lined with geometric figures of animals extending for miles. Not only do some of the lines run for more than 5 miles, but they are also perfectly straight; as much as even our modern aerial surveyors are capable of. These drawings are only visible from the air, leading us to the conclusion that flight has been rediscovered. Recent research has even indicated that this is true. The Nazcas wove a very fine, black cloth which was apparently used for hot air balloons. When a Nazca member died, they were put into a basket under the balloon. As the balloon was filled with hot air, the black color kept the heat in, and their body was carried out to sea in a ritual dedicated to the sun god. Actual experiments using the same materials available to the Nazca have proven successful for hot air flights (Chittick, p. 73). One of my favorite examples of a changing world or extremely intelligent ancestors are the accurate maps showing what the land looks like under the polar ice caps. Only in modern times have we been able to determine this, and only with high tech equipment. Either men had drawn these maps shortly after the Flood, before the Ice Age hit, or they possessed amazing technology. By the way, man should not have been around prior to the Ice Age according to evolution.

Often times it is said that ancient man could not travel as well. However, the Polynesians had boats capable of traveling across the entire ocean before the time of Christ. *Readers Digest* records the fact that the Americas were not discovered by Columbus. In Rio De Genera, ancient stones with inscriptions giving a date of 531 BC describe the Sidonians traveling to what is now the Americas. While comparing ancient Egyptian Hieroglyphics with writings of an old Indian tribe from the East Coast of the United States, it was discovered that many words were identical (Oakland, Ancient Man). This fits well with the spreading of people at the Tower of Babel. Further evidence is seen at the archaeological site near Santiago, Tuxtla where a sculpture over 2,000 years old, appears to be negroid. No black people were believed to be in the New World until slave trade began, yet this is "rock hard" evidence suggesting otherwise. In Mexico, an Egyptian figurine was found showing Egyptian influence in the western hemisphere. At the pre-Inca site of Tiahuanaco in Bolivia, faces of every racial background are carved into a stone wall (Chittick, p. 77). All these examples show that men of all races had contact with one another, and therefore, they could travel far beyond what was previously thought. Could these people have migrated out from the Tower of Babel? They certainly were intelligent beings.

Another fascinating fact about the ancient people is that they were obsessed with the observation of the stars and planets. Often times they would build temples and ziggurats on hills to worship the "gods." All over the world, evidence of such demonic worshipping has been found. What I find interesting is that this answers why civilization has declined. The Bible tells us of many occasions where God destroyed entire cities due to the worshipping of false gods. The ancients worshipped everything as a god, whether it be wind, rain, sun, moon, rivers or hills. Today, with the new age movement growing rapidly, history is repeating itself. Everything and everyone is a god, according to the new age. We are no longer physically evolving, but rather spiritually moving upward to a higher level of consciousness. If God destroyed past civilizations because of their turning to satanic practices, will He not do it again? The Bible clearly tells us, yes!

Even more recent findings show that man was not stupid. In 1992, a Stone Age "ice man" was discovered well preserved in a glacier in the Alps of Italy. If by chance the C-14 date could be trusted, it showed that he lived about 1000 years before Abraham on a Biblical scale. Yet many signs of intelligence were seen. He had boots that were insulated by grass, a bow and arrow using ballistic principles, tattoos (1300 years earlier than scientists had expected), neatly trimmed hair, well-made clothing with stitched patterns, plants that may have been used as medicine, and a copper ax which was before its time, according to evolutionary thinking (Von Fange, pp. 164-165).

Archaeological finds go completely against the traditional views of evolution. The Bible clearly shines as truth with over 25,000 identified sites which match the Bible. The Tower of Babel, part of the continuation of satanic worship, was just one of the many sites in which God showed man who was in charge. After being spread throughout the world, much technology was lost, but much was taken with them as well. Too many similarities between cultures and languages exist for evolution to be true, not to mention the extreme sophistication involved as well. At the time of creation, man must have used 100% of his brain compared to the small percentage used today. What amazing evidence for a man made in God's image at God's Creation. Just think how much more we would know if evolutionists would spend less time trying to trace mankind back to apes and, instead, trace them back to a more advanced people preceding even the Egyptians.

Population Crunch. . .Not

Given the six billion people on earth today and the 2% growth rate per year, it would only take 1100 years to reach this point from one pair of human beings. This fits relatively well with the Biblical model, taking into consideration Noah's Flood and the mass destruction of civilizations because of satanic worship and the judgment put upon them as a result thereof.

If evolution is true, on the other hand, we have millions of years to account for. As mentioned when discussing the lack of human bones in the fossil record, in only 1 million years there should be 10^{8600} people on the earth today.

That is far beyond what is considered mathematical impossibility, and then certainly more evidence of human bones should be found in the fossil record. Going backward to see what the growth rate must be if the earth is only 1 million years old and has a current population of six billion people, we find that it should be 0.002%. This is far below what all of history has ever recorded or would allow.

The problem is also compounded when we consider that today we are living in a period of mass murder (abortions), wars, violence, birth control, and a growing number of diseases. Therefore, if we still have a growth of 2%, the ancient civilizations should have at least the same rate, if not more.

Evolution has also been teaching us that the world has become overcrowded and that something must be done about this problem. The following headline appeared in the August 14, 1994, issue of the *Los Angeles Times*: "Earth Feels Crunch of 5.5 Billion People" This article explained how the present population of 5.5 billion people is twice that which the earth is capable of maintaining for a long period of time. Paul Ehrlich of Stanford University has been studying this topic for some time and is considered to be one of the leading experts in population research among the scientific community. Ehrlich has concluded that "We want to reduce the impact so there's hope of getting over the top and bringing the population back down." In order to reach this goal, it is believed that both social and political reform are necessary, ultimately closing the gap between the upper and lower class, male/female stereotypes, and industrial versus agricultural countries. Removing these gaps would maximize cooperation among individual and national groups. In addition, Ehrlich states, "There's [much] evidence that equity between the sexes can lower the fertility rate," which shows that women in the work field no longer have time to have children, thereby slowing down the growing population problem.

This proposed plan to bring the population down seems, at first, somewhat innocent; however, in the book, The Population Bomb, also by Ehrlich, abortion, too, is viewed as a praiseworthy means of population control. Ehrlich views abortion as "a highly effective weapon in the armory of population control," and recommends "compulsory birth regulation" by means of government regulated "temporary sterilants to water supplies or staple food" (Ehrlich, Bomb, pp. 88, 135). In addition, Ehrlich desires that "federal laws make instruction in birth control methods mandatory in all public schools" (Ehrlich, World Population, p.9). As one can see, population control encompasses a wide range of religious consequences. No longer is it simply a matter of how to provide food or water to the people, but rather how to alter our lifestyles and keep ourselves from growing in numbers, even if it means taking the lives of the yet to be born children of God.

Psalm 127:4-5 states, "Like arrows in the hands of a warrior are sons born in one's youth. Blessed is the man whose quiver is full of them." Also Genesis 1:28 which reads, "God blessed them and said to them, 'Be fruitful and increase in number; fill the earth and subdue it. Rule over the fish of the sea and the birds of the air, and over every living creature that moves on the ground."

Scripture clearly tells us that children are a blessing and God desires us to procreate and nurture our children in the admonition of the Lord. Yet, most importantly, we have the promise that God will always provide for our needs as well as our children's, no matter how many people are on the earth.

Ehrlich and others make children a curse and take away from God's command to "fill the earth." Perhaps our job is done; maybe we have overfilled the earth because of our promiscuity and sinfulness. Indeed, this excess is what many would like us to believe; however, the population scare is simply another ploy to herd unsuspecting citizens into following, and even depending upon, the government for comfort and support. Claire Chambers, who has followed the population control movement since 1977, states, "Since its inception, the UN has advanced a worldwide program of population control, scientific human breeding, and Darwinism" (Chambers, p.3). One can already sense the evolutionary ideas of Darwin and Hitler brewing in the minds of many proud and powerful men who hold to the belief that certain races are weak and, therefore, unwanted or unnecessary. One need not look far to see other examples of such UN support for anti-Christian means of population control.

In calculating the population of the entire earth, one discovers that all the people could easily fit in the state of Iowa without its becoming any more densely populated than Tokyo, Japan. Vernon Walters, former ambassador to the United Nations under Ronald Reagan, validates a relatively sparse worldwide population when he shows that, "if the United States were as densely populated as Belgium, we would have 3 billion people." He went on to add, "Have any of you ever seen an undernourished Belgian" (*St. Louis Post*, 1994)?

One way to solve this overpopulation problem is to attempt to find another planet or moon to live on. In order to test this possibility, the Biosphere which covered 3.15 acres in Arizona tried to isolate a living environment that would self-supply everything needed to sustain life. It proved impossible to sustain only eight people. After 1.3 years in 1991, the oxygen level was too low, 19 of the 25 vertebrate species became extinct, as did most of the insects, the water and air were polluted and temperature control failed as well. Joel Cohen and David Tilman were quoted, saying, "No one yet knows how to engineer systems that provide humans with the life-supporting services that natural ecosystems produce for free. . . earth remains the only known home that can sustain life" (*Science*, 1996). In short, nobody can give what God has already given and promises to give.

The overpopulation myth has engulfed our society, promoting evolution to diminish Christianity and dependence upon God, replacing Him with the infamous Big Brother. We must stand firm on our foundation of Christ, our Redeemer and Savior, our Leader and Protector. While evolution makes life without purpose and reduces our physical bodies to that of an animal, abortion and other population control methods flourish uninhibited, without a hint of reason or remorse. Though equality among the roles of men and women, too, are explained away with sociological jargon, Scripture is clear regarding how we are to lead our lives. Stand firm in the faith and praise God from whom ALL blessings flow.

CHAPTER 13
THE "VERY GOOD" PRE-FLOOD WORLD

The Firmament

Keep in mind while reading this chapter, though interesting, is making only a *theory* about the unobserved past. There is no way to describe for certain anything about the past, but scientific experiments today are suggesting that much of this is indeed possible. Scripture certainly describes a world that was much different prior to the Flood of Noah, so be sure, there was a very good pre-Flood world, but as to why, we can only theorize.

There is vast Biblical and scientific evidence showing a primordial paradise. Legends and traditions record that some people did not experience helpless old age, everything was there. The Sumerians and Egyptians record that there was no sin on earth, the crocodile did not seize prey and the serpent did not bite. Even in China it was said that perfect virtue existed and the birds and animals were led about without restraint (Oestreicher, Impact 192). How could such events take place? The Bible clearly tells us they did and science certainly shows the earth to be much better in times past.

One of the major reasons this paradise existed was perhaps the firmament or expanse created by God on the second day. "And God said, 'Let there be an expanse between the waters to separate water from water.' So God made the expanse and separated the water under the expanse from the water above it. And it was so" (Genesis 1:6-7). During creation there was both a vertical and horizontal separation of water. The "horizontal" separated the dry land from the water and the "vertical" separated water from water thus creating the firmament. Therefore we have an indication that water was involved in this canopy. We do not know for sure what form of water it was made of, but other possible clues come from the Hebrew word for firmament or expanse, which is *raqiya* (raw-kee'-ah). *Raqiya* means to flatten out and extend a solid vault or canopy.

Another point about *raqiya* is that it also seems to refer to metal. For years Hebrew scholars have not known what to do with this definition of "firmament" so it has generally been accepted as just being a water vapor canopy. However, Josephus, a famous Jewish Historian records that the firmament was indeed crystalline (Josephus, Antiquities) as do other modern scholars (Harris, no. 862). There also seems to be some scientific evidence that supports a metal in the firmament.

An interesting characteristic of most metals is that they are clear in their pure form. In fact, when man went to the moon the visors on their helmets had a thin layer of pure, transparent, gold (*National Geographic*, 1969). Water is

H_2O, meaning two parts hydrogen and one part oxygen. When pure H_2O is compressed in experiments done today, under extremely cold conditions the oxygen appears bluish, but the two parts of hydrogen are crystallized. At first the crystals appear transparent (can see through) and later they become opaque (can't see through). Since *raqiya* means to flatten or compress together and spread out, the water (H_2O) may have reacted in a similar way as seen in the above experiment, creating a firmament with hydrogen crystals (Baugh, Symphony).

Taking this a step further, microscopic examination of this crystalline, metallic hydrogen shows that a vast majority is transparent, allowing light to shine through. However, also present in smaller amounts are areas of opaque metallic hydrogen that are superconductive (*Popular Science*, 1989). This is important for two reasons. First, light would shine through only those "veins" in the firmament which were transparent (Mao, p. 1463). But most importantly, the opaque, superconductive material would serve as a means to hold the firmament in place. Recent experiments of superconductive material shows that it will suspend a magnet in the air. NASA showed a photograph of a man holding superconductive material between his fingers and above the material was suspended in mid air, a magnet. This would work both upside down and right side up (NASA, 1988). Keeping in mind that the earth is like a great big magnet and the firmament perhaps having a superconductive metallic hydrogen, the firmament would be held in place (*Discover*, 1991). However, the above theory can not be tested today and, therefore, we can not say for sure this happened. In fact, some believe this to be scientifically inaccurate.

Hydrogen when excited by energy glows pink. This could perhaps explain why plants in the pre-Flood world grew much more abundantly than today (by hundreds of feet). This is not to say that the earth would appear pink but rather pink light would be given off. It would be similar to looking through a pair of pink sunglasses where the world does not appear pink but rather all colors seem more vivid. Research has shown that plants grow better in pink light, which fits exactly in the firmament model (Moses, p. 88).

Still, yet another fascinating result of such a firmament is that it solves much of our problem with C-14 dating. As mentioned earlier, C-14 comes from N-14 being bombarded by cosmic radiation. The firmament would have filtered out the harmful, short wave, radiation received from the sun and, therefore, C-14 would not be produced (even if the canopy was just water vapor). This means that living organisms before the Flood would have little or no C-14 in their bodies and, therefore, would appear extremely old according to the C-14 dating method.

The filtering out of the harmful, short wave radiation is **one** of the causes for life's longevity in the pre-Flood world. Studies of the average age of people on a geographical basis shows that people today live shorter lifespans near the equator (Brown, Secret, p.92). Also, it is a well known fact that the sun causes us to age much faster than normal. Recently on the Oprah Winfrey show someone asked if there was anything to stop the aging process. The answer was that the best thing you could do was to never (summer or winter) go outside without sun screen on. The deadly, short waves of the sun are known to cause over 60 diseases today, all of which would be prevented because of the firmament (Peterson, Longevity). Keep this in mind as we will return to this subject soon.

Another beneficial effect of the firmament would be greater air pressure with higher oxygen (higher oxygen without the higher air pressure would be harmful). Before the Flood, evidence shows we had roughly twice the atmospheric pressure and from 30-35% oxygen (compared to the current 21%) as seen in air bubbles trapped in fossilized amber (Berner, p. 1406). However, new evidence has caused creationists to feel this is too high because oxygen poisoning would result and, therefore, a better estimate may be from 23 to 28%.

Higher air pressure is also what we would expect to see with the firmament because all of the atmospheric gases, which NASA shows have escaped nearly 200 miles into outer space (as far as gravitational pull would allow) would have been compressed underneath this canopy. At present our bodies are under about 14.7 pounds of pressure per square inch, but being born into this world we normally feel nothing from this pressure. Although, when there are weather changes often times joints ache due to the change in pressure. Today, greater air pressure with higher oxygen is of great benefit to our bodies as we see from replication of such an atmosphere in hyperbaric chambers. A hyperbaric chamber is something that allows us to adjust the oxygen and air pressure in a controlled environment. Amazing things happen in hyperbaric oxygen treatment (HBO). Normally it takes from 7 to 21 days for an open wound to heal and 53 days to completely heal. However, with HBO this healing time can, on average, be cut in half, depending on the severity and type of problem (Fife, 1994). Dr. William Fife is head of the HBO lab at Texas A & M University where more research exists on this subject than in any other non-government center. Some of the current research at Texas A & M suggests that HBO treatment may cure Chronic Fatigue Syndrome, Post Polio Syndrome, and heal migraine headaches within 30 to 40 minutes. Other near miraculous healings of gas gangrene and ear drum problems, have been treated within one to two hours (Fife, 1995). In a few cases, people have shown near miraculous healing from arthritis and carbon monoxide poisoning. It was reported that one man was brought into a hospital brain dead as a direct result of carbon monoxide poisoning. This man was an organ donor so they wanted to try and purify his organs. They wheeled him and his life support system into the chamber and three days later the organs were purified because the man walked out of the hospital completely recovered with complete memory (Baugh, Battle).

Increased air pressure has solved another problem. Paleontologists have struggled with the idea of animals such as the *pteranodon* actually being capable of flight despite their 20 foot wingspans. The size and weight of this creature indicates that to become airborne it would need to run at least fifteen miles an hour and by appearance, they could not run at all. However, as airline pilots will attest, it is easier for heavy airplanes to take off at lower elevations because of the greater air pressure. With twice the atmospheric pressure before the Flood, which science (even evolution, but not on same time frame) is now supporting, the *pteranodon* would be able to take to flight with only a slight breeze.

Larger animals such as the *brachiosaur* have been criticized too, because how could they get enough food for their huge bodies when plants were the only thing on the menu? With higher air pressure animals have an increased metabolism and oxidation allowing them to receive maximum energy from the food they eat. Therefore, less food would be required.

It has even been suggested that as a direct result of higher pressure and oxygen that mosquitoes would not even bite before the Flood. Today, it is the female mosquito which bites in order to receive nutrients from the oxygen in your blood. However, in the pre-Flood atmosphere the higher oxygen content and air pressure may have kept this annoying pest satisfied (Baugh, Symphony). Again this is something theorized about the unobserved past so we can not be sure, but it would make sense with what the Bible says about a "very good" world.

The amount of carbon dioxide in the air is much less today than during the pre-Flood era (Walker, p. 164). It has been proposed that we had eight times the amount we currently have today (from 0.026% to .25%) which again fits perfectly with the creation model due to the vast quantity and quality of plants giving off carbon dioxide (Zimmer, p.32).

The higher pressure and carbon dioxide content also explains why such lush, huge vegetation is seen in the fossil record. At K O University in Tokyo, Japan, Dr. Kei Moris did some fascinating studies on a cherry tomato plant (the kind that get about 2-3 feet tall and live about 2-3 months with cherry size tomatoes). He wanted to maximize the potential of this tomato plant's growth so he put it into a cylinder by which he could pump up the air pressure. His reasoning behind this was to enable the plant to take in more carbon dioxide quicker, but inadvertently he was recreating a pre-Flood atmosphere. Dr. Moris wanted to also get rid of the harmful rays of the sun so he brought sunlight to his basement through fiber optics, again inadvertently recreating the proposed pre-Flood world. After two years had passed Kei Moris had a cherry tomato plant that stood over 14 feet tall and had 903 tomatoes that were grapefruit size (Brown, Secret,p 159). Today, this plant is still living after 15 years and is over 40 feet tall bearing 15,000 very large tomatoes (Baugh, Symphony). Being created as vegetarians (Genesis 1:29-30), this fits well into the "very good" world that God made.

Genesis 2:5 mentions that it did not rain until the time of the Flood and, therefore, natural streams watered the earth. With a firmament, a sub tropical climate would be expected all over the world because it would serve as a greenhouse, holding in the heat but not getting too hot. High and low air pressure systems would not form which would not allow clouds to form, which would not allow rain. This also explains why there was no rainbow before the Flood.

One final adjustment of our thinking about the pre-Flood world involves the electromagnetic field of the earth. Scientists have measured the electromagnetic field of the earth's atmosphere for over a century and we now know that the it has declined nearly 7% in only 130 years (McDonald, p. 14). Not only does this present a better atmosphere but also a young one. Accordingly, if we could go back in time only 15 to 20,000 years ago, we would have the electromagnetic field of a neutron star and atoms could not hold together; the planet could not exist. (Likewise, in the next 2,000 years the field will cease and life will not be possible either (Rees, Robin p. 14).

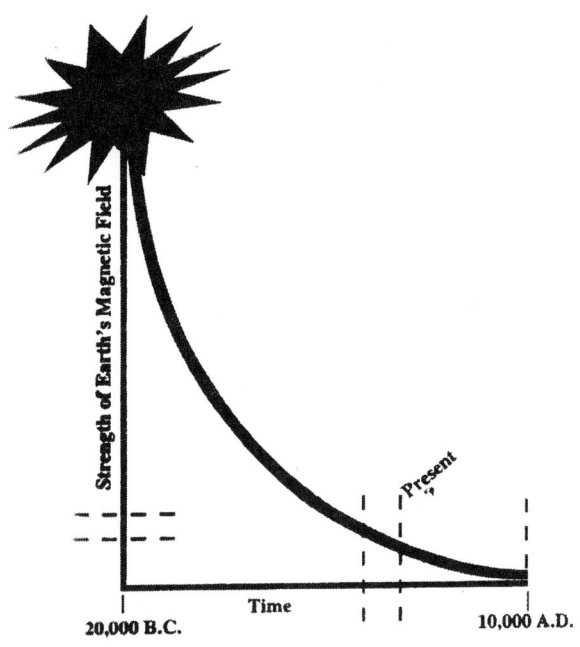

Figure 35: The Magnetic field of the earth would have been too strong for the planet to exist only as far as 20,000 BC. Likewise, it will be too weak for life at 10,000 AD

Further evidence shows that the electromagnetic field influences the body in incredible ways. In fact, it affects everything from molecules to man, and without it, cells can not divide during the process of mitosis (Dubrov, p. 61). Evidence is also present showing that this much needed field was not only stronger in the past but may have even held steady before the Flood, thereby creating a better atmosphere. How and why could this be? Answer: the firmament held the energy in place.

My favorite example of the benefit of the higher electromagnet currents on our bodies has to deal with snakes. Today, if one is bit by a rattlesnake, a long process of treatment and pain is the outlook, unless a person has a stun gun. Yes, a stun gun. I myself have one which delivers only 36,000 volts of DC current. If I were bitten, I would take the stun gun and zap myself near the bite, again perpendicular to the first zap, and a third time just because it felt good. I

Figure 36: Rattlesnake bites can be cured by electrical shock treatments.

probably would not even go to the hospital after this. New evidence is showing that electricity can be a cure for all kinds of venomous bites, including bees, spiders, mosquitoes and snakes. Snake venom is made up of mainly proteins and enzymes which are chemically bonded together, and therefore, making them impossible for your body to assimilate in any beneficial way. However, electricity breaks those bonds allowing your body to take in the protein and it turns out to be beneficial to you. So in the pre-Flood world, after the curse, if you were bit by a snake, it may not have affected you because of the higher electromagnetic field. Also, the wound from the bite may have healed much faster because the higher oxygen and pressure would aid in that, just as in HBO treatment today. I have given lectures where doctors have not heard of such a thing while in other places I have had doctors in the audience who have actually used this treatment. Nonetheless, it has been documented and proved to work in most cases.

The Brown Recluse spider is one of the most dreadful of all spiders. A Brown Recluse bite literally rots our flesh down to the bone. One 10 year old girl bit by a Brown Recluse Spider (Fiddle back) was zapped on top of the bite while being grounded underneath the bite (under the arm). In 24 hours, all was gone.

In fact, the Oklahoma State Medical Journal recorded that from September of 1988 to September of 1989, 21 cases were confirmed where a Brown Recluse Spider bite had been "zapped" for treatment and all cases were cured within one treatment (Osborn, p.9).

Regarding snakes, Dr. Ronald Guderian, a missionary doctor from Seattle, has successfully treated more than 60 humans with snakebites by electric shock. Tests have shown that the enzymes in snake venom are destructive to human tissue but when these enzymes are first "zapped" and then put in test tubes with human flesh, they no longer destroy the tissue (Mueller, p.66-68).

One farmer was stung by a bee and was deathly allergic to bee stings so he began running to his house. On the way he felt his chest beginning to tighten and in his preoccupied state, he tripped over the electric fence. Need I say more? He was cured (Meuller, p76).

Many other examples have been recorded showing us what a great world the pre-Flood world must have been. If the world was like this, how come we are just discovering this now? We aren't discovering it, rather rediscovering it today! Ancient batteries have been found in Egypt showing not only the intelligence of man, but perhaps also past medical treatments. For years scientists did not know what these batteries were used for but new findings show much historical evidence relating electric shock to medicine. Electric fish were used for medicinal purposes by the Greeks and Romans while bronze and iron needles with electrical devices have been found in Seleucia, which may have been used for acupuncture (already a standard practice in China). The ancient Scribonius Largus wrote, "For any sort of foot gout, when the pain comes on it is good to put a living black torpedo fish under his feet while standing on the beach, not dry but one on which the sea washes, until he feels that his whole foot and ankle are numb up to the knees" (Down, p.12). All of this points to a forgotten age where memories of higher electric fields once aided in the fighting of diseases and other common ailments.

Combine all of the evidence above and we may have the answer to why not only plants were larger in the fossil record but animals as well. It appears nearly everything was better in the past. In the fossil record some dragon flies had wing spans up to 60 inches, cockroaches were a foot long, bison stood 10 feet at the shoulders and the Saber tooth tiger stood 6 feet at the shoulders. (Meanwhile plants which are only 20 inches today were 120 feet as seen in the fossil record. Sounds like a cherry tomato plant doesn't it?).

Longevity of Man

The graph below shows the ages people were living before and after the Flood. Adam had lived 930 years while Methuselah topped out at 969 years, but after the Flood, immediately the life span drops. Enoch, of course, was taken to heaven alive and therefore we can ignore him for our purpose here. The bottom line shows the age at which these people were having children, and again we see a sharp drop after the Flood. Notice the people who do have children at an old age must be disqualified from our example because God granted Abraham and Sarah a child in their "old age," which already at that time was considered to be a miracle. As we have shown above, the firmament collapsed as a result of the

Figure 37: Longevity greatly and quickly decreased after the flood as the top line indicates. The bottom line shows the age in which pre and post flood people had children.

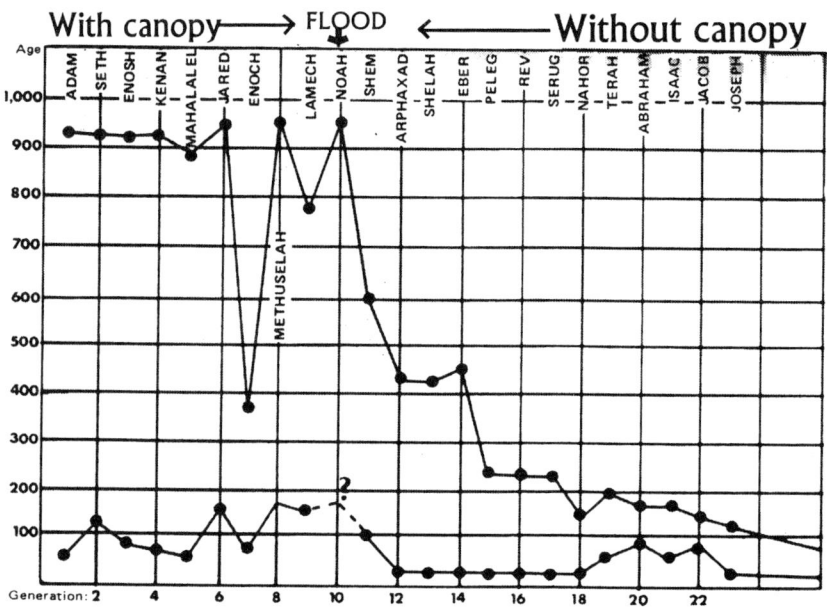

Flood and no longer did we have this much needed, "very good,"protective device. After this, short wave radiation, lower air pressure, less carbon dioxide, less oxygen, and a lower magnetic field all contributed to a sharp drop in longevity. All of this not to mention the fact that Adam and Eve were created genetically perfect until after the curse, when things changed and genetic mistakes were passed down through the generations allowing for more disease, etc. After solar radiation was more prevalent post-Flood, these genetic mutations would occur on a faster basis. (A very pure genetic make-up answers how Cain could marry his close relative and still have healthy children). Note: If dinosaurs lived as long as people, this could explain why some would be so large because many reptiles today never stop growing as long as they live, therefore, a 900 year old dinosaur could get very large.

Later on the graph, at the time of Peleg, another sharp drop in lifespan occurs. As mentioned earlier, this may be the time at which the earth was divided and perhaps the Ice-Age occurred. The cold, damp climate associated with this period may have contributed to the evidence of rickets that we see in the bones of Neanderthal Man.

All fits well into the Biblical picture. So there you have it! We now may know why people were able to live longer in the pre-Flood world. One thing is for sure, they did live longer because the Bible tells us so.

CHAPTER 14
NOAH'S ARK

What Happened?

In order to fully grasp the importance of the Ark today one must understand the importance of it in the past. In the days not long after creation, the Bible tells us, "The LORD saw how great man's wickedness on the earth had become, and that every inclination of the thoughts of his heart was only evil all the time. The LORD was grieved that he had made man on the earth, and his heart was filled with pain. So the LORD said, 'I will wipe mankind, whom I have created, from the face of the earth--men and animals, and creatures that move along the ground, and birds of the air--for I am grieved that I have made them'" (Genesis 6:5-7). It was because of man's rejection of God that the Flood came (The same destruction by other means can happen today, too). This disaster did not come without warning as Noah was given 120 years in which to build the Ark and for people to repent (Genesis 6:3). However, people continued to reject God so His anger came down upon the people of the earth. It began to rain for 40 days and 40 nights as the firmament collapsed and the fountains of the deep were broke open, covering the highest mountain by over 20 feet (Showing it to be a global Flood, not a local one). Before this, the land was watered by natural streams (and perhaps heavy dew as a result of the firmament) because it had never rained before (Genesis 2:5) and, therefore, rain itself must have been terrifying (Also explains why no rainbow before the Flood). One hundred and fifty days later, after the waters began to abate, the Ark rested on Ararat still surrounded by water. Seven more months would pass before Noah and his family could set foot on dry ground. Two and one-half months after resting on Ararat, the tops of the nearby mountains were visible. Forty days after this Noah released a raven which never returned (Ravens are scavengers and it would not bother them to get into the muddy, wet surroundings). Seven days following, a dove was sent out and returned, perhaps not wanting to rest on unclean surfaces. After another seven days, another dove was sent out and brought back in its beak an olive leaf. Three hundred seventy-one days had passed from the onset of the Flood until the end where the Ark is said to rest to this day on Ararat. Of much importance was the rainbow that God set in the sky as a covenant that He would never again send such a Flood to destroy the earth. Not only is this a wonderful promise but it also shows the Flood to be a global event. If it was just a local flood, God would have never promised not to send another Flood like it. But we know in fact, that it was a mountain covering deluge (II Peter 3:3-6) which was even given its own name to distinguish it from other floods in the Bible (*mabbul*-Hebrew, *kataklusmos*-Greek). The fact that the lifespan of man declined sharply thereafter, as well as numerous other proofs, also show this to be anything but a local event.

  The vast geological evidence corresponds with the Biblical and historical record. The September, 1977 issue of *Reader's Digest* states, "With variations, the Bible account of a great universal flood is part of the mythology and legend of almost every culture on earth. Even people living far from the sea. . . have legends of a great flood washing over the land, covering the tops of mountains and wiping out virtually all life on earth" (p. 129). As earlier mentioned, many historians believe that legends so widespread have much truth in them.

17th Day of Nisan Not a Coincidence

Careful note was given to explain that the Ark landed on Ararat on "the seventeenth day of the seventh month" (Genesis 8:4). Henry Morris gives a possible explanation for this detail as being a topological reference to Christ's deliverance. Dr. Morris writes, "The Lord Jesus Christ rose from the dead also on 'the seventeenth day of the second month.' The seventh month of the Jewish civil year (and this is probably the calendar used here in Genesis 7 and 8) later was made the first month of the religious year, and the Passover was set for the fourteenth day of that month (Exodus 12:2). Christ, our Passover (I Corinthians 5:7), was slain on that day, but then rose three days later, on the seventeenth day of the seventh month of the civil calendar" (Morris, Record, p.209). As Noah was delivered from the bondage of the Ark, we too have been delivered from the bondage of sin.

The 17th day of the 7th month is the 17th of Nisan on the Jewish Calendar, corresponding to our April 17th. Also, *deliverance* first came on the 17th of Nisan through the Ark of Noah. However, a **second** deliverance came on the same day (17th of Nisan) years later, at the parting of the Red Sea. About this time, the Passover was first instituted as the 14th of Nisan where God said, "This is a day you are to commemorate; for the *generations to come* you shall celebrate it as a festival to the LORD--a *lasting ordinance"* (Exodus 12:14). The Israelites left Egypt the following day (15th of Nisan) and camped that evening at Succoth. On the 16th of Nisan they traveled again as far as Ethan and finally on the 17th of Nisan they reached Migdol and the Red Sea (Num 33:1-8).

Before the Exodus, a **third** deliverance on the 17th of Nisan is the entrance into Egypt and the deliverance from a famine. We know about this event because Scripture tells us that the above exodus occurred on the exact day 430 years earlier when the Israelites entered Egypt through Jacob's family. We read, "Now the length of time the Israelite people lived in Egypt was 430 years. At the end of the 430 years, to *the very day*, all the Lord's divisions left Egypt" (Exodus 12:40-41).

Also a **fourth** deliverance occurs on this same day about 40 years later after the Israelites wandered in the desert before being allowed to enter the promised land. After crossing the Jordan, the Passover was celebrated (always on the 14th of Nisan). On the 15th day, "The day after the Passover, that *very day,* they ate some of the produce of the land: unleavened bread and roasted grain" (Joshua 5:11). On the 16th day, "The manna stopped the *day after* they ate this food from the land; there was no longer any manna for the Israelites, but that year they ate of the produce of Canaan" (Joshua 5:12). That now brings us to the 17th day of Nisan again where Joshua went to check out the walls of Jericho and saw a man with a drawn sword. Joshua asked him if he was a friend or an enemy, where upon this "man" replied, "Neither . . .but as commander of the army of the LORD I have now come" (Joshua 5:14). Joshua then received detailed instructions of how to conquer Jericho. Jericho itself did not fall until seven days later due to the seven days of marching around the city walls, but one can say that the same day the angel gave Joshua those instructions was the same day in which Jericho was doomed to fall.

A **fifth** deliverance on this day occurs about 800 years after the entrance into the promised land. After the period of the judges, (Saul, David and Solomon) the kingdom was divided and a series of evil kings ruled Israel causing worship in God's Temple to cease. One of the last evil kings, Ahaz, was replaced by his son Hezekiah, a righteous man who cleansed the Temple and restored worship therein. 2 Chronicles 29:1-28 gives us the chronological events climaxing on the 17th day of Nisan. Here we see that on the 16th day of Nisan the cleansing of the Temple is complete. Worship and sacrifice then begins on the 17th of Nisan. A most important day in Jewish and Christian history because their salvation is again restored.

Yet a **sixth** deliverance occurred on this notable day. The book of Esther contains a story about the entire Jewish race being nearly wiped out by Haman, who was under King Xerxes command. Through a long process of Godly intervention, the Jews again are saved on the 17th day of Nisan. Haman had tricked King Xerxes into signing a edict to kill all of the Jews. Esther 3:12 tells us that this signing took place on the 13th of the first month, that being the month of Nisan. Immediately after Esther heard of this decree she had the entire Jewish community fast and pray for three days. When finished on the 16th day of Nisan (Esther 5:1) Esther went to the king and invited him and Haman to a banquet the following day, the 17th of Nisan. At this banquet Haman's evil tricks were exposed. He was executed by the King and the Jews had been delivered once again.

As mentioned at the beginning of this section, by far the most important of all the events that took place on the 17th of Nisan was the resurrection of Christ. A **seventh** deliverance for all mankind. Christ was crucified on the 14th of Nisan, the day the Passover began. After remaining in the grave for three days, Christ rose from the dead on the 17th. If one calculates the odds of so many important events occurring on any given day you come up with 1 in 783,864,876,960,000,000 chances that such events could take place. From this alone it is clear that God controls the world and He watches over His people. Isn't it wonderful to have a personal relationship with such a loving and powerful God, who has promised heavenly dwellings for all who follow Him. Certainly, nothing stands in the way of this promise, not even Satan himself.

Did Giants Really Rome the Earth?

We read in Numbers 13:33 (KJV), "And there we saw the giants, the sons of Anak, which come of the giants: and we were in our own sight as grasshoppers, and so we were in their sight that the people living in Palestine at that time were giants." Also, Genesis 6:4 (KJV) states, "There were giants in the earth in those days; and also after that, when the sons of God came in unto the daughters of men, and they bare children to them, the same became mighty men which *were* of old, men of renown." These giants seem to be one of the causes for the wickedness of the world for which God sent the Flood. For many today, the popular opinion has been that the giants came about because Godly men married worldly women. The key to understanding this question comes from the phrase, "sons of God." As strange as it seems, these people may have been angels, not the good ones, but evil angels like Satan. The book of Job seems to support this interpretation. While rebuking Job for his pride, God asked Job where he was when the earth was created: "Whereupon are the foundations thereof fastened? Or who laid the corner stone thereof; when the morning stars sang together, and all the **sons of God** shouted for joy?" (Job 38:6-7 KJV). Obviously, Godly men were not around when the foundation of the earth was laid so the sons of God must be good angels because they were the only ones created at this time. Again we read from Job, "Now there was a day when the **sons of God** came to present themselves before the LORD, and Satan came also among them. And the LORD said unto Satan, whence comest thou? Then Satan answered the LORD, and said, from going to and fro in the earth, and from walking up and down in it." (Job 1:6-7 KJV). Here too, we see that the only possible explanation for this term is evil angels. This is not hard to understand when we remember that Satan took one-third of the angels with him when he was cast out of heaven. The Hebrew word used here is *bene elohim,* and is found only one other time (Job 2:1) in the Old Testament besides the above mentioned. Related words such as *bar elohim* (Daniel 3:25) and *bene elim* (Psalm 29:1; 89:6) are also used, but again are interpreted as angels, possibly making the passage in Genesis to be taken as angels also. Even Josephus and the Septuagint interpret Genesis 6:4 this way.

How could someone of the spiritual world have children with those of human flesh? Many theories have been given to explain this phenomenon including the idea that angels in the flesh with male bodies had sexual intercourse with the women of those days. However, I find it more probable (though not for certain) that simple demon possession could well have produced these effects. The New Testament records a variety of cases in which normal human beings were changed physically as a result of demon possession. The man possessed by Legion in Matthew chapter eight had extraordinary strength, while others foamed at the mouth. Why then could these angels not possess men, women, and children of that day, and make them giants or "mighty men." After all, during sexual intercourse, the two become one flesh.

A "giant" jaw was found near Java which remained in the American Museum of Natural History for some time. Dr. T. Weidenreich called it a "jaw of a giant" (Moore, p. 249). *National Geographic* had a recent article about a giant found in South Africa, "At 5 feet 4 inches tall, the boy from Turkana was surprisingly large compared with modern boys his age; . . . This find combines with previous discoveries of *homo erectus* to contradict a long held idea that humans have grown larger over the millennia. Our ancestors on the African savanna may have been much taller than we ever imagined" (*National, Geographic*, p. 629).

Who were these giants? They *may* have been none other than Satan's angels themselves who had nearly taken over the world with their deceitful ways. But as God had promised, he delivered Noah and his family to continue the line by which the Messiah would come.

What About All That Water?

Another common hang-up for people who try to reason out the Flood is the question of where the water came from and where it went. This is actually a simple question to answer and has been answered somewhat in the chapter dealing with Pangea. To first explain where the water came from we need only go to the Bible where it reads, "In the six hundredth year of Noah's life, on the seventeenth day of the second month--on that day all the *springs of the great deep burst forth*, and the *floodgates of the heavens were opened.* And rain fell on the earth forty days and forty nights" (Genesis 7:11-12). The fountains which were watering the ground with the absence of rain broke open and the firmament collapsed, changing the earth forever. We also need to remember as discussed in earlier chapters, even Biblical evidence seems to suggest that the mountains were probably not as high as they are now, nor were the oceans as deep. But even so, today the earth is 2/3 water so ample amounts are certainly present.

Where did the waters go? As just mentioned the Bible indicates that the mountains were raised and valleys were deepened, allowing for the water to run off the slopes. We read, "Thou didst cover it with the deep as with a garment; the waters stood above the mountains. At thy rebuke they fled; at the sound of thy thunder they took to flight. The mountains rose, the valleys sank down to the place which thou didst appoint for them. Thou didst set a boundary which they should not pass, so that they might not again cover the earth" (Psalm 104:6-9 -RSV). In addition to this, the Bible tells us that the wind dried up the land. The Hebrew word for wind is *ruach* which can be translated also as Spirit, depending upon the context. Therefore either the wind or intervention from the energizing Holy Spirit may have aided in the waters recession because in Genesis 1:9 the "Spirit of God was hovering (literally vibrating) over the face of the deep." An interesting connection to say the least.

The Ark Itself

Noah received direct instructions from God as to how big the Ark should be and how to build it. First of all it was to be made of gopher wood, which many have interpreted to be Cyprus wood. However, many scholars today believe that gopher wood is not a type of wood, rather a process of laminations similar to our plywood today. Combined with the pitch coat, we have a better understanding of the Ark's watertight seal (Genesis 6:14). The dimensions were given in cubits, which is to some extent unclear today. A cubit has been estimated to be from 18 to 22 inches depending upon who was king at the time. Normally a cubit was the distance from the finger tip to the elbow, thereby allowing for variance. However, most scholars, upon doing much research, believe the cubits of the Ark to equal a ship measuring 450 feet long, 75 feet wide and 45 feet tall. New evidence seems to have brought this size to be even larger, but for our purposes here we will use the smaller measurements. In any case, the Ark was a tremendously stable ship, in fact, the battleship US Oregon was actually designed after the measurements given for the Ark (same proportion but only 1/7 smaller than the Ark) and this ship proved to be one of the most seaworthy ships ever (Cummings, p.77-78). Other replicated models have been put in wave simulators that show the Ark to be stable with waves well over 500 feet, something we would expect from a Flood of this magnitude.

A window was to be constructed on top of the Ark as well. Hebrew scholars really didn't know how to use this word, but many eyewitness accounts tell us that it was just that; a window that ran along the entire length of the ship. We will discuss this further later on.

The size of the Ark is very important because many people do not believe that all the animals could fit on the Ark when the exact opposite is true. Again, using the lower limit of the cubit, the Ark would hold 1,400,000 cubic feet and hold over 40 million tons. Putting this into perspective, a standard railroad box car would hold 240 sheep and the Ark would hold 522 of these boxcars. That means the Ark would hold the equivalent of 125,000 sheep (Morris, Genesis Record, p.181). I realize sheep are small, but if we use this size as an average it fits well with what we would expect the ship to have to hold. For example, according to the fossil record the average size of the dinosaurs is that of a chicken to a lamb. We only get to hear about the large dinosaurs because they are the ones that interest us and we are the ones that provide funding for these digs, but most dinosaurs were small as evolutionists admit. We must also consider why Noah was to take these animals on the Ark -- to reproduce after the Flood. As earlier mentioned, most reptiles never stop growing throughout their entire lives. If dinosaurs were reptiles and they lived for hundreds of years like people, they would naturally get bigger. So then, would Noah take a huge, old, worn out dinosaur that would not produce young after the Flood was over, or would he take a small, young, healthy, strong dinosaur that could fill the earth again? Obviously the small, young one, so much of the problem of available space is taken care of right there.

To take this a bit further, the number of animal "kinds" on the earth may surprise you. As we go through this keep in mind that a "kind" does not mean one of every dog that was in existence, but rather only one pair of dogs would be needed to get ALL of those in existence today. It has been estimated that there are fewer than 18,000 kinds of animals today (amphibians, reptiles, mammals, birds etc.). Using this figure, let us be generous and double it to allow for those which have become extinct, bringing us to 36,000 animals. However, God said take "two" of every kind so we need to double this again, bringing us to 72,000 animals. We will then make this 75,000 because Noah was to take an additional five of every clean animal for sacrificial and eating purposes later on (Morris, Record p.185). Even at 75,000 animals we only take up about 60% of the Ark's capacity of 125,000 animals as shown by the railroad cars. This means 40% of this huge ship would be left over for food and supplies for both the animals and the eight people on board.

The Mountain of Ararat

Before one goes in search of the Ark there are a number of things to consider prior to leaving. It seems as if God does not want the discovery of the Ark to be confirmed. One must battle nature, political unrest, animals, and the mountain itself.

Mount Ararat is not just a little hill to be conquered in one day, in fact, it took Ed Davis (eyewitness of Ark) three days to reach the Ark. The base of the mountain itself covers 400 miles while the base of the snow capped area of the mountain (Aghri Dagh) covers 17 miles and stands an awesome 17,000 feet tall. Since Ararat is a volcanic mountain it is primarily made up of scarred, volcanic material, snow, and ice. An interesting but expected feature is the pillow lava which is formed from magma cooling under deep water. On June 20th, 1840, an earthquake caused what is now called the Ahora Gorge, a great chasm that reaches one and a half times the depth of the Grand Canyon. Its now rocky slopes and steep cliffs make the mountain very difficult to climb, let alone search out the Ark.

Also present on the mountain are snakes, wild dogs, mountain lions, and bears. In 1970, Eryl Cummings woke up finding mountain lion tracks in the fresh snow outside his cave. Apparently this animal came to "sniff" him out and left shortly thereafter. Eryl felt that God was watching over him (Cummings, p. 315-316). Perhaps one of the most aggressive animals on the slopes however, are the ferocious wild dogs, which will not hesitate to attack.

The weather makes it extremely difficult to search for the Ark as well. Almost daily there are storms somewhere on the mountain with blistering winds and heavy snowfall. John Morris, who has led many expeditions on Mount Ararat, was struck by lightening high in the clouds that surrounded the mountain (Morris, Ark, p.36). This "shocking" event took place on his first trip, yet he lived to go back several more times thereafter. When Ed Davis saw the Ark, a storm cut his trip short as well. In 1943, after a three day journey up to the Ark, it snowed all night until the snow was belt deep. He naturally had to go back down the mountain while he could, but even then it took him five days to get back down because of the weather (Davis, 1995).

Finally, the political unstability of the area makes this quest a rather difficult one. Since Ararat rests in Turkey, one must get special permission ($$$) from the government to even set foot on the mountain. Even after this your trip is not guaranteed, for in many cases the expeditions, even after beginning, have been called off prematurely. Political unstability is why Ed Behling was never able to take a picture of the Ark. His guide would not allow him to take a camera since Ed was American and he was Turkish. If anybody stopped them and saw the camera, they could have been accused of being spies (In Search of Ark, 1993).

Eyewitness Accounts

There are well over a dozen eye witness accounts of people who have claimed to have seen and even photographed the Ark. The problem is that the pictures always seem to disappear and people seem to die just before the proof is made conclusive. For this reason, I believe God simply does not want the Ark to be discovered yet, but some day He may show it to us, according to His purpose. The late editor of *National Geographic*, Melville Grosvenor once said, "If the

Figure 38: Russian man recalls seeing this picture taken in 1917

Ark of Noah is ever discovered, it would be the greatest archaeological find in human history, the greatest event since the resurrection of Christ, and it would alter all the currents of scientific thought" (Grosvenor, 1976). I believe to some extent this would be true. Surely many Christians would find a renewed faith and some may even turn to Christ as a result. At the least, it should allow people to recognize God's righteous judgment upon sin and the followers thereof. Romans 6:23 tells us "the wages of sin is death" and therefore we have been warned but the verse continues "the gift of God is eternal life through Jesus Christ our Lord." Remember this because despite the doom and gloom of the story of Noah and God's judgment, it brought deliverance and eternal life to those who follow Christ. However, when the Ark is actually found, a vast majority will still deny the Ark's existence and its significance to the Gospel, and scramble for alternative answers. If evolution is believed with all of its inconsistencies, I am sure an alternate explanation for the Ark won't be hard to find. Nonetheless, we turn to look at the evidence that is before us at present, which I believe is quite fascinating.

Important to realize before going into these accounts is that the people noted have had nothing to gain from their stories nor did they know each other. In some cases, the people did not even know what Noah's Ark was as they were not Christian. The sightings have, however, produced a great spiritual strengthening for these people and they now live a life dedicated to serving our Lord.

In 1905 a shepherd boy named Jacob saw the Ark as he was going after his goats which had strayed away. A picture drawn from his minds eye showed a box like structure sticking out of an icy glacier on a rocky, "step like" ledge.

In 1916 a Russian pilot was testing a new high altitude airplane engine near Mount Ararat. While looking down he saw a large boat high on the mountain slopes. He landed the airplane and told his commander about what he saw. Within days, a group of 150 soldiers and scientists climbed the mountain up to the Ark. In fact, they went inside and measured the ship, took photographs and documented everything. Unfortunately, the revolution started at the same time this was going on and the country was overrun with communism and the anti-religious Bolsheviks. The pictures, documentation, and in many cases, the soldiers, were destroyed. It wasn't until years later that a man surfaced in the United States who claimed that he had pictures that were taken during this documentation. Again, before the pictures

Figure 39: Mr. Green's friend recalls seeing this photo.

could be revealed, the man died and the pictures were lost. One man who saw the pictures, however, drew a sketch of a box-like barge sticking out of the ice and having a door on the end.

In 1953, a man named George Green took pictures of the Ark from an airplane. Naturally, he was very excited and showed various people his findings. George planned to go back with a special team to explore the Ark but died

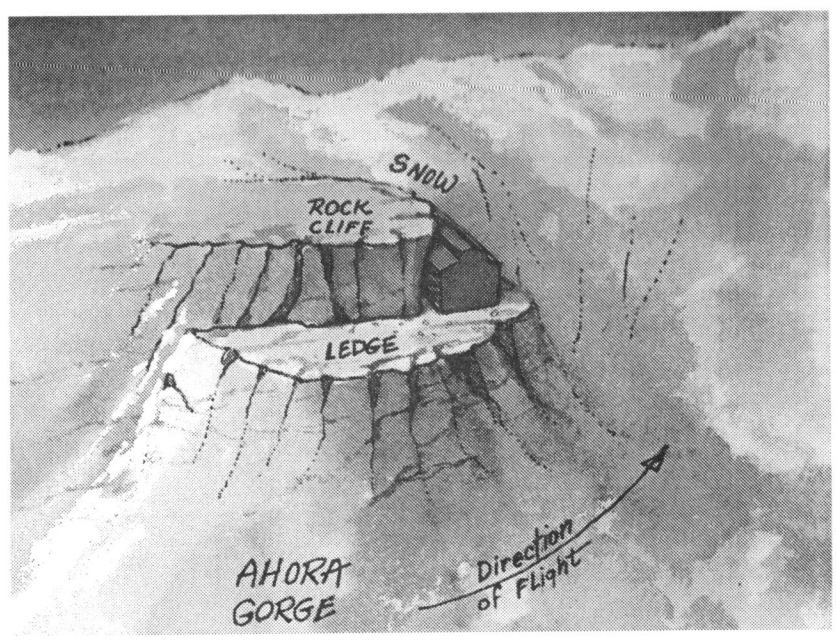

Figure 40: Mr. Shapell's sketch from Navy plane.

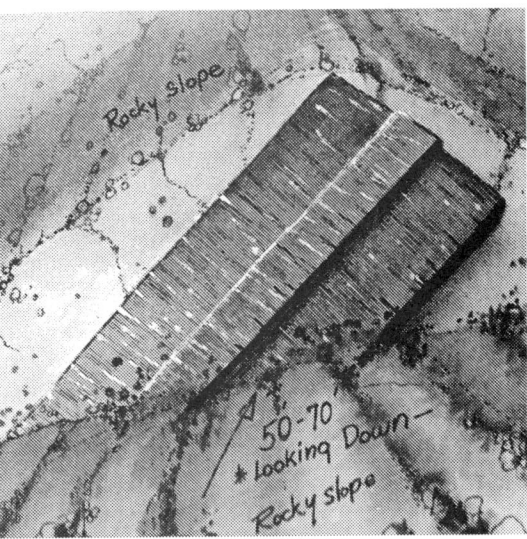

Figure 41: Ed Behling's sketch of his sighting.

before this could materialize. You guessed it, the pictures disappeared but friends recall what the pictures showed. Sketches showed a portion of the "boxy" Ark sticking out of the side of a cliff and resting on a small ledge leading to another steep cliff.

In 1974, a man by the name of Albert Shappell was flying a mission for the Navy over Turkey and was taking many pictures. While flying over Ararat, he noticed this huge boat and naturally photographed it extensively. Albert was not a Christian at the time and, therefore, had no idea what he was photographing. A few years later, after becoming a Christian, Mr. Shappell realized what his pictures were of. When he returned to the Navy to view the pictures, his mission and the photographs were denied existence.

Other people working in the Pentagon have also claimed that files exist, which are labeled "Noah's Ark," but unfortunately our government is unwilling to cooperate on this matter.

Also in 1974, Ed Behling was taken up Ararat by an old shepherd who lived on the mountain. This rare occurrence was only made possible because of a friendly relationship with a Turkish man. However, Behling had to agree not to take a camera along. The shepherd man explained that a Turkish person seen with an American and a camera could raise suspicion and unneeded danger. After extensive hiking, Ed Behling looked down below and saw the Ark protruding out of the side of the mountain upon which he was standing. Upon telling this story to John Morris of ICR, a missing puzzle piece seemed to have been discovered. By putting wood in a glacier it would be preserved, but it would not petrify. Many accounts have claimed that the wood was petrified and Ed Behling described the Ark as being buried in what appeared to be rock. Understanding that Ararat is a volcanic mountain and is made up of volcanic matter, it would be conceivable that the Ark could be covered with ash, which would petrify wood. This does not contradict those accounts having snow on the Ark for two reasons: 1) the Ark has split so there are two pieces, one being higher than the other (many accounts confirm this); and 2) snow could cover the rocks which surround the Ark. Mr. Behling also explained that he could not get down to the Ark without a rope and, therefore, was unable to get inside.

During World War II, Ed Davis also saw Noah's Ark. Ed was stationed in Iran and the government was using native boys to help drive supplies for Russia during the war. They were going to make a supply sergeant out of one boy, but he wanted to remain a driver so he asked Ed if he could get him transferred. Ed went to the sergeant and asked him if he'd transfer this boy but the sergeant said he couldn't because if he did, everyone would want to be transferred. Sometime after, Ed and the boy went down to the rock quarry to get a load of rock where Ed looked over and saw Mount Ararat. The mountain could be clearly seen this day, and Ed said, "that's where the Ark is." The boy nodded and told Ed that his folks (who he claimed were descendants of Noah) knew where the Ark was and they went up there frequently. After Ed mentioned that he would like to see it, the boy told him that someday when his dad came over to see him he'd tell him that. It wasn't long after when the boy brought his dad over to introduce him to Ed. The father said the Ark was not exposed at that time, but when it melted off he'd come get Ed and take him up. A couple of months later he came back and said part of it was showing and now was the time if he'd like to go. So Ed went to the company commander and asked permission to leave, but was refused because of the danger involved outside the camp. But, as Ed started to leave, the commander changed his mind and allowed him to drive a supply truck to the base of the mountain. That morning they left and arrived at a village near the base of the mountain in late afternoon. They went to bed for a short time until someone came to get them and then they drove the rest of the night. Finally, sometime after daylight they came to another village where they ate breakfast. From here they started off on horseback and then that evening camped overnight in a cave. Someone took their horses back, while they ate supper and went to bed. The next morning they left on foot and it took three days to go up the mountain (Along the way they stayed in different caves). The next morning it was raining and snowing so they stayed in the cave until around noon, but when it cleared up they continued up to where they could see the Ark. After a few moments, the sun broke through the clouds and shined on it. Ed recalls the front end being broken off and it had slid against the mouth of some caves. Inside the broken half he could see both large and small pens on each of the three levels. He described it as looking like a huge piece of blue rock shaped like a boat. The next day they planned to lower themselves down on ropes to get in the Ark, but that night it snowed until it was belt deep so they were forced to leave while they could. As a result of the snow, it took them five days to go back down the mountain.

During my interview with Ed Davis he also shared other fascinating insights about the people who took him up the mountain. Ed claimed that his guides were Kurdish and they told him their descendants have taken care of the Ark ever since it landed on Ararat because it was a precious, religious relic. The Kurds claimed that at times it had been under ice for a hundred years, and that's when they like it best so that nobody could damage it. Also, during Ed's visit to one of the villages he was shown artifacts kept in a locked room. After the Ark broke in two, some things were scattered on the ground so the Kurds collected them, consisting of sheep staffs and tools that were used to construct the Ark.

Since 1986, the Turkish government has not allowed anyone to enter what is known as Davis Canyon (named because of Ed Davis's description of the Ark's location). On one expedition, the Turks allowed an airplane to fly around the mountain on a cloudy day when they thought nothing could be seen. However, it was possible to get above the clouds where it was clear in places to see the mountain top and into parts of Davis Canyon. Afterwards, pictures revealed what is believed to be the *rock* that Ed Davis described standing on as he looked down on the Ark. No Ark can be seen from this picture however. Perhaps it is covered with ice or it is from the wrong angle. The plane could not get very low and was moving very fast.

One of the most remarkable pictures was taken by Bob Garby. Mr. Garby was trying to see into Davis Canyon (This is before he knew of Ed Davis) but could not get into it because of the difficult terrain. He climbed around to the top of another canyon hoping to see down inside Davis Canyon. Unable to see and somewhat disappointed, he got down on his belly over a rounded edge and held out his camera to take a picture. Not being able to see what he was photographing he left the sight. This remarkable picture showed a striking resemblance of other sketches of the Ark. Because this site photographed has yet to be examined, we cannot say that this is the Ark of Noah and some suspect it is not, however, it will be interesting to see what further expeditions reveal.

Figure 42 Mystery Object taken by Bob Garby

Another scientist from Texas has recently also photographed what is believed to be the Ark of Noah. Satellite imagery also seems to confirm the photograph; hence, an expedition is mounting to "confirm what has already been discovered" as some believe. These photographs again show exactly what sketches and accounts have been describing all along.

Many more sightings have been recorded but I feel those written about are sufficient to raise curiosity and interest. When God is ready for this discovery to be announced, the evidence above will be confirmed once and for all, but until then, we must simply believe that God's Word is true and that the Ark rested on Mount Ararat.

Furthering this testimony are the many archaeological sites on Ararat which have not yet been excavated. One would assume that after Noah got off the Ark that he would stick around in the area for a while and therefore signs of civilization should be found. Well, as a matter of fact much evidence is there. In a direct route down the mountain from
where the Ark is believed to be is a cave dated back before the Hitites judging from pictures carved into the wall. The same picture is seen in a wood sketch displayed in an ancient book. This sketch shows the cave when the entrance was still closed.

Not far below the cave rests what appears to be an altar. As you recall, immediately after leaving Noah's Ark many animal sacrifices were

Figure 43: Eight Sumerian crosses carved in rock.

made to God. Even more fascinating is a rock below the altar showing eight Sumerian crosses carved into the stone. Eight people on the Ark and eight crosses, who knows? Also present is PRE-cuneiform writing (oldest writing ever known) which experts believe to be talking about a flood, however, because of the minimal amount of writing it is difficult to decipher.

Finally, further below the altar is a shrine filled with crosses inside and out. Local shepherds call this the "House of Shem" but this probably is not the case. Nonetheless it evidences an ancient civilization in a location where the Bible suggests one should be found. Remember the rainbow (Genesis 9:13) and for that may God be praised!

As a last note, some have claimed that the mound, shaped similar to a boat on Mount Ararat, is Noah's Ark. Soil samples and later research has shown this to be false so don't get to excited if you hear about this.

Figure 44: Pre-Hitite cave. Note carvings of priests on either side of entrance. See wood carving in Figure 46.

Figure 45: Ancient wood carving showing cave in direct route down from mountain.

CHAPTER 15
HUMANS BY CHANCE
OR DESIGN?

Romans 1:20 clearly states that the entire world is an intricate design and that those who fail to see God's power are deliberately denying God's existence. How can any medical doctor view our intricate cells, DNA, muscles and organs and believe in the chance formation of such a great design? Why is it that when we see a car, far less complex than the human body, it would be absurd to think that it was a product of chance and random processes. Has anyone ever thought Mount Rushmore was a product of natural erosion? Have you ever read a book where the letters on the pages may have randomly come together to form words? Of course not, books need an intelligent writer to shape and organize meaningful information. Next, we examine the human body and its complex systems, most of which doctors cannot understand.

The function of the human brain alone, the most complex system in the universe, is beyond our comprehension. Consisting of over 100 trillion cells and sending over 100 million separate signals throughout the body every second, the brain is like a computer *far beyond* the world's largest and most sophisticated technology. The brain's capacity is phenomenal -- if a person learned something new every second, it would take three million years to fill the brain with information. Every cubic inch of your brain contains over 100 million nerve cells and is interconnected with 10,000 miles of fibers. "I will praise You, for I am fearfully and wonderfully made; marvelous are Your works, and that my soul knows very well" (Psalm 139:14).

DNA material stores all the information necessary for our life, enough to fill 1,000 books of 500 pages each with small print. Even more fascinating is that all this information is replicated word for word you might say, in only twenty minutes. DNA consists of two long strands of information wrapped around each other in a spiral shape. Between each of these strands are rungs which attach to both sides. Evolution states that this complex system evolved by random chance, yet the odds of forming the combination needed for just ONE of these rungs of information for reproduction is 1 in 10^{87} power. To put this calculation into perspective, evolutionists argue that the universe is about 4.6 billion years old - - rendered in seconds 10^{25} power (Origin of Life). The Bible tells us that we only need to look at nature to see that God exists. With such an intricate system made for our benefit, nature is persuasive evidence. The Psalmist tells us that man was created, "A little lower than the heavenly beings and crowned him with glory and honor. You made him ruler over the works of Your hands; You put everything under his feet" (Psalm 8:5).

All of this aside, how could man evolve without the intricate reproductive system in both the male and female. In order for the "evolved species" to procreate, there would have had to be both male and female subjects evolving almost simultaneously, at the same place on earth with the proper reproductive system involving all the above mentioned DNA, prepackaged.

Some people question how Adam could have named all the animals and still remember them the next day. According to evolution, the human mind has grown more complex along with the physical body. Yet the Bible states that Adam named all the animals shortly after being created himself (Genesis 2:19-21). Adam was pure and living in a new world untouched by the destructiveness of sin. Therefore, Adam could have had the capacity to process and understand far more information than we can today. Science tells us only 10-20% of our brain is being used today. What happened to the other 80-90%? The answer from the Bible is the consequences of sin. Of course, evolution tells us that we are getting smarter but real science doesn't support this contention. For this reason we cannot scientifically answer how Adam could name so many animals but the Bible does record the answer.

Since many times God has given His prophets information to pass on to others, quite possibly the Holy Spirit also granted Adam extraordinary knowledge. It is a pseudo belief to assume that we are somehow smarter than people were years ago. We may not know why, how, or even what the ancients did but we can be sure they were not stupid. A few miles north of Ur, Abraham's first dwellings, the Weld-Blundell Expedition uncovered what is called the Weld Prism. The Weld Prism contains historical writings composed by a man named Nur-Ninsubur around 2100 BC. Often recorded are the names of kings who lived before the Flood. Rene Noorbergen writes concerning this find, "In his account he records the list of ten pre-Flood kings and ends his writing with the sad words, 'and the flood overthrew the land.' The Sumerians and later the Babylonians and Assyrians further recognize the pre-Flood era as a source of superior literature. One Babylonian king recorded that 'he loved to read the writings of the age before the Flood.' Assurbanipal, who founded the great library of Nineveh, also referred to the great 'inscription of the time before the Flood.' It must be remembered that the reason the pre- and post-Flood civilizations advanced at a more rapid rate than our own today is that they were using their brains to their fullest capacity, whereas we, according to the physiologists, are using only one-sixth of ours" (Noorbergen, p. 26).

Dr. William Spear writes, "Why are we reluctant to believe this [ape-man, mentality of ancient man] as a possibility? The effects of the Fall are enormous. Our understanding was darkened (Ephesians 4:18; I Corinthians 2:14), our hearts became deceitful (Jeremiah 17:9-10), our mind and consciences were defiled (Genesis 6:5; Titus 1:15), and our wills were weakened (Romans 7:18). It is no wonder that we do not understand, and even willfully reject, the record of creation from the Bible. Today, fallen, sinful, human nature dupes us into thinking that we are at the pinnacle of our success and progress. We wrongly and arrogantly think that we know more than the first man knew and have better developed intellectual abilities than he did. But, even though arrogant about, deceived by, and ignorant of many things, we are held accountable for the truth we do know. As Christians, we should not casually dismiss information from the Bible simply because it does not "fit" with our present technological ideas or our present-day secular explanations of science.... Should we not be profoundly thankful to God because He has chosen to redeem and eventually restore our abilities through the grace and love of our Lord Jesus Christ?" (Spear, Impact).

CHAPTER 16
THE BIBLE: DIVINELY INSPIRED AND AUTHORITY

Josh McDowell once had a difficult time believing what is found in the Bible. His book, <u>Evidence that Demands a Verdict</u>, was started to seek and prove the Bible a fraud. To his amazement he discovered that the Bible was truth and he became a Christian. Many others, too, have become Christians by searching the Holy Scriptures because God's Word works through the power of the Holy Spirit. Vast archaeological and historical evidence also validates Biblical truth. Following is scientific and Biblical evidence of Christ's authority here on earth; however, the only real proof is found through personal reading of the Bible with an open mind. Before you begin, pray that the Holy Spirit will open your heart and mind. When you finish, I have complete confidence that no doubt will remain regarding the historical and spiritual reality of this Book.

The Bible's accuracy is sure. Evidence for the New Testament manuscripts is more abundant than that of any other historical, ancient book. In addition, the New Testament has been copied more than any other ancient manuscript. Around 5,000 Greek manuscripts have been discovered consisting of 76 papyri, 250 uncials, 2646 minuscules and 1,997 lectionary manuscripts (Metzger, pp 31-33). The following chart shows the accuracy of the many New Testament translations (Hall).

The New Testament contains nearly 20,000 lines with only 40 doubtful lines. By comparison, the Iliad contains nearly 15,600 lines with 764 doubtful ones.

Literally hundreds of eyewitness accounts were available to validate Christ's resurrection and the information contained in the New Testament. Over 500 people witnessed Christ's return after the resurrection, including Mary Magdalene (John 20:1); Lalome and Joanna (Luke 24:10); Mary, the mother of James (Matthew 28:2); various women from Galilee (Luke 23:55); Peter (Luke 24:34); Cleopas (Luke 24:13-32); the ten apostles in Jerusalem (John 20:24); Thomas and eleven others (John 20:26-29); seven disciples on the Sea of Galilee (John 21:1-24); eleven disciples on a mountain in Galilee (Matthew 28:16-20); five hundred others at once (I Corinthians 15:6); brother James (I Cor. 15:7); and finally, the disciples on Mount Olives (Acts 1:4-12). Clearly there were enough witnesses to back up the resurrection claims in the Bible, for Christ appeared at least ten different times in forty days.

(ANCIENT TEXT COMPARISON)

Author	Date written	Earliest copy	How many	Accuracy of
Caesar	1st Cent BC	900 AD	10	---------------
Livy	1st Cent BC	------------	20	---------------
Tacitus	c. 100 AD	100 AD	20	---------------
Thucydides	5th Cent BC	900 AD	8	---------------
Herodotus	5th Cent BC	900 AD	8	---------------
Demosthenes	4th Cent BC	1100 AD	200	---------------
Mahabharata	----------------	------------	--------------	90%
Homer	9th Cent BC	------------	643	95%
New Test.	1st Cent AD	c. 130 AD	5.000	99% +

Some critics have made unfounded claims that these people had hallucinations. Hallucinations usually occur when one already believes something will happen; yet the disciples saw him with initial disbelief (John 20:25; Luke 24:15; Matt 28:17). Since the disciples and others had visited closely with Jesus beforehand, recognizing Him should not have been a problem, especially since many visits were relatively lengthy. Also, Jesus Himself added evidence of His resurrection by performing miracles after His return (John 20:30; Acts 1:3).

Others claim that New Testament writers had bad memories and could not possibly keep track of all the events that took place. However, one must remember that in Jesus' day memory was much more important and more developed because many laws and books were passed down orally. Also, the events written down occurred over a period of years and would certainly be engrained deeply into memory. Finally, we must not forget that Jesus Himself promised that He would grant His disciples the ability to remember His teachings (John 14:26).

Archaeology

Archaeology fervently supports the Bible. More than 25,000 sites mentioned in Scripture have been located and identified. Furthermore, reputable archaeologists have stated that no archaeological find has ever contradicted the historical facts found in the Bible (Geisler, p. 322). Paul and Luke record historically accurate titles such as Gallio, the proconsul of Achaea, Lysanias- the tetrarch of Abilene, a temple warden, politarchs, and even references to Caesar and Herod. For example, Luke's reference to "Lysanias, the tetrarch of Abilene" was for some time denied historically because Lysanias was not known. However, now Greek manuscripts show him to be the tetrarch between AD 14 and 29. Luke refers to him at the time of John the Baptist's ministry, which was AD 27, in direct agreement with historical records (Geisler, p.325).

Places such as the Pool of Siloam (John 9:7-11), the judgment seat near Corinth (II Corinthians 5:10), and many more have been found. Near the theater at Corinth an inscription states, "Erastus in return for his aedileship laid the pavement at his own expense" (Geisler, p.326). Could this be Paul's coworker (Acts 19:22)?

Historical Records

Secular historical records corroborate the history found in Scripture. The Jewish Historian Josephus, (AD 37-100) records information about "the brother of Jesus, the so- called Christ, whose name was James. . ." (Antiquities XX (9:1). Similarly Josephus writes, "At this time there was a wise man who was called Jesus. . .Pilate condemned Him to be condemned and to die. And those who had become His discipled did not abandon His discipleship. They reported that He had appeared to them three days after His crucifixion and that He was alive; accordingly, He was perhaps the Messiah concerning whom the prophets have recounted wonders (Antiquities XVIII.33, Arabic text).

The Greek recorder, Lucian, stated, "The man who was crucified in Palestine because he introduced this new cult into the world. . .. Furthermore, their first lawgiver persuaded them that they were all brothers, one of another after they have transgressed once for all by denying the Greek gods and by worshipping that crucified sophist himself, and living under his laws" (On the Death of Peregrine).

The Roman historian, Suetonius (AD 120) wrote, "As the Jews were making constant disturbances at the instigation of Chestus [Christ], he expelled them from Rome" (Life of Claudius 25:4). Suetonius also recorded, "Punishment by Nero was inflicted on the Christians, a class of men given to a new and mischievous superstition" (Lives of Caesars, 26.2).

Pliny the Younger (AD 112) wrote how he persecuted Christians as he attempted to "make them curse Christ, which a genuine Christian cannot be induced to do. . . .They were in the habit of meeting on a certain fixed day before it was light, when they sang in alternate verse a hymn to Christ as to a god, and bound themselves to a solemn oath not to do any wicked deeds, and never to deny a truth when they should be called upon to deliver it up" (Epistles X. 96).

The Samaritan historian Thallus (AD 52) made some remarks about a strange eclipse at the time of Christ. It was strange because a solar eclipse does not take place when there is a full moon. Christ died at the paschal full moon. We see from Julius Africanus' (AD 221) mention of Thallus' writings, "Thallus, in the third book of his histories, explains away this darkness as an eclipse of the sun--unreasonably, as it seems to me."

A letter (AD 73) in the British Museum from a father to his son in prison reads, "What advantage did the Jews gain from executing their wise King? It was just after that that their kingdom was abolished. . . . But Socrates did not die for good; he lived on in the teaching of Plato. Pythagoras did not die for good; he lived on in the statue of Hera. Nor did the wise King die for good; he lived on in the teaching which he had given" (Bruce, p. 14).

Finally, the Jewish Talmud (finished by AD 500) refers to Christ saying, "On the eve of Passover they hanged Yeshu (of Nazareth) and the herald went before him for forty days saying (Yeshu of Nazareth) is going to be stoned in that he hath practiced sorcery and beguiled and led astray Israel. Let everyone knowing aught in his defense come and plead for him. But they found naught in his defense and hanged him on the eve of Passover" (Sanhedrin 43a).

These are a few of the many records regarding the validity of the Bible; others have not survived through time.

Scriptural Evidence

Since the Bible is accurate and true, Scripture shows Christ's deity accurately also. First, we must clearly understand that the name Jehovah (JHWH, the same word also translated LORD) is above all names in the Old Testament. In fact, so sacred is JHWH that many Jews would not even let this word come from their lips. Exodus 3:14 shows Jehovah to be the great "I AM". Also in Isaiah 44:6 Jehovah Himself states, "I am the first and I am the last; apart from Me there is no God." Further, Isaiah 42:8 states, "I am the LORD; that is My name! I will not give My glory to another or My praise to idols." Geisler writes, "In view of the fact that the Jehovah of the Jewish Old Testament would not give His name, honor, or glory to another, it is little wonder that the words and deeds of Jesus of Nazareth drew stones and cries of 'blasphemy' from first century Jews. The very things that the Jehovah of the Old Testament claimed for Himself, Jesus of Nazareth also claimed as the following verses reveal: Jesus said 'I am the good shepherd' (John 10:11), while the Old Testament declared 'Jehovah is my shepherd' (Ps.23:1). Jesus claimed to be judge of all men and nations (John 5:27f and Matt. 25:31f) but Joel, quoting Jehovah, wrote: 'for there I will sit to judge all the nations round about' (Joel 3:12). Jesus said, 'I am the light of the world' (John 8:12) whereas Isaiah says, 'Jehovah will be unto thee an everlasting light, and thy God thy glory, saying, Father, glorify thou me in thy own presence with the glory which I had with thee before the world was made.' But Isaiah quoted Jehovah vowing, 'My glory will I not give to another' (42:8). Jesus spoke of Himself as the coming 'bridegroom' (Matt. 25:1), which is exactly how Jehovah is depicted in the Old Testament (cf. Isa. 62:5; Hos. 2:16). In the book of Revelation John quotes Jesus: 'I am the first and the last' (1:17), which are precisely the words Jehovah used to declare that there was no other God besides Himself (Isa. 42:8). . . .Perhaps the strongest and most direct claim of Jesus to be Jehovah occurs in John 8:58 where He said to the Jews, 'Truly, truly, I say to you, before Abraham was, I am" (Geisler, p.331). Immediately after that claim, the Jews picked up rocks to stone Jesus because they recognized He was claiming to be the "I AM" of Exodus 3:14. Many other examples can be cited where Jesus exercises power which only God alone is said to have. In Mark 2:5 He forgives sins which God alone has power to do (Jeremiah 31:34). Jesus raised many from the dead (John 5:25) yet God alone is able to give life and raise the dead (I Samuel 2:6; Deuteronomy 32:39; Psalm 2:7). God created the world (Genesis 1; Isaiah 40) and Jesus too, created the world (John 1:1-5; Col. 1:16-17). No one but God is to be worshipped, (Exodus 20:1-4; Deuteronomy 5:6-9) yet Jesus is worshipped nine times without ever giving rebuke (Matthew 8:2; 9:18; 14:33; 15:25; 20:20; 28:17; Mark 5:6; John 9:38; John 20:28). Finally, Jesus requested that people pray in His name (John 14:13; John 14:14; John 15:7; John 14:6; I Corinthians 5:4; and Acts 7:59 where Christ's disciples actually pray to Jesus).

There are some claims that Jesus was not equal to God based on key verses where Jesus states, "My Father is greater than I (John 14:28); Christ's admittance that He did not know when the second coming would occur (Mark 13:32); or His prayer on the cross where Christ said, "My God, My God, why hast Thou forsaken me" (Mark 15:34). Geisler explains, "The Father was greater than Jesus in office but not in nature. Jesus claimed equality with God in essence (John 5:18; 10:30); it was only in His function as Son that he was less than the Father" (Geisler, 335). Concerning his knowledge of the end times, Christ did not know with His human nature as Son. It is interesting to note that though He claims ignorance on knowing the time of the end in Mark 13 while He has a human nature, He does not claim the same ignorance when questioned about the end after His resurrection and in His glorified state (Acts 1:6-7). Regarding Christ's prayer on the cross, there are many examples elsewhere that show one part of the Trinity conversing with the other. For example, in Psalm 110:1 we read, "The LORD said to my Lord, 'Sit at My right hand, Till I make Your enemies Your footstool.'" When one views the above verses with the rest of Scripture in mind, Jesus clearly is one with God and the Holy Spirit.

What is the point of taking so much space and effort to explain Jesus' Deity? C.S.. Lewis says it best: **"I am trying here to prevent anyone saying the really foolish things that people often say about Him: 'I'm ready to accept Jesus as a great moral teacher, but I don't accept His claim to be God.' That is the one thing we must not say. A man who was merely a man and said the sort of things Jesus said would not be a great moral teacher. He would either be a lunatic--on a level with the man who says he is a poached egg--or else he would be the Devil of Hell"** (Lewis, pp.55-56).

We shall close this section then with final evidence of Christ being the Messiah, not a mere mortal or a simple teacher of morals. It is with the understanding that Jesus is the Messiah that the Old Testament and the New Testament really come alive and fit together as one continued story. In fact, the Old Testament's focus is to point us to the coming Messiah and God's plan and intervention in bringing this about. The Old Testament is filled with prophecy which Jesus fulfilled with His coming as the Messiah. Amazingly, or shall we just say prophetically, these predictions were made hundreds of years before they actually took place. So important is this message that Matthew writes His entire Gospel book with the emphasis of fulfillment of Old Testament prophecy. Because of the extent of passages, I refer you to the chart below.

New Test. Text	**Old Test. Text**
Prophecy Fulfilled	
Matthew 1:17	Genesis 12:3; 22:18
Jesus was to descend from Abraham	
Matthew 1:23	Isaiah 7:14
Virgin birth	
Matthew 2:6	Micah 5:2
Birth in Bethlehem	
Matthew 2:10-11	Isaiah 60:1-6
Many coming to worship birth of Jesus	
Matthew 2:15	Hosea 11:1
Fleeing to Egypt	
Matthew 2:18	Jeremiah 31:15
Crying in Ramah	
Matthew 3:3	Isaiah 40:3
John's voice in the wilderness	
Matthew 3:16	Isaiah 11:2; 61:1
Holy Spirit descending upon Jesus	
Matthew 4:11	Psalm 91:11-12
Jesus' protecting Angles	
Matthew 4:15-16	Isaiah 9:1-2
Jesus going to Galilee of the Gentiles	
Matthew 8:17	Isaiah 53:4
Taking our infirmities	
Matthew 9:13	Hosea 6:6
Jesus desired mercy not sacrifice	
Matthew 10:35	Micah 7:6
Jesus sent to divide house	
Matthew 11:5	Isaiah 35:6
Blind receive sight	

Matthew 11:5b	Ps 72:2-13; Zec 11
Good news is preached to the poor	
Matthew 11:10	Malachi 3:1
Messenger sent ahead	
Matthew 12:7	Hosea 6:6
Mercy, not sacrifice	
Matthew 12:18-21	Isaiah 42:1-4
The servant of the Lord	
Matthew 12:18	Isaiah 11:2-3
Putting Spirit on Him	
Matthew 12:40	Jonah 1:17
Jesus- 3 days and 3 nights buried	
Matthew 13:14-15	Isaiah 6:9-10
Seeing but not perceiving	
Matthew 13:35	Psalm 78:2
Speaking in parables	
Matthew 15:8-9	Isaiah 29:13
Hypocritical worship prophesied	
Matthew 16:27	Proverbs 24:12
God's fair judgment	
Matthew 17:10-11	Malachi 4:5-6
Elijah comes	
Matthew 21:5	Zechariah 9:9
Jesus' entry on donkey- Palm Sunday	
Matthew 21:9	Psalm 118:26
Shouts of Hosanna	
Matthew 21:12	Malachi 3:1
Jesus would cleanse the Temple	
Matthew 21:13	Isaiah 56:7
Temple turned into den of thieves	

Matthew 21:16	Psalm 8:2
Children praising God	
Matthew 21:42	Psalm 118:22-23
Jesus, the rejected cornerstone	
Matthew 22:32	Exodus 3:6
The living God of Abraham	
Matthew 22:44	Psalm 110:1
Jesus, the Son of David	
Matthew 24:15	Daniel 9:27, 11:31
Abomination of desolation	
Matthew 26:21	Ps 4; 55:12-14
Jesus betrayed by a disciple	
Matthew 26:31	Zechariah 13:7
Jesus being struck	
Matthew 26:31b	Zechariah 13:7
Disciples fleeing at Garden	
Matthew 26:38	Psalm 22:14
Jesus overwhelmed with sorrow	
Matthew 26:60	Psalm 27:12
False witnesses accuse Jesus	
Matthew 26:63	Isaiah 53:7
Jesus remained silent	
Matthew 26:67	Isaiah 50:6
Jesus spit on	
Matthew 26:67b	Lam. 3:30; Mic 5:1
Jesus struck at His trial	
Matthew 27:9-10	Zechariah 11:13
Jesus betrayed for 30 pieces of silver	
Matthew 27:34	Psalm 31:6-7
Jesus drinks nothing for His pain	

Matthew 27:35   Psalm 22:18
Dividing Jesus' garments by lots

Matthew 27:38   Isaiah 53:12
Crucified between two robbers

Matthew 27:40   Psalm 22:7; 109:25
People shake heads and insult Christ

Matthew 27:46   Psalm 22:1
"My God why have You forsaken Me"

Matthew 27:57-60   Isaiah 53:9
Jesus buried in a rich man's tomb

John 19:33   Ps 34:20; Ex 12:46
Not a bone would be broken

Galatians 4:4   Genesis 3:15
Messiah to be born of a woman

Luke 3:23; Hebrews 7:14   Genesis 49:10
Messiah to be of the tribe of Judah

I Peter 2:7   Psalm 118:2
Jesus would be rejected by the Jews

Luke 23:33   Ps 22:16
Jesus' hand and feet are to be pierced

Luke 23:34   Isa 3:12; Ps 109:4
Jesus would pray for his persecutors

John 19:23   Psalm 22:18
Jesus' side would be pierced

Acts 2:31; Mark 16:16   Psalm 2:7; 16:10
Jesus will rise from the dead

Acts 1:9   Psalm 68:18
Jesus will ascend into heaven

Hebrews 1:3   Psalm 110:1
Jesus will sit at the right hand of God

The Bible is Inspired by God

We have already shown that the Bible as a whole is a reliable, historical, and archaeological record. But what about authorship, was the Bible truly inspired? Although difficult to comprehend, Jesus Himself recognizes the Old Testament as God's Word divinely inspired through men. One thing to keep in mind while reading the New Testament is that the words contained therein were not mere diaries of the apostles, rather written records of what Jesus had taught and, therefore, it is God's Word.

We generally contribute the first five books of the Bible to Moses who regarded his writings as God's Word (Exodus 20:1; Leviticus 1:1; Numbers 1:1; Deuteronomy 1:3). The readers of these books recognized God's divine hand in these words (Joshua 1:8; I Samuel 12:6; Daniel 9:12; Nehemiah 13:1). Later in the days following Jesus, Paul referred to the entire Old Testament as the "oracles of God" (Romans 3:2). Jesus spoke of the Old Testament as history and authority, and in many cases His refuting the Pharisees and Saduccess depends upon the historical truth of the Old Testament. Jesus says, "And so upon you will come all the righteous blood that has been shed on earth, from the blood of righteous Abel to the blood of Zechariah, son of Berekiah, whom you murdered between the temple and the altar" (Matthew 23:35). Though not realized by the average English speaking population, Jesus claims all of Scripture to be true and historical. Abel was murdered in Genesis (first book of the Bible) and Zechariah was killed in II Chronicles (last book in the Hebrew Bible -- all other books are not missing, but rather between Genesis and II Chronicles). Jesus, a Jew, would have used the Hebrew Bible, therefore, saying that every word from A to Z, from beginning to end, is accurate. In addition, Christ cites from all of the Books of Moses, eleven other Old Testament books, plus the minor prophets. Jesus includes mention of things such as creation (Matthew 19); Noah's Flood (Luke 17:27); Jonah (Matthew 12:40); Abraham and other patriarchs (Hebrews 11:8); Sodom and Gomorrah (Luke 17:29); the exodus from Egypt (I Corinthians 10:1-2); Jericho (Hebrews 11:30); and many more events. In Matthew 5:17 Jesus teaches that the Law and the Prophets shall never pass away and Luke 16:16 shows how the information contained in the Law and Prophets was complete up to the days of John the Baptist.

Jesus also claimed that His words were from the Father (Matthew 11:27; John 8:26-28) and that His Word was authority (Matthew 28:18-19). These verses are precisely why Timothy takes the stand that, "All Scripture is God-breathed and is useful for teaching, rebuking, correcting and training in righteousness, so that the man of God may be thoroughly equipped for every good work" (2 Timothy 3:16-17).

Should we expect to receive more divinely inspired work in the future? Scripturally speaking, the current 27 books of the New Testament end the revelation of Christ. Jesus' life and His ministry fulfilled all things and we now wait for the last hour (I John 2:18; Luke 24:27, 44; Matthew 5:17). Hebrews puts it best when declaring that God spoke to His people through prophets during Old Testament times, "but in these last days He has spoken to us by a Son" (Hebrews 1:2). The end is near and we have Christ as the last word, for Daniel is told to "close up and seal the words of the scroll until the time of the end. Many will go here and there to increase knowledge" (Daniel 12:4), but John in Revelation, is commanded to, "not seal up the words of the prophecy of this book, for the time is near" (Revelation 22:10). Finally, the authorized people to write the books of the Bible are now all dead. Jesus commissioned the twelve apostles and gave them special power and authority. This is not to undermine our roles as the priesthood of all believers (I Peter 2:9) but as Geisler writes, "Through the apostles' hands the early believers receive the Holy Spirit (Acts 8:14,15) and to the apostles were committed the 'keys to the kingdom' (Matt. 16:19; cf. 18:18). The early church was built on the foundation of the apostles. . . (Eph. 2:20), it continued the 'apostles' teaching. . .' (Acts 2:42), and it was bound by apostolic decision (Acts 15)" (Geisler, p.369). It is for the reasons just mentioned that Paul himself had his credentials screened by the apostles (Galatians 2:2-9).

Hebrews states the written message, "was confirmed to us by those who heard Him" (Hebrews 2:3). Even though some New Testament books such as Mark, Luke, Paul and James were written by men other than the apostles themselves, each was backed by an apostle and walked with them at some point. It seems that credentials for apostleship are laid out in Acts 1:21-22 where we read: "Therefore it is necessary to choose one of the men who have been with us the whole time the Lord Jesus went in and out among us, beginning from John's baptism to the time when Jesus was taken up from us. For one of these must become a witness with us of his resurrection." A witness 1) had to have been with the apostles from day one of Jesus' ministry and 2) witnessed the resurrection. Therefore, when all eyewitnesses ceased, so did the writings of God.

How then can we decipher false writings when they are said to be "new revelations?" First and foremost, because Christ and His witnesses were the last word, but a general rule outlined by Geisler asks these eight questions:

1) Do they claim to have a new revelation from God or mankind? If so, we know it to be from a source other than God. Examples would include Edgar Cayce and Jeane Dixon of whom Jesus may be referring to when He warns, "beware of false prophets" (Matthew 7:15).

2) Do they have a different revelation for mankind? Some have revelations which seem religious but yet have a different angle of looking at things. John writes, "do not believe every spirit, but test the spirits to see whether they are from God; because many false prophets have gone out into the world" (I John 4:1). Even more to the point Paul warned, "not to become easily unsettled or alarmed by some prophecy, report or letter supposed to have come from us. . ." (II Thessalonians 2:2).

3) Is Christ as God Incarnate in human flesh acknowledged? Many false denominations claim that Christ was not a true Godhead and that He was merely an angel or just a great moral teacher. I John 4:3 shows us that this is the Spirit of the Antichrist.

4) Do they obtain revelations from angels or spirits? It is because Christ is the last revelation that Paul **warns** us of revelations from an "angel from heaven" (Galatians 1:8) or from a "spirit" (II Thessalonians 2:2).

5) Do they use objects of divination to obtain their prophecy? For example, Jeane Dixon used a crystal ball and Joseph Smith used a stone in a hat. Deuteronomy clearly states, "Let no one be found among you. . . who practices divination. . . Anyone who does these things is detestable to the LORD" (Deuteronomy 18:10-12).

6) Is Christ the center of the prophecy? "Every spirit that does not acknowledge Jesus is not from God" (I John 4:3). Need more be said.

7) Do they ever utter false prophecies? "If what a prophet proclaims in the name of the LORD does not take place or come true, that is a message the LORD has not spoken" (Deuteronomy 18:22). Many prophets such as Edgar Cayce and Jeane Dixon have been wrong more often than right, yet God says if at any time they are mistaken they are not of Me.

8) Are they official or confirmed prophets of God? Every prophet from Moses on, was laid up before the Lord (Deuteronomy 31:24-26; Joshua 24:26). Later their names were registered (Ezekiel 13:9) and they all performed miracles in God's name (Geisler pp. 372-376).

These eight above guidelines help readers detect false teachings even though they may sound good, even religious. Some say that the book of Matthew alone expresses sufficient knowledge for salvation; we have all that is needed in the knowledge of Christ crucified.

Conclusion

An overwhelming list of proofs and evidences of creation and a young earth indicate a wonderful and caring God, who by grace, sent His Son for us, that we may be forgiven and have the opportunity for eternal life with Him in paradise. It seems that scientific evolution is an oxy-moron. I hope and pray that this book has given you the desire and motivation to search Scripture for answers to all questions in your life, but most importantly, I pray that it has either restored, strengthened or given you new faith in God's inerrant Word. I encourage you to take a stand for Christ and His Word. At times the answers are not all there, but it is during those times that this faith becomes essential. May

God bless you richly in your studies through the Holy Spirit and may we meet one day at the foot of our Savior's throne. Hallelujah, Hallelujah, He is Risen!

CHAPTER 17
UPDATES

I Do Believe in Evolution!

Don't worry. I haven't fallen off of the deep end. But it is true. I do believe in evolution. If someone asked you if you believed in evolution, what would you say? My response is, "what do you mean by evolution?" Today we throw out the term "evolution" and we automatically think of molecules mutating to man. However, the word "evolution" simply means change over time. I guess the real question then becomes what is meant by "change?" This is precisely what we will look at in this chapter to clarify and help you defend your stand on creation.

Indeed, we cannot deny that change does take place. Cars wear out, animals shed their fur, skin etc. and babies grow up. So is this evolution? Yes, just not the definition one normally thinks of. Therefore, to say we don't believe in evolution would be a lie. However, if we say we do believe in evolution we must clarify that it isn't the Darwinian definition. There are two terms that we need to look at: microevolution and macroevolution. Understanding these two terms will give you a clear understanding of many so-called "proofs" of evolution that are thrown at Creationists.

The term *microevolution* is unfortunate because, as we said, the very word "evolution" makes people think of ape turning into man. However, microevolution has nothing to do with such fairy tales, but it is a scientific fact.

Microevolution is a result of random errors in DNA replication. It doesn't include genetic variations such as differing eye color or different shapes and sizes of related animals, etc. It never displays increasing complexity or order, nor does it produce beneficial change.

Years ago fruit flies were bombarded with radiation to increase mutations which were to speed up the "evolutionary" processes. The results showed absolutely no NEW information, only corrupted OLD information causing crumpled, oversized, undersized or extra-winged flies. In addition, they were blind, sterile, weak, diseased, deformed, or dead. The key here is that mutations do not cause new species (which needs new information) to evolve. Even Paul Grasse, a leading evolutionist, said in <u>Evolution of Living Organisms</u> (1977), "Some contemporary biologists, as soon as they observe a mutation, talk about (macro) evolution... this logical scheme is, however, unacceptable: first, because its major premise is neither obvious nor general; second, because its conclusion does not agree with the facts. No matter how numerous they may be, mutations do not produce any kind of evolution."

One example of microevolution is seen in a recent study done on the *Vibrio cholerae* bacterium that causes cholera. Research has shown that this germ became more powerful and dangerous not because of new information being added but because of a loss of information. When the 2nd law of thermodynamics does its thing this germ loses *chemotaxis*, an ability to move when there are chemical changes. (*New Scientist*, 4 May 2002, p.9.) This is strong scientific evidence of creation, not evolution. The process of variety among a species and other bacterial resistance to antibiotics is evidenced with this study. Evolutionists love to use these things as examples of macroevolution in process but these studies prove otherwise.

Macroevolution is what is often referred to when people talk about "evolution." This requires increased complexity and NEW information to be added into a species (something never seen in nature or even in a laboratory). Scientists have tried to identify a mechanism for evolution to take place. During the time of Darwin some suggested the frequent use of an appendage would cause them to get larger (the giraffe getting a long neck by stretching out all the time to get leaves in the trees). This was disproved. Now, scientists are hoping mutations would provide the mechanism for evolution. First, doesn't this seem strange to you? Why are people so upset when nuclear radiation is placed near them? Shouldn't we be excited that we can now pass on our "mutations" to our children and grandchildren to move forward in the evolutionary race? Logic and first hand scientific evidence shows us radiation causes mutations and this is NOT beneficial. Secondly, mutations never add information, they only corrupt existing information. Macroevolution requires new additional information and mutations cannot provide that. Another dead-end for evolutionists.

Natural selection is often cited as a mechanism for macroevolution. Natural selection is a term used to describe how an animal may survive or go extinct usually based upon environmental changes. In other words, the ability to adapt to an environment or "survival of the fittest." This is technically what we would call *genetic variation*. Indeed we see "adaptations" and "survival of the fittest" in nature but does this provide the necessary mechanisms for macroevolution? NO! Natural selection "selects" existing genetic information from a gene pool that comes from an original "kind" of animal. In other words, we see two different sizes of dogs that have the same genetic information, either one dog has lost information or it has had some of it rearranged, but no NEW information was added to the dog.

Many evolutionists have tried to use bacteria becoming resistant to penicillin as an example of macroevolution. This is not an example of macroevolution but of natural selection. Sometimes an undetected characteristic reappears making something look as if it were new. An example would be two black haired parents having a red-headed child where a recessive gene was selected. This "red-haired" gene wasn't new, it already existed within the DNA but was previously unused or detected. In other cases, resistant bacteria were already a variation of the same kind of bacteria but were the minority. In other words, both types of bacteria were already in existence but the resistant strain was fewer in number and harmless. As medicine was taken the "weak" bacteria was killed off, leaving the resistant ones behind to prevail (survival of the fittest). Was new information added to the bacteria? NO! As a matter of fact, we have found the same resistant varieties of bacteria in the ice man found in the mountains showing these varieties are not new, just now more dominate because we killed the others off with penicillin.

Darwin's finches are still used as "proof" of macroevolution. However, these finches all display common genes with no NEW information. Therefore, the finches are only another example of genetic variation, not macroevolution. Natural selection may explain the extinction of the less fit and the survival of the most fit, but it DOES NOT explain the ARRIVAL of the fittest.

Dr. Royal Truman, an organic chemist states, "There is no evidence that DNA mutations can provide the sorts of variations needed for evolution... The sorts of variations which can contribute to Darwinian evolution, however, involve things like bone structure or body plan. There is no evidence for beneficial mutations at the level of macroevolution, but there is also no evidence at the level of what is commonly regarded as microevolution."

When God created the animals He put in them the full genetic information. The dog had the capability for long hair or short hair. In some cases this information has been lost and in other cases, even short-haired dogs still have the genetic information for long hair. The point is that genetics have limitations. You can breed bigger dogs, but you will never get a dog bigger than a horse because that information was never in the animal. You can get stronger mosquitoes, but they will never get so strong that you can't squish them. Neither genetic variation nor microevolution can allow for macroevolution to take place. We keep breeding faster horses. Why don't they just breed wings on them? The obvious answer is that they can't because this involves new information being added. (This is also why when we see mutations you might have an extra head on a cow, but it is never a horse or dog head). The same information was just corrupted or misplaced. You may have an extra leg on a calf, but it is still a calf leg. Never have we seen a calf leg on a horse, etc.

We discussed earlier how some believe sickle cell anemia is an example of a beneficial mutation because if you have this disease you won't get malaria. This is like saying that if you cut off your foot you won't get athletes' foot. There is no such thing as a beneficial mutation. A mutation is a mistake that always brings about more disorder or loss of information.

EVOLUTION IS NOT EVEN A THEORY!

According to the scientific method the systematic approach to problem solving goes like this:
1) Make an observation
2) Gather evidence
3) Make a hypothesis
4) Build models to support hypothesis
5) If the hypothesis can explain observations and make predictions without contradictions it becomes a theory.
6) A theory is "established" and agrees with all known experimental evidence. It must be falsifiable (some possible experiment that could prove the theory untrue).
7) Becomes a Law of Nature like the Law of Gravity, Biogenesis, and Motion. (These laws will disprove evolution and will be discussed in greater detail later).

Number six states that a theory must be falsifiable. For example, evolution is said to be supported by transitional fossils and by the lack of those same transitional fossils. Therefore, it is not falsifiable because both evidence, or lack of evidence, is said to support the theory.

Therefore, macroevolution cannot even be a theory according to the scientific method. Not only isn't it falsifiable, but no one has been able to observe it or even build a model to support the hypothesis. Macroevolution, therefore, can remain only as a hypothesis and a poor one at that.

The 2nd Law Buries Evolution

We hear a lot about the 2nd Law of Thermodynamics and how it supports Creation, not evolution. But what do evolutionists say about it? Is this a one-sided argument? This section will show you that it is indeed a final nail in the coffin for evolution. The Second Law of Thermodynamics comes from the Greek word *Therme* (heat) and *Dynamis* (Power). Evolution states that things are moving in an upward manner towards more complexity. Technically, both the first and the second law bury evolution. Both laws are considered empirical Laws of Nature and are not questioned by anyone today.

The first law states that matter can neither be created nor destroyed because matter is being conserved. In other words, nothing is coming into existence and nothing is leaving. Now think about that. If matter and energy are not being made nor destroyed, where did the original matter come from? Since there is absolutely no known scientific process that has been able to defy this Law, evolution must be called a faith. In his book, Origins and Destiny, Dr. Robert Gange, an evolutionist, writes, "The First Law teaches that a natural process cannot bring into existence something from nothing.. . .the universe had a beginning, which seems to be scientifically accepted, then one conclusion is that something unnatural created the universe... taken at face value, this conclusion is consistent with the total sum of evidence before us." (Gange, p. 18).

The Second Law states that energy goes from a state of usable energy to a state of less usable energy for doing work in an isolated system. It also states that entropy (losing the ability to do work) always increases in the universe. One example of this Law can be seen with a cup of hot water. The hot water has molecules moving quickly and, therefore, has a high level of energy. However, heat always flows to cold so the heat (available energy) will slowly disappear into the air causing the air temperature in the room to rise slightly. But now this heat has become unusable energy because that heat will never cause the water to become hot again. Eventually the room temperature will match that of the water temperature and an equilibrium will have been met. Even the famous evolutionist, Isaac Asimov, said of this Law: "The universe is constantly getting more disorderly! Viewed that way, we can see the second law all about us. We have to work hard to straighten a room, but left to itself it becomes a mess again very quickly and very easily. Even if we never enter it, it becomes dusty and musty.. .In fact, all we have to do is nothing, and everything deteriorates, collapses, breaks down, wears out, all by itself – and that is what the second law is all about." (*Smithsonian Institute Journal*, June 1970, p.6).

If everything is wearing out, then the universe had to have a beginning, and that beginning had to have a high level of energy and available work. It must have been much better than what we see today.

What do evolutionists say about this? They claim (rightly so) that there are three types of systems: open, closed and isolated.

* An open system can have matter and energy added or taken away. For example: energy is constantly being added to the earth from the sun. Another example would be a cow eating the grass that energy from the sun helped grow.

*A closed system can have energy added or taken away but not matter. For example: a thermos with hot water will have energy lost as it cools down but the water will remain.

* An isolated system cannot receive or lose matter or energy. The only *theoretical* isolated system is the universe because nothing comes in and nothing goes out.

Therefore, an evolutionist would say that the second law only applies to an isolated system and that the earth is an open system since energy (sunlight) can be added to the earth. Therefore, evolution could occur. Then they will state examples such as a seed growing into a full grown tree or a fetus growing into an adult. Isn't this increased complexity? NO.

Evolutionists conveniently leave out vital information. In order for life to have formed and to have become more complex you would need 4 requirements: 1) An open system like the earth, 2) A source of energy like the sun, 3) A mechanism to capture and change the energy into a useful form. (A plant uses photosynthesis to use the sun's energy), and 4) Something to use this converted energy for useful, metabolic work. Evolutionists always speak of the first two steps but always leave out the other two. No matter how much energy is added, unless it can be captured, stored and transformed to a usable energy, it is useless. This can be clarified by picturing your home computer being torn apart. Now try typing on your keyboard. Nothing will happen if there is no mechanism (hard disk, memory etc.) to capture the energy put in. Likewise, DNA and biological mechanisms have much more complexity than a hard disk. All cells can capture, store and transform energy. If this wasn't available what good would adding energy (sunlight) to an open system like the earth be in the process of evolution? Where did this information in the cells come from? Isn't this putting the cart before the horse? How could it evolve? Not only that, but what good would captured energy be if you don't know what to do with it? That would be like wiping everything off your hard drive on the computer and just typing on the keyboard. Though energy is being put into the computer, the energy cannot be decoded into useful information. So again the question must be asked: Where did the information come from to direct the use for stored chemical energy into complex processes seen in cells today? This is what evolution would produce: 1) The sun provides energy for work and increased complexity. 2) There is nothing to capture the energy so we need to have something evolve to do so. 3) We have no energy to do this because there is no way to capture and use the sun's energy. Go back to step 2. Go to step 3, then 2, then 3, then 2. See the circular logic? Therefore, simply adding energy to a system cannot cause something to evolve.

Let's turn back to the seed turning into a tree and a fetus growing to adulthood. In both cases, there was already a mechanism to capture, convert and use energy in the tremendous amount of information stored in its DNA. So where did DNA come from? Also, all this information is present from the start. No new information is ever put into the DNA of any living thing. In addition, from the moment of conception every cell begins to deteriorate and use its available stored information and energy until eventually the second law wins and death occurs.

We can even take the basic components of a cell and lay them out in the sunlight (or add any kind of energy you wish) and they will do nothing but decay, just as the second law says. Simply adding energy to an open system is not enough to overcome the second law of thermodynamics. You first need information.

Other evolutionists will say that ice crystals overcome the second law because they are very orderly. However, simple order is nothing. An ice crystal could be compared to a book of nothing but AFAFAFAFAFAF. There is no *information* in AF, it is just a repeated pattern. In addition, ice crystals actually show increased entropy (usable energy moving towards unusable energy) because it is at a lower energy level due to the lack of heat (energy). Therefore, as ice forms, energy is being *lost* and the opposite is required to form complex molecules in life.

Everything we have discussed can logically prove that God exists. If you ask an evolutionist were the original matter came from to begin the universe in the big bang they may ask you where God came from (eternal God or eternal matter argument). If so, ask them if something can create itself. (Remember, the first law says it cannot). They will have to say no. Then ask them if nothing can create something. They will again have to say no. Then say, if something cannot create itself and nothing cannot create something, the only possible answer to where the original matter came from is that somebody or something OUTSIDE the universe created it. As Christians we know that somebody to be GOD. God is self-existing. The evolutionist may then say matter is self-existing, however, matter cannot self-exist because the second law tells us that if matter were eternal, by now we would be at a standstill because everything wears out according to the very law of science. However, since God is OUTSIDE of the universe He is also outside of its laws and He CAN be self-existing. The second law will only apply to things within the universe.

Clearly, it took outside intelligence to put the necessary information into this universe. It also could not have started simple and worked its way up because that goes against the second law. If the universe is becoming less organized as this law says, then the initial energy, organization and complexity originated with our Creator - Jesus. "In the **beginning** was the Word, and the Word was with God, and the Word was God. He was with God in the beginning. Through Him **all things were made;** without Him **nothing** was made that has been made. In Him was **life**, and that Life was the Light of men. The Light shines in the darkness, **but the darkness has not understood it**" (John 1:1-5).

Evolution and Similar Characteristics

According to evolutionists similar characteristics indicate a common ancestor. Time and time again we keep hearing that dinosaurs evolved into birds as scientists try and point out the nesting habits of certain dinosaurs. Apparently, if dinosaurs nested, they must be related to birds. Isn't that good scientific logic? Science and logic are two different things, never mind the fact that the above example is neither scientific nor logical.

Indeed we find many similarities among animals. Frogs, bears, lions, dogs and cats all have four legs. Giraffes, cows, horses and deer all have hair and noses. A chicken, duck, and even the platypus of Australia have beaks but are they related? Absolutely not! Fords, Chevy's and Nissans are all cars with wheels, windows and doors but they are not related. They are simply different cars from different designers with the same purpose. The reason all of them have four wheels is because the *law of physics shows that a car will run much better that way.* Cars are made the way they are because they all fall under the same universal laws.

The above cars could be compared to the different kinds of animals God created. Though there are many types of birds, they are all birds but made from a common Designer who created them to function under the universal laws He created.

Evolutionists are not scientists! They are more like philosophers who imagine what they want to believe. You have heard the phrase, "I wouldn't have believed it if I hadn't seen it." Well, evolutionists wouldn't see it if they didn't believe it. Remember, if you learn everything you can about one side of an issue you have been indoctrinated. Learn everything on both sides of an issue and you are educated. Evolutionists look at these similarities from a one-sided perspective. For example, Carl Sagan, a prominent evolutionary astronomer wrote in his book, <u>Intelligent Life in the Universe</u>: "The inner workings of terrestrial organisms—from microbes to man – are so similar in their biochemical details as to make it highly likely that all organisms on the earth have evolved from a single instance of the origin of life." (p.183).

On the contrary, Mr. Sagan, similarities indicate a common design, not evolution. If a man's chemical composition was not similar to that of a plant or animal the only thing we could eat would be one another. But God created us to breathe the same air and drink the same water so that we could live together under the same scientific laws on the same earth.

Another problem with similar characteristics supporting evolution is that it is only the similarities that evolutionists point out, clearly because of their agenda in brainwashing society with evolutionary propaganda. Dr. Enoch in his book, <u>Evolution or Creation</u>, shows how when the cytoplasm of cells is put into a centrifuge little jelly -type pellets are formed. In these pellets the chemical formula for the cells of different species are all different. This is, of course, never mentioned in evolutionary textbooks because it shows dissimilarity. The specific gravity of human blood indicates that man is closer to a frog and a snake than a monkey, but again, most people don't know this because it goes against the philosophy of evolution. Had the test results shown the gravity of blood to be close to an ape this would be on the front page of the newspaper. According to milk glands, we are closest to the donkey, not an ape. Our eye is closest to the octopus and our heart is closest to the pig. When was the last time you read about an "ape" to human heart transplant? According to cytochrome C tests we are closest to the sunflower, but nobody is saying we are related to the grass.

Can you see the problem? This one-sided thinking of evolutionists is a dead end philosophy. EVERYTHING is pointing to a Designer. This is one reason why so many people (even atheists) are believing in Intelligent Design. Sure, many do not accept this intelligent being to be the one and true God, but it does show that the evidence is pointing away from the childish fairy tales of evolution. As a Christian who has been left with the Bible as validated evidence of Creation and the origin of life I know my Creator is my Redeemer, Jesus Christ of Nazareth. Living Lord and Judge of the universe. He created me among many other things with similar characteristics because He made the world under the same laws of science (of which He too, created).

A Common Textbook Lie

Stanley Miller has done an experiment to try to create a single amino acid. The building blocks of life are amino acids, sugars, and bases. The amino acids form the protein, which assists towards life. Similarly, DNA needs bases and sugars for its existence. The experiment constitutes only an amino acid, a substance distant from the necessary components of life. The results of this experiment have been put in textbooks all over the world, despite the fact that it was a flop (though students aren't told that). One high school textbook states, "The idea that an organic soup could originate from a primitive atmosphere was tested in the laboratory by Stanley Miller in 1953. This demonstrated that complex organic molecules could have been produced by inorganic ones". These "complex organic molecules" talked about are amino acids, which really are not all that complex, plus the acids produced in this experiment were the wrong type (which the textbooks don't mention). The very next page of this same textbook states, "These primitive cells could have flourished," giving the impression that Miller had created an actual cell, but an amino acid is far from any type of cell. In this experiment, Dr. Miller used methane, ammonia, water vapor and hydrogen because he said these were the initial elements in the first atmosphere billions of years ago. How did he know? Because these were the gases that he thought were needed for life; therefore, he had a prior answer to his question before he started, to ensure success - mere circular reasoning. Sometimes creationists are accused of using the Bible as the starting point for everything. That is where we base our assumptions; however, evolutionists base their assumptions on the fact that evolution has occurred. What a difference! The Miller experiment (despite the fact we must admit eternal God or eternal matter) assumes that the materials suggested existed, but how were they preserved when ultraviolet rays from the sun destroy methane and kill any living organism? The only reason we can live today is that the 21% of oxygen in the atmosphere and ozone protect us from the UV rays. Why doesn't Dr. Miller propose oxygen in his primitive ozone? Because oxygen stops the chemical reactions needed to form the bases, amino acids and sugars. Furthermore, all the above mentioned chemicals would be burned up because of the oxygen. In other words, you need oxygen to create your product, but once it exists the oxygen destroys the thing it creates. Knowing this, Dr. Miller chose not to use oxygen in his experiment, something Carl Sagan even admits is a big problem. One reason that oxygen cannot be objectively left out is because scientists have found it in rocks which, according to evolutionary theory, have been dated over 3.4 billion years old, suggesting oxygen was always in the atmosphere. This being the case, the oxygen would never allow amino acids to form, hence life could not form. But letting Miller have this "minor" detail, he then went on to conduct his experiment by heating up the hydrogen, water vapor, ammonia, and methane in a flask. As the materials were heated, they rose through a tube into an electrical chamber (to simulate lightning). From here the gases went on to be cooled and the end product was trapped in a separate chamber, while the rest of the materials kept circulating through the entire process again. The important thing to remember here is that the end product was not allowed to get back to its original flask. Why? Because if it did, the heat source there would kill the product. Like the oxygen, heat is needed to form the product but it also destroys it.

Furthering the problem of amino acids is that they come identified as left handed and right-handed. In order to produce life, 100% of them must be left-handed, but in nature there is a 50% mixture of left and right handed amino acids. Natural evolution cannot produce the needed 100% left-handed amino acids. Let's put this into a different perspective: the chance of getting struck by lightning is 1 in 600,000; the chance of winning the lottery is 1 in 30 million; the chance of getting 400 amino acids all left handed in a sequence is 1 in 10^{78000}, which is far beyond mathematical impossibility. Also, the chances of getting ONE ecoli bacteria (in the intestinal tract to aid in digestion) would be 1 in 10 hundred billion. According to astrophysicists the number of atoms it would take to FILL the entire universe would only be 10^{80}. This gives you some idea of the ridiculous numbers involved in forming one amino acid or cell. Even if this could be done, still no life exists; therefore, any logical person should be able to realize that the Law of Biogenesis is that life cannot come from non-life. Dr. Stephen Meyer of Cambridge University has stated in an article *Mere Creation: Science, Faith and Intelligent Design*: "Thanks largely to Miller's experimental work, chemical evolution is now *routinely presented in both high school and college biology textbooks* as the accepted scientific explanation for the origin of life. Yet chemical evolutionary theory is now known to *be riddled with difficulties*, and Miller's work is understood by the origin of life research community itself to have *little if any relevance to explaining how amino acids, let alone proteins or living cells, could have arisen on the early earth.*" (1998, p 118 emphasis mine).

God alone can create life! If this is not true, and life can be formed by chemicals in a laboratory, then God lied, because Genesis 2:7 clearly tells us, "the LORD God formed the man from the dust of the ground and breathed into his nostrils the breath of life, and the man became a living being." As a creationist, I know God can be trusted and He never lies. Jesus alone is my Redeemer and Giver of Life: "For the bread of God is He who comes down from heaven and gives life to the world" (John 6:33).

WHICH CAME FIRST- THE CHICKEN (DNA) OR THE EGG (RNA)?

Many evolutionists believe that either DNA or RNA were the first things to have evolved. Not only is that impossible but DNA actually supports a Creator. DNA is the most complex molecule in the universe with nothing even close to compare. The average human has over 50 trillion cells. All the DNA in these cells would only fill about two tablespoons. If all the information in the chromosomes from just one person were stretched out and laid next to each other side by side it would go to the moon and back 5 million times. The information in just one person's chromosomes would make enough books to fill the Grand Canyon 40 times. Each of the 15,000 cells in an infant is more complex than the Space Shuttle. One can only resound with the Psalmist, "I will praise thee; for I am fearfully and wonderfully made" (Psalm 139:14).

DNA (Deoxyribonucleic Acid) is two strands coiled together into a double helix that carry information for any living organism to make all the molecules needed for life. It even stores all the information for cells to divide. RNA (Ribonucleic Acid) is a single strand that puts the genetic information found in the DNA to use by building proteins. These proteins cannot arrange themselves without the help of the DNA or RNA. Proteins are like the machines in a wood shop and the RNA/DNA would be the blueprints or instructions to construct the machines. (See "Unlocking the Mysteries" video on our web site).

RNA is also very unstable and will only last from about 30 minutes to a few hours, whereas DNA is very stable. This stability is why information is stored in DNA. In short, DNA stores information and then passes it on to RNA, which reads and decodes the information to make proteins.

The challenge to any evolutionist is to answer the question of where life came from. With DNA, one must answer the question of where did all the information, stored within itself, come from? In other words, how could the process of natural selection or microevolution gain and pass on information to increase complexity? Today, very few scientists believe DNA could have been the first molecule to evolve because of its extreme complexity.

The genome of a mammal has about 2-4 billion symbols of information, that, if put in a book, would be about 1000 volumes of 1000 pages each. Now imagine copying all that information symbol for symbol without any mistakes. This is exactly what DNA does as it duplicates and checks itself for errors in 20-80 minutes leaving a cat a cat, and a dog a dog. How could evolution use multiple chance mutations (mistakes) to add information to DNA when all cells have a built in code to prevent change from occuring in the DNA?

The catch-22 comes in when we see that in order for DNA to replicate it must use a protein (DNA polmerase) of only left-handed amino acids.

Remember, proteins cannot be made without DNA and now DNA cannot reproduce without proteins. This means God had to have created DNA and proteins simultaneously. (And RNA makes the proteins so it, too, has to be there at the beginning).

Evolutionists have suggested that it must have been the RNA that evolved first because it is only a single strand and DNA is far too complex. Let us examine this logically. RNA must be able to reproduce itself, but how can it do this without the instructions from the DNA which hasn't evolved yet? RNA is unstable with a half life of only 44 years (much too short for evolution). Also, if temperatures get above 100 degrees Celsius the half life goes down to 70 minutes. This sure throws logic out the window for those evolutionists claiming life evolved in the hot hydrothermal environments. All this and we still haven't even answered the question of how RNA came to be. How could lifeless, unordered chemicals without any information come together to form a complex molecule with huge amounts of information and order? TIME is the answer for evolutionists. Given enough time anything is logical. Right? WRONG! Earlier, when discussing the 2nd law of thermodynamics we saw that the greater the time the more the decay. But again, this is only what a known LAW of science states. I guess we could ignore it if it doesn't fit our faith. (Sorry, I couldn't resist the sarcasm).

Evolutionists have therefore suggested that RNA could provide its own self-replication to start life. How? Dr. DeDuve, a Nobel prize winning biochemist states in the *American Scientist*, "with considerably more foresight and technical support than the prebiotic world could have enjoyed- an RNA molecule capable of catalyzing RNA replication *have failed so far*" (1995, emphasis mine).

To even further compound the problem we see that nature is mixed with both left-handed and right-handed amino acids. However, ribose sugars in DNA and RNA are ALL right-handed. This is simply ignored as yet another "mystery" but in reality makes evolution impossible and illogical. In order for RNA to evolve you not only need to select ONLY the proper parts (right-handed amino acids) but you also then need to arrange them in ONLY the proper order (without error as DNA does). This would be like filling a hat with 26 English letters, 22 Hebrew letters and 24 Greek letters all in both small and capital letters. Now mix them up and draw out the phrase, "WHERE DID I COME FROM?" You must not only get the right letters but they also must be put in the right order. Because DNA and RNA use only right-handed amino acids they must also be all capital letters. Anytime a small letter, a wrong letter, or an out-of-order letter was picked you have to start all over. The odds of this happening with this short phrase are impossible. Now consider that the phrase for DNA would have billions of characters all in the right order, how much logical sense does it make to say that DNA or RNA came about by chance?

Another question we may ask is, "What is faith?" According to the dictionary it is a "Belief or trust in somebody or something; especially without logical proof." Does this sound like evolution to you? There is no logical explanation to the origin of life and certainly no proof. The only logical explanation is that there is an Intelligent Designer who put it all together. As the Bible clearly has been telling me for centuries, long before it was even a debate,

Jesus Christ is that Creator: "In whom we have redemption, the forgiveness of sins. He is the image of the invisible God, the firstborn over all creation. For by him all things were created: things in heaven and on earth, visible and invisible, whether thrones or powers or rulers or authorities; all things were created by him and for him. He is before all things, and in him all things hold together" (Col. 1:14-17).

DNA is so complex it is a trillion times more efficient in storage than the best computer chip technology available today. The Microsoft Windows operation system contains about 700 million bits (characters of information). How much information is in each one of these bits of 0's and 1's? Absolutely none. They are merely numbers by themselves. What makes the operating system so special is the arrangement of these parts. How did these pieces of information get arranged into meaning? Outside intelligence. We could wait for trillions of years and we would never get these individual numbers to arrange themselves into meaning. Likewise, we could lay all the basic components of DNA and RNA out in the sun to receive energy and nothing but decay would take place because there is no mechanism to capture the energy. Secondly, there would be no mechanism (machine) to convert the energy into a usable form. Matter + Energy + Time does NOT = Life. However, Matter + Energy + Outside Intelligence does = Life.

Probability states that any number greater than 10^{50} (1 with 50 zeroes after it) is impossible. In order to get just 10 sequential steps in order the probability can be found by taking 10 X 9 X 8 X 7 X 6 X 5 X 4 X 3 X 2 X 1 which is 3,628,800. When it comes to genetics this means you have 3,628,799 wrong ways that will mess things up and only 1 right way. Straight forward math and probability tells us that the odds of getting one cell together with all information in the right order is $10^{40,000}$. This is even more remarkable when we realize that astrophysicists estimate that the number of atoms in the UNIVERSE is 10^{80}. Harold Urey, a Nobel prize laureate said, "All of us who study the origin of life find that the more we look into it, the more we feel it is too complex to have evolved anywhere. We all believe as an *article of faith* that life evolved from dead matter on this planet. It is just that its complexity is so great, it is hard for us to imagine that it did." (*Christian Science Monitor*, Jan 4, 1962 emphasis mine). Werner Gitt, the Director and a Professor at the German Federal Institute of Physics and Technology also states, "The question is 'How did life originate?' Isn't it amazing that reproduction goes on billions of times each day without notice. The information in the DNA causes bacteria to reproduce an exact copy of itself in about 20 minutes. On the other hand complete regeneration in a human is about 25 years. This begs the question of why bacteria would want to "evolve" into a human when it has a better reproduction system for survival. There are 87 genes encoded on the DNA of *Haemophilus influenzae* that deal with reproduction of the DNA. The statistical odds of getting this right is 1 in 10 with 170 zeroes behind it. Even the lottery has better odds than this."

Food for Thought

In recent newspaper headlines we have been hearing a lot about botched abortions or in the case of Nancy Crick of Queensland, Australia, a botched assisted suicide. After bowel cancer surgery years earlier, Nancy was told the cancer was back. This time she opted to go with euthanasia and took a fatal mix of drugs to die peacefully, rather than let her cancer take her through a road of suffering. An autopsy after her death revealed there was no cancer in her body. Many pro-lifers were quick to bring this to public attention to try and show why euthanasia was wrong. However, think about this. If she had cancer would it have been okay then? Not at all! The issue isn't whether someone is going to suffer or not. The issue is do we have the right to take life into our own hands? If life is a product of chance chemicals coming together I suppose we have that right. If God created us in His image and He has commanded us not to kill then we must answer differently. Likewise, the issue of abortion isn't that sometimes it doesn't work. The real issue is that life comes from God and when we shed innocent blood, we will be punished.

Creationists have long suggested scientific evidence that the speed of light has been slowing down (another example of the 2nd Law of Thermodynamics), but only to receive severe criticism. Now scientists like Alan Guth are proposing something called "inflation" where the universe may have gone through a rapid growth stage. However, in order for this to take place the speed of light needed to be faster in the past. To support this they showed that the speed of light from quasars measured in 1999 has slowed down today. (*New Scientist*, 19 January 2002. P.4).

It has been a long supported belief that coral reefs such as the Great Barrier Reef of Australia took 20 million years to form. Recent drilling there showed that it could be no older than 600,000 years old. In fact, the scientists have said that all the reefs may have been formed at a time of a "global reef initiation event" where the melting glaciers flooded the oceans. (*Geology* **29**(6): 483-486, 12 June 2001). Isn't it amazing that one study can reduce the age over 96%. I'm not proposing that reefs have taken this long, as the Bible indicates the earth is only 6,000 years old but one more study could bring the 600,000 down to the 6,000. I also believe I know what the "global initiation event" was; Noah's Flood.

The great peppered moth story of how the number of peppered moths grew with the industrial revolution has been debunked. Earlier in this book we showed how this could not be an example of evolution no matter what. Even L. Harrison Matthews, a famous biologist, admitted this. Now, however, it has been revealed that the moths were already dead when the pictures that appear in textbooks were taken. These moths were glued onto trees, producing faulty evidence of what wasn't truly evidence to begin with. Yet this information still appears in many public school textbooks. One such example is the Holt Biology 2001 text which says, "A hypothesis explaining the replacement of light moths by dark moths can be formed using Darwin's theory of evolution by natural selection. Dark peppered moths are common in industrial areas where tree trunks are darkened" (p. 291). Not only did this not occur but they also mislead you into thinking that natural selection is evolution. As of May, 2002 these pictures remain in the Tulsa Zoo. This is a classic case of false evidence brainwashing our children. Almost every textbook misleads students by asking questions like, "Do you think humans are still evolving?" Can you see the problem? There is no right answer. To say "No," means they once were. To say "Yes" means they still are.

In October of 2000 Russell Vreeland, from West Chester University in Pennsylvania, made a startling claim that he and his team had revived bacteria that had laid dormant in salt crystals 2,000 feet below ground in Mexico. Supposedly these crystals were to be 250 million years old. According to laboratory studies, DNA should last no more than 100,000 years. The idea was that this bacteria was trapped and could not get energy from the outside environment so it turned itself off and became dormant. The problem is, then it could not repair itself either when normal deterioration takes place (2nd Law). As a result, this bacteria could not be millions of years old and this salt deposit cannot be this old either. Even evolutionary critics are saying something could remain dormant only a few thousand years, which fits nicely into the Biblical model. The same problem occurs with the DNA found within dinosaur bones. How can something supposedly so old still be here today, unless of course, it really isn't that old. If the earth is only 6,000 years old then we have our answer. (*Nature* **407** (6806): 897-900, 2000). How can evolutionists be so blind? The famous Christian author, C.S. Lewis was even taken in by the lies of so called science and believed in theistic evolution for a time. But near his death he said, "I wish I were younger. What inclines me now to think you may be right in regarding it [evolution] as the central and radical lie in the whole web of falsehood that now governs our lives is not so much your arguments against it as the fanatical and twisted attitudes of its defenders." (Lewis, C.S., Private letters, 1951).

In Australia scientists have found a way to transform sediments into hard stone within a few days using only natural processes. This shows that rocks do not take millions of years to form, but a catastrophe such as Noah's Flood could have made the sedimentary rocks we have today in a short time (*Creation Magazine*, May 2002 p. 38).

About 500 giant fossilized oysters have been found at the 13,000 foot level of the Andes Mountains. Some were 12 feet across and would have weighed over 650 pounds. Evolutionists have claimed that these are about 200 million years old. This poses a problem because if the Andes are really that old, they should have eroded by now. From a creationist perspective we see that Noah's Flood would have deposited these oysters. This also fits well with the cattails over 60 feet tall, grass-hoppers over 2 feet long, and other large insects seen in the fossil record. We explained why things were larger in the past on the section dealing with the Pre-flood world and its environment.

Did you know that the hair from a bacteria is like a complex motor, much more sophisticated than anything made by man. This motor is so small that 8 million of them would fit in the cross section of a human hair. It also rotates at 100,000 rpm's. How could something like this evolve?

The Law of Angular Momentum poses an interesting problem for evolution. This law can be illustrated by picturing a merry-go-round. If you spin kids on it they have a lot of fun. However, if you spin it faster, the kids begin to get scared. Spin it faster yet and they will begin to hang on as their feet swing out. Spin it even faster and they will fling off, moving in the same direction that the merry-go-round was spinning. Likewise, the theory of the Big Bang is that an atom-sized particle was spinning at great speeds and all the energy of the universe was bound in that particle. Then it exploded. Why then do Venus, Uranus, and six of the 63 moons rotate backwards? The Law of Angular Momentum states they should all be spinning in the same direction they were before the explosion. This shows the Big Bang did not happen. 2 Peter 3:10 gives us the Biblical perspective of the Big Bang showing it hasn't happened, rather it is coming: "But the day of the Lord will come as a thief in the night, in which the heavens shall pass away with a great noise, and the elements shall melt with a fervent heat, the earth. . . shall be burned up."

Critics have said that there is no way Noah's Ark could have been a real boat because the largest wooden boat that we could make with any stability was 300 foot. This can be proven wrong with simple historical records. Ussher said that Leontifera had 1600 rowers (800 on each side), along with 1200 fighting men. He records this boat being 400-500 feet long. Athenaeus tells of Ptolemy Philopator's ship (244 BC) being 420 feet long, 57 feet wide and 72 feet high. Before World War II, there was a Roman boat from the time of Caligula found. It was well over the 300 foot range as well. In fact, we even have pictures of this awesome boat. Unfortunately, the boat itself was destroyed in the war and is no longer in existence.

Our God is an Awesome God!

One of my favorite Scripture verses is Romans 1:20 which states, "Since the creation of the world, God's invisible qualities, His eternal power, and His divine nature have been clearly seen through that which has been made so that men are without excuse." One need not search high and low to see God in His creation. In fact, if you simply walk to the mirror one of the most amazing evidences of a loving God will stare you right in the face.

I listened to a tape by Tom Hignell once who shared many examples of why evolution was a lie. While man goes on boasting about what he has and does, Tom decided it better to boast of what God has and does. Did you know that the body has over 75 trillion cells. When God forms the body in the womb He makes two sets of 23 chromosomes come together with all the DNA information to make a human being. There are only about 1 million seconds in eleven days and a trillion seconds in 32,000 years but the body has over 15 trillion cell divisions with each one having meaning and purpose. How could something like this evolve?

During embryonic development another fascinating divine evidence of God is seen. A heart is split with a right side and a left side with the right side of the heart taking blood from the body and sending it to the lungs to get oxygen. The blood then returns to the left side of the heart and sends it out to feed the body until it returns to repeat the process. A baby, however, doesn't use its lungs to breath while in the womb so God has designed a hole in the top chamber of the heart that has a flap so that blood from the mother bypasses the lungs and goes directly to the body. When the baby travels through the birth canal and breathes the first breath the pressure in the lung changes and the flap goes over the hole. That flap heals and seals in a matter of a couple of days leaving the blood now going to the lungs of the baby.

There is an estimated one oct-tillion (1 and 27 zeroes) of atoms in the average human body. Tom put that in perspective by showing that if you covered the earth with peas 4 feet deep and then do that to 250,000 other planets you would reach one oct-tillion.

The average human body has 10 gallons of water, enough carbon to make 9,000 pencils, enough phosphorous to make 2,200 matches, enough iron to make a medium nail, enough potassium to shoot off a small cannon, enough lime to white wash a chicken coop and enough sulfur to rid one dog of fleas.

The body is also so symmetrical that twice the distance around your wrist is the distance around your neck. Twice the distance around your neck is the distance around your waist, the length of your foot is about the same as your face. The distance from finger tip to finger tip with your arms outstretched is the same as your height. But of course this is all an accident if you believe in evolution.

The average person will blink 330 million times in a lifetime, make 25 million finger clenches, 2.5 billion heartbeats, pump 350 million quarts of blood, make 740 million breaths, laugh 540,000 times and cry 3,000 times. The average male has 400 billion sperm at conception that travel an equivalent of 5 miles and you're one of them. The kidney filters 40 gallons of blood a day. You will grow 60 feet of fingernails, 350 miles of hair and have 45 miles of nerves that send impulses at over 325 mph. There are 8 million red blood cells produced every second. You have about 6 lbs. of skin that would cover 20 sq. ft. You will make 1 billion steps covering about 77,000 miles with each step landing on the bones of your feet with a force three times your body weight. You will breath in about 78 million gallons of air which is enough to fill the Hindenburg one and a half times. You have 20 feet of small intestine which covers about 100 sq. ft. of surface area and 6 feet of large intestine which is five times the area of the bodies skin. The villa in the small intestine increase the surface area 600 times so that without it, the small intestine would need to be 2 miles long instead of its 20 feet. Your intestines will squeeze out over 4 tons of food in 70 years.

The human brain weighs about three lbs and produces enough energy for a 20 watt light bulb. It holds enough information for 500,000 sets of encyclopedias which, if stacked, would be 442 miles high.

You will have about 2,100 gallons of blood pumped over 62,000 miles of blood vessels each day. You have about 125,000 hairs in your scalp with a loss of about 45 per day (Inverse for me). Each follicle will grow about 30 feet in a lifetime. When you sneeze you cannot keep your eyes open and the air will travel out your mouth at about 100 mph. Blood can reach any part of your body in six seconds. Your fingertips are so sensitive that four- one hundred thousandths of an inch depression can be felt. Your eyes can see a candle lit 30 miles away on a crisp evening. You can taste 4/100 gram of salt in 530 quarts of water. The eye can see 300,000 color variations and the ear can hear three- one hundred thousandths of a second difference from one ear to the other. Every person has a unique and special voice print, finger print, iris print and body odor yet of course, evolution caused all of this instead of a Creator who makes everyone special.

Other amazing facts outside human kind testify to God's creation and not evolution. A cheetah can go from 0 to 65 mph in 3 ½ seconds while a corvette will take 5 ½ seconds. Isn't it interesting that man-made things are not as well done as God's creation? A large elm tree will grow 6 million leaves and pump water 150 feet an hour. In one summer day it will use 1 ton of water. Salmon can return to spawn in the same place each year by recognizing impurities in the water. Bees dance to tell the rest of the hive where nectar is. It only took humans 7 years to figure out the dance, how did evolution program this in? Birds never fly into one another and dolphins never swim into each other. The bombardier beetle shoots out a gas at over 212 degrees Fahrenheit. There are over 100 billion galaxies with each one having 1 trillion stars. Astronomers say holding one grain of rice up against the sky covers 1500 galaxies. Our Milky Way galaxy is said to be 500,000 light years across and yet God is concerned about each human on this tiny planet.

So what is the point of all these facts? Though amazing, these facts don't even scratch the surface of the intricacy of God's creation and the human mind and spirit. Tom went on to explain that even more amazing than God's great power was His ability to restrain His power.

When Peter cut off the ear of the high priest's servant Jesus said, "Do you think I cannot call on My Father, and He will at once put at My disposal more than twelve legions of angels? But how then would the Scriptures be fulfilled that say it must happen in this way" (Mat 26:53-54)? Philip showed us that Jesus, "was led like a sheep to the slaughter, and as a lamb before the sheerer is silent, so He did not open His mouth" (Acts 8:32). When taunted by the soldiers on the cross Jesus withheld His power, "'He saved others', they said, 'but He can't save Himself! He's the King of Israel! Let Him come down now from the cross, and we will believe in Him'" (Mat 27:42). Why did Jesus do this? His answer is, "For I have come down from heaven not to do My will but to do the will of Him who sent Me" (John 6:38). But Jesus went on to say, "And this is the will of Him who sent Me, that I shall lose none of all that He has given Me, but raise them up at the last day" (John 6:39). Did you catch that? The God of all power withheld His power so that He could take care of each tiny individual in this tremendous space. Our Lord wants us to be with Him on the last day. It's our choice! The creation speaks of God's existence and power as Romans 1:20 tells us. If we reject that knowledge we are "without excuse." What does that mean? If we reject God and His son, our Redeemer, the last day will bring only hell, fire and destruction for an eternity. This is not God's will, but He is a just God and will not change His mind. May we walk in God's will and glorify His Name.

CREATION PUTS AN END TO PRO-CHOICE

Many people still question why teaching Creation (a six, 24 hour day creation with an earth only a few thousand years old) is so important. Romans will show us it is vital in understanding right from wrong, Christianity from Islam and other false religions. But without creation, true repentance will never come to this country and the September 11th tragedy will only be the beginning.

Romans makes a clear connection between the creation, the Creator, and our choices in life: "The wrath of God is being revealed from heaven against all the godlessness and wickedness of men **who suppress the truth** by their wickedness, since **what may be known about God is plain to them**, because God has made it plain to them. For since the creation of the world **God's invisible qualities**--His **eternal power** and **divine nature**--have been **clearly seen**, being **understood from what has been made**, so that men are without excuse. For although they knew God, they neither glorified Him as God nor gave thanks to Him, but their **thinking became futile** and their foolish hearts were darkened" (Rom 1:18-21). Notice that simply by viewing the creation we can see God's qualities, power and nature. If we fail to recognize God's attributes we are without excuse because they stare us right in the eyes every time we open our eyelids and view the creation. The well known Psalm 139 states, "I praise You **because** I am fearfully and wonderfully made; Your works are wonderful, I know that full well" (Psa 139:14). I am perplexed at the ability of a doctor to see the developing fetus and the intricate body, but yet deny that a Designer created it all. But what strikes me even more is what God states will happen to people who willingly deny God's hand in Creation.

Let us see how the above Romans passage continues: "For although they **knew God**, [no such thing as an atheist] they neither glorified Him as God nor gave thanks to Him, but their thinking became futile and their foolish hearts were darkened. Although they **claimed to be wise, they became fools**" (Rom 1:21-22). Does this sound familiar? How can a doctor claim to be so wise with his degrees but yet be so foolish? The answer lies in the continuing verses where we see that God will blind them.

"**Therefore** [because they rejected God as Creator] God **gave them over in the sinful desires of their hearts** to sexual impurity for the degrading of their bodies with one another. They exchanged the truth of God for **a lie**" (Rom 1:24-25). But wait, there is more: "Because of **this**, [because they rejected God as Creator] **God gave them over to shameful lusts**. Even their women exchanged natural relations for unnatural ones. In the same way the men also abandoned natural relations with women and **were inflamed with lust for one another**. [Homosexuality comes from rejection of the Creator]. Men committed indecent acts with other men, and received in themselves the due penalty for their perversion" (Rom 1:26-27). Oh, but we're still not done, "**Furthermore**, [because they reject God as Creator. . .get the point?] since they did **not think it worthwhile** [sound like our opening question] to retain the knowledge of God, He **gave them over** to a **depraved mind** [must have this to agree with abortion], to do what ought not to be done. They have become filled with every kind of **wickedness, evil, greed and depravity** [all justifications of abortion]. They are full of envy, **murder,** strife, deceit and malice. . .[and the list goes on]" (Rom 1:28-30).

One need not think too deeply to understand that if we reject God as our Creator that leaves us with no one to tell us what to do because, after all, we are just accidents. You want to practice sexual immorality? Go ahead if that is your *choice*. . . your opinion. You want to have an abortion? Go ahead if that's your *choice*. . .your opinion. Can you see how the very word pro-**choice** is a rejection of our God as Creator and Rule Giver? The Bible leaves us with no choice or opinions but only an absolute truth. If we believe in pro-choice (no matter what those choices may be) when God has left us with a set of commands who are we going to have to answer to when we disobey those commands to follow our choices or opinions? God, our Creator! The only real choice we have is to decide whether we accept God's Word and Him as Creator and Rule Giver or reject God as Lord and Master of our life. When we reject absolute truth and choose to say black is white and wrong is right, God "gives us over to" . . . .(you fill in the blanks, because it is your choice).

Our society has been given over to abortion and other immoral acts because of "pro-choice," an anti- submissive philosophy to our relationship with God. He isn't our Creator who has the authority to set the rules for life, but rather a mere spiritual guide, teddy bear, or suggestion box. We have become like the Israelites in the book of Judges where it says, "In those days Israel had no king; everyone did as he saw fit" (Judg 17:6).

Even worse, rejecting God as Creator means the next natural step is to reject God as Savior. When we reject God as Savior we reject the only means of hope and a cure for abortion givers and receivers. If the Genesis account of origins isn't true, than Adam and Eve aren't real people. This means the Fall into sin isn't literal either. Therefore, death (the curse of sin) isn't a result of the fall. Now we are in trouble. If death is natural, as an evolutionist would say, it can have no purpose or meaning. If death has no purpose or meaning, Jesus' death can have no purpose or meaning either. In fact, why would Jesus have needed to come to earth? He could have just stayed in heaven if dying wasn't absolutely necessary. But death DOES have meaning and purpose. It was the *curse* of our sin, and Jesus took that away from us by conquering death: "Where, O death, is your victory? Where, O death, is your sting? The sting of death is sin, and the power of sin is the law. But thanks be to God! He gives us the victory through our Lord Jesus Christ. [through His death and resurrection] (1 Cor 15:56-57). This is why Muslims and Buddhists have no hope of heaven because Jesus seen through creation is the only one who can conquer death (John 14:6). If, in my "pro-choice" attitude of life, I *choose* to believe that death is natural and the fossil record merely came about by animals dying without death having any meaning before Adam and Eve existed, then Eve's fall into sin can't be the cause of death since death was already in existence. If death was in this world before Adam and Eve and, therefore, has no purpose or origin (wasn't the curse of sin), then Jesus' death can have no purpose either. There was no "sting of death" to be taken away, therefore, Jesus was not the cure for death because there can be no cure if there is no disease.

On the other hand, if my Pro-LIFE attitude towards God accepts death as a result and disease of sin, I can also accept the life giving cure He has given me through the death and resurrection of Jesus Christ by which the sting of death was taken away. Though pro-choices of the past may have left scars, the pro-life of Christ offers forgiveness and an eternal cure that is only available through our Creator. Therefore, teaching creation is vital to the heartbeat of every child, born or unborn because it will not only provide the absolute law that says that heartbeat needs to keep beating but it also assures the life of that child eternally. In addition to that, those who have gone astray cannot experience the necessary healing that comes about from the love and forgiveness of Jesus Christ, the Creator of the Universe. "Through [Jesus] all things were made; without Him nothing was made that has been made. In Him was **life**, and that life was the **light** of men. The light shines in the darkness, but the darkness has not understood it." (John 1:5). Have you understood the Light and why creation is so important?

What Makes a Choice?

Should I have an abortion or not? This is a question tormenting many women today, not because of a poor "choice" a month or so earlier, but because they were trained with a humanistic philosophy. Unfortunately, even among many Christians the thought of an abortion is not completely ruled out because God has simply been added to their humanistic foundation in their education. As a result, we don't completely think like Christians and, therefore, we are not making choices consistent with Christianity and our actions betray our Christian identity.

How has this mind set come about? A major factor has been the removal of God as Creator from our schools, churches and families. If God created you, then He sets the rules. If we don't abide by those rules we will have to answer to our Creator. What if evolution was true? Then we are a product of chance by lightning striking primordial soup millions and billions of years ago. If we came about by chance, each biological "accident" has their own opinion as to what truth is. For some, truth may be abortion, the practice of homosexuality, or even premarital sex. Our educational systems that have been founded upon humanistic philosophies are teaching us that we need to tolerate everyone's opinion, in fact, when it comes to such things as homosexuality, students are often encouraged to experiment to find out their true identity. So who is to say what is the right choice? Is there only one choice? Not according to our society.

Today abortion depends upon many circumstances: age, health, time, convenience, and often times, the dad. With every person having different circumstances, opinions and beliefs, abortion may seem right in some circumstances if this is the way we have been trained to think. But again, who is to say when those circumstances merit murder: YOU are, according to society. To be consistent one must question whether or not it was wrong for some disgruntled students to shoot their classmates. They had been teased and wronged by others while at the same time had been taught to stand up for what they believed in, life revolved around their happiness, everyone's opinion and beliefs were acceptable. These kids simply did what they were taught. They stood up for what they believed in. . . revenge. Now, because the majority of the populace believes murder is wrong, we say their opinions don't measure up as being acceptable. Majority rules when it comes to morality I guess. What happens when the growing number of practicing homosexuals becomes the majority? What happens when the majority believe third trimester abortions are okay? What happens when the majority feel that old people have nothing to offer and they only suffer anyway so why not kill them? What happens when the majority feel their race is superior to another as the majority in Germany did during the Holocaust? What happens when a majority reject God as Creator? The answer is that we become like Israel, "In those days Israel had no king; everyone did as he saw fit" (Judg 17:6). Today, our king (God as Creator and rule giver) has been dethroned and we do as WE see fit.

    The Bible clearly tells us that a baby becomes a human being at conception and, therefore, abortion is not a question of timing, but is simply murder at any developmental stage: "Surely I was sinful at birth, sinful from the time my mother conceived me" (Psa 51:5). But because many see their self-serving circumstances more a standard of truth than God's Word, we kill these sinful creations of God, (who need a Savior,) as we see fit.

    If our world had no standard for the right measurement of a yard, everybody's measurement would differ. That is exactly what has happened with our moral fabric of society. We see it being unwound and we sit back and wonder why, as our children are being taught there are no absolutes.

    So how do we make decisions in our life, whether it be abortion, church relations, or daily moral living? There can be only one absolute, and God is that standard by which we measure right from wrong. There is no gray area when it comes to truth, we can't all be right. God's Word clearly tells us that the Bible is that standard and gives us answers to every moral dilemma. Perhaps that is why Proverbs states, "Every word of God is flawless; He is a shield to those who take refuge in Him" (Prov 30:5).

    The problem is that people need to have faith in something to follow it. How many people read the Bible enough to know it and quote it as the Bible encourages, "and how from infancy you have known the holy Scriptures, which are able to make you wise for salvation through faith in Christ Jesus" (2 Tim 3:15). Instead we read all kinds of self-help books and watch different programs with all kinds of opinions. James says, "Such wisdom does not come down from heaven but is earthly, unspiritual, of the devil. For where you have envy and selfish ambition [a big circumstance for abortion], there you find disorder and every evil practice. But the wisdom that comes from heaven is first of all pure; then peace-loving, considerate, submissive, full of mercy and good fruit, impartial and sincere" (James 3:15-17). Does abortion fit any of the attributes of "wisdom from heaven?" I would encourage everyone to train their children in the truth and then put these things into practice because one must be trained to think Biblically before they will act in a Biblical way: "Whatever you have learned or received or heard from me, or seen in me--put it into practice. And the God of peace will be with you" (Phil 4:9); "But if a widow has children or grandchildren, these should learn first of all to put their religion into practice by caring for their own family and so repaying their parents and grandparents, for this is pleasing to God" (1 Tim 5:4).

Many people have confronted me about how I know that what I teach is right, after all, it is only my interpretation. I can boldly say that my teachings are right because my teachings are not my own. As long as I do not stray from God's Word and let God's Word interpret itself, there is no problem. It is only when my wisdom interferes with what Scripture says. I can't understand how Jesus walked on water or how the Red Sea was parted. Science can't explain it, my mind doesn't understand it, but my faith believes it. If we can't think outside the realm of our reality, what good is your faith? One must either have faith that God is who He says He is or that man's wisdom is all what he thinks it is. I know me and my mind, and I wouldn't trust it to be infallible for anything.

Is it okay to have an abortion? NO, is the clear answer that comes from the book of Truth, our standard. We must put Christ into practice in our daily life. My prayer is that I may say as Paul once did, "And we also thank God continually because, when you received the word of God, which you heard from us, you accepted it not as the word of men, but as it actually is, the word of God, which is at work in you who believe" (1 Th 2:13).

Genesis: Revelation foretold!

There many connections between Revelation and Genesis. Perhaps that is why Scripture seems to make reference to a future restoration of Edenic principles: "The LORD will surely comfort Zion and will look with compassion on all her ruins; He will make her deserts like Eden, her wastelands like the garden of the LORD. Joy and gladness will be found in her, thanksgiving and the sound of singing" (Isa 51:3). A *small* sample of such connections follows:

1. There is gold in the new city (Rev 21:21) and the Garden of Eden (Gen 2:12).
2. A river flows from the throne (Rev 2:10) and from the garden (Gen 2:10). The Tree of Life resides in both Eden and in the city (Gen 2:9; Rev 22:2).
3. Both the garden and the city have been specially prepared for man (Gen 2:8,9; Rev 21:2).
4. The garden was a type of paradise with no sin and the city is a paradise with no sin.
5. God walked with man in the garden as He will in the new city (Gen 3:8; Rev 21:3).

Further we see that in Genesis the terms Eden and the Garden of Eden are often used interchangeably. However, in Genesis 2:8 we see that the Garden was planted on the east side of the *land* of Eden, hence the Garden OF Eden. Once the fall came, Adam and Eve were driven out of the Garden and must have gone through an eastern gate, because after they left, God put a cherubim there to keep everyone out. The cherubim were only placed on the east suggesting that this was the only place the Garden was accessible. In fact, the ancient word "paradise" even means "an enclosed garden." Let's take this one step further; when Cain was driven away he went further east (Gen 4:16) and, therefore, further away from God and His paradise. This is also why the Tabernacle always had its entrance from the east side. The only way to enter our paradise (heaven) is from the east. In Ezekiel 47:1-2 we see the River of Life flowing from the throne, and it appropriately flows east. The Wisemen who came to see the baby Jesus came from the east (Matt 2). Likewise, the Jews have the Eastern Gate cemented shut in Jerusalem because only the Messiah is able to go through that gate. It is believed that when Christ returns He will go through the Eastern Gate or sometimes called the Golden Gate.

    We see further evidence that the Garden of Eden foreshadows our heavenly home when we look at the River of Life that flowed DOWN from the center of Eden and separated into four other rivers. This means the Garden was a mountain. As a matter of fact, even Ezekiel calls Eden a mountain when talking of Satan: "You were in Eden, the garden of God; every precious stone adorned you: ruby, topaz and emerald, chrysolite, onyx and jasper, sapphire, turquoise and beryl. Your settings and mountings were made of gold; on the day you were created they were prepared. You were anointed as a guardian cherub, for so I ordained you. You were on **the holy mount** of God; you walked among the fiery stones" (Ezek 28:13-14). This is why God makes so much of mountains in Scripture. For example, Isaac was nearly sacrificed on Mount Moriah where the temple was later built. The Ten Commandments were given on Mount Sinai. Jesus was Transfigured on a mountain, tempted on a mountain, ascended from a mountain, and gave His Sermon on the Mount from a mountain. Elijah called down fire while on Mount Carmel. When sin came into the world, Adam and Eve were restricted from the Mountain of God. Likewise, only Moses, the priests and the 70 elders were later allowed to meet God on Mount Sinai, and even then only after making atonement through a sacrifice (Exo 24). Anyone else who touched the mountain would die. Clearly mountains represent not only the Garden of Eden, but heaven, the very thing Eden symbolized. We read in Revelation: "And he carried me away in the Spirit to a **mountain great and high**, and showed me the Holy City, Jerusalem, coming down out of heaven from God" (Rev 21:10). That is also why we read in Hebrews: "But you have come to **Mount** Zion, to the heavenly Jerusalem, the city of the living God. You have come to thousands upon thousands of angels in joyful assembly" (Heb 12:22).

    We also read of the rivers and the surrounding area of the Garden: "The name of the first [river] is the Pishon; it winds through the entire land of Havilah, where there is gold. (The gold of that land is good; aromatic resin and onyx are also there)" (Gen 2:11-12). Note that there are three articles found here: gold, resin and onyx. First let us address the onyx. In Exodus 25:7 and 28:9-12 we see that the High Priest was to wear two onyx stones with the names of the 12 tribes of Israel on them. The purpose of these stones was explained, "Fasten them on the shoulder pieces of the ephod **as memorial stones** for the sons of Israel. Aaron is to bear the names on his shoulders as a memorial before the LORD" (Exo 28:12). A memorial of what? The only time we see this stone prior to this is in the Genesis account of Eden. When the people looked at the priest they were to see a Holy Man like Adam in heaven. We will examine the priest in a moment, but for now realize that God wanted the people to see that He was going to restore them to the Edenic paradise once again.

Second, we deal with the resin or *bdellium*. Later on we see that the Israelites received manna from heaven while in their desert wandering. We read, "The manna was like coriander seed and looked like resin" (Num 11:7). The word for resin is the same Hebrew word (*bedolach*) used in Genesis for resin and is used nowhere else in Scripture. In Exodus we are told the color of the manna eaten by the Israelites: "The people of Israel called the bread manna. It was white like coriander seed [same Hebrew word for resin] and tasted like wafers made with honey" (Exo 16:31). Therefore, if the manna was white and it looked like resin, the resin in Genesis must also be white. That makes clear the reference in Revelation: "He who has an ear, let him hear what the Spirit says to the churches. To him who overcomes, I will give some of the hidden **manna**. I will also give him a **white** stone with a new name written on it, known only to him who receives it" (Rev 2:17). This resin in the Edenic paradise foreshadowed the white stone to come, where we will receive a new name which only comes by being made new in the spirit. It is also worth noting that the references to resin and onyx were made to the Israelites while they passed through the area believed to be Havilah, the general location of the Garden of Eden.

Thirdly, the gold was significant. We know that the Temple foreshadowed heaven: "They serve at a sanctuary that is a copy and shadow of what is in heaven" (Heb 8:5). That is why the Temple was covered in gold (Ex 25, 1Kings 6). The clothing of the High Priest was also layered with gold (Ex 28). It should be no surprise then, that so many Old Testament passages use the imagery of precious stones to foreshadow salvation. A few examples follow:

- "Herds of camels will cover your land, young camels of Midian and Ephah. And all from Sheba will come, bearing gold and incense and proclaiming the praise of the LORD" (Isa 60:6).
- "Surely the islands look to me; in the lead are the ships of Tarshish, bringing your sons from afar, with their silver and gold, to the honor of the LORD your God, the Holy One of Israel, for He has endowed you with splendor" (Isa 60:9).
- "O afflicted city, lashed by storms and not comforted, I will build you with stones of turquoise, your foundations with sapphires. I will make your battlements of rubies, your gates of sparkling jewels, and all your walls of precious stones" (Isa 54:11-12).

It should be no surprise then that Revelation describes our paradise in such a way: "The wall was made of jasper, and the city of pure gold, as pure as glass. The foundations of the city walls were decorated with every kind of precious stone. The first foundation was jasper, the second sapphire, the third chalcedony, the fourth emerald, the fifth sardonyx, the sixth carnelian, the seventh chrysolite, the eighth beryl, the ninth topaz, the tenth chrysoprase, the eleventh jacinth, and the twelfth amethyst. The twelve gates were twelve pearls, each gate made of a single pearl. The great street of the city was of pure gold, like transparent glass" (Rev 21:18-21). Gold was significant not only in the beginning but also in the end.

Earlier I said I would discuss the Holy Priest who foreshadowed the redeemed man. The priest was to wear white linen (Exo 28) just as in heaven we, too, receive white linen to wear: "Fine linen, bright and clean, was given her to wear. (Fine linen stands for the righteous acts of the saints)" (Rev 19:8). Furthermore, we see that part of the curse was sweat, "By the sweat of your brow you will eat your food until you return to the ground, since from it you were taken; for dust you are and to dust you will return" (Gen 3:19). That may be why no clothing was to be worn that made the Holy man sweat, "They are to wear linen turbans on their heads and linen undergarments around their waists. They must not wear anything that makes them perspire" (Ezek 44:18). In heaven, the curse is wiped away, and as a model of the redeemed man, no curse should be found. Also on the priest's chest was a gold plate engraved with the words, "Holy to the Lord" (Ex 28:36) showing the symbolic removal of the curse upon the priest. We already discussed how his breastplate was covered with gold and precious stones.

The garden was also abundant in vegetation, another symbol of prosperity. In more places than I have time to mention, trees are used in reference to Godly men (Gen 18:4-8; 30:37; Jud 3:13; 4:5; 1 Kings 19:5; John 1:48 etc.). We see that every blessed man is seen as having his own vine or tree for protection and comfort. We read of these blessings, "During Solomon's lifetime Judah and Israel, from Dan to Beersheba, lived in safety, each man under his **own vine** and fig tree" (1 Ki 4:25). Likewise our heavenly home is described with such blessing: "In the last days the mountain of the Lord's temple will be established as chief among the mountains; it will be raised above the hills, and peoples will stream to it. Many nations will come and say, 'Come, let us go up to the mountain of the LORD, to the house of the God of Jacob. He will teach us His ways, so that we may walk in His paths.' The law will go out from Zion, the Word of the LORD from Jerusalem. He will judge between many peoples and will settle disputes for strong nations far and wide. They will beat their swords into plowshares and their spears into pruning hooks. Nation will not take up sword against nation, nor will they train for war anymore. **Every man will sit under his own vine and under his own fig tree, and no one will make them afraid,** for the LORD Almighty has spoken" (Mic 4:1-4). We also read in Zecheriah, "In that day each of you will invite his neighbor to sit under **his vine and fig tree**, declares the LORD Almighty" (Zec 3:10). It is for the purpose of showing blessings that planting and flourishing is almost always used in reference to God's work throughout Scripture. Psalms states, "He is like a tree planted by streams of water, which yields its fruit in season and whose leaf does not wither. Whatever he does prospers" (Psa 1:3). In Jeremiah we read, "But blessed is the man who trusts in the LORD, whose confidence is in Him. He will be like a tree planted by the water that sends out its roots by the stream. It does not fear when heat comes; its leaves are always green. It has no worries in a year of drought and never fails to bear fruit" (Jer 17:7). Isaiah writes, "In days to come Jacob will take root, Israel will bud and blossom and fill all the world with fruit" (Isa 27:6). Even the lampstand in the Temple was described as a tree with branches, and yet, pure gold (Exo 37:17). The Cedar walls within the temple [a model of heaven] were carved with flowers, palm trees and vines (1 Kings 6:15-36), all showing God's abundant blessings through Edenic symbolism. In celebrating the Feast of Tabernacles or the Feast of Booths the Israelites were to make booths of foliage and palm branches to symbolize God's protection. During this time they were to leave the security of their homes and walled cities to live out in the open in unprotected booths. God promised that He would protect and watch over them; they didn't need to trust in walls or other means of security: "Three times a year all your men are to appear before the Sovereign LORD, the God of Israel. I will drive out nations before you and enlarge your territory, and no one will covet your land when you go up three times each year to appear before the LORD your God" (Exo 34:23). This feast should have reminded them of the Paradise of Eden and the Paradise to come. During this time they were told to sacrifice 70 bullocks (Num 29:12ff) to symbolize the original 70 nations of the earth in Genesis 10. Therefore, they were celebrating the gathering of the nations into God's eternal Kingdom when atonement would be made for them. Interestingly enough, the Israelites forgot about this feast and did not practice it until their return from Babylon (Neh 8:13-18). It would be through Israel that Christ would come (Rom 9:5) to redeem and restore His people for a paradise much better than that of Eden, this time it would be heaven. As Jesus said, "In My Father's house are many rooms; if it were not so, I would have told you. I am going there to prepare a place for you. And if I go and prepare a place for you, I will come back and take you to be with Me that you also may be where I am" (John 14:2-3). Revelation is not a separate book from the rest of Scripture, it is merely the conclusion of Genesis, the last act, and without it the story of salvation is incomplete.

What if Heaven Wasn't That Great?

I know this isn't really about Creation, however, it is about our Creator and your relationship with Him. This challenging thought may reveal more than you care to know.

Many of us have suffered a great deal in our life and need to experience true healing, not just a bandage to cover up our emotional pains. How do we move from this heartache to healing? The answer to that question lies in building a deeper relation with our Creator. Bill Gillham makes an interesting analogy in His book <u>What God Wishes Every Christian Knew</u>. (I would highly recommend reading it). He forces us to look at our motivations for believing in and following Christ by imagining a hellish heaven.

Have you ever asked yourself the question whether or not it is Christ you love, or the possibility of getting to heaven? What if heaven was "hellish?" What if heaven consisted of a scarcity of food, dry and hot weather, hard labor, no entertainment, and it was a heavily over populated area? Each day, however, you could work side by side with Jesus. What if you also lived with Jesus and would come home after each long day of work to share an apartment with Him and eight other people, but you could spend those evenings talking with Jesus and He would answer every question you had?

On the other hand, what if hell was "heavenly?" What if it was beautiful with flowing streams and green palm trees, mountains and pleasant aromas? What if there was no work and you could have any material possession or do anything you wanted? You could have plenty of friends, however, Jesus wasn't there because He was in heaven. Where would you want to go? This is a hard question because it makes us ask ourselves whether we are in love with heaven or Jesus.

Consider it another way. Let's say your spouse was diagnosed with a disease and the doctors said the only way he/she could live was to move out into a secluded desert. Would you tell your spouse, "Go on ahead, I think I will stay here and take care of the house and yard to make sure it doesn't get run down?" You would promise to call him/her every night before bed and before every meal. You would also agree to meet once a week on a hard park bench for one hour to visit. Would this be a desired marriage relationship? Certainly not! You would give up all you had to be with the one you love. Sometimes, however, this is exactly how we treat Christ. Rather than living *with* Him and building our relationship and knowing Him more, we simply pray before meals and bed, and once a week we meet Him at church for a short time before going home to do our own things. We *visit* Christ when we should, as Scripture tells us, *live* with Him. We should love Christ as we love our spouse; desiring to know Him fully. Heaven is not a *place* as much as it is a marriage *relationship*. We read in John, "We know also that the Son of God has come and has given us understanding, *so that we may know Him* who is true. And we are **in** Him who is true--even in His Son Jesus Christ. He is the true God **and eternal life**" (1 John 5:20). Note that we are IN Christ and that Christ IS eternal life. Therefore, we don't inherit a place of eternal life, we fully inherit the person; Christ Jesus. Believe me, this is no small matter to understand that we are in Christ and can do nothing without Him. Have you lost joy in this life because of something you have done in the past? A relationship with Christ will help your heart to accept what your head already should know. . .Jesus forgave our sin, forgot it, threw it away and will never let it count against us. In John we read, "If anyone does not remain *in Me*, he is like a branch that is thrown away and withers; such branches are picked up, thrown into the fire and burned. If you remain *in Me* and My words remain in you, ask whatever you wish, and it will be given you. . . .I have told you this so that My joy may be in you and that your joy may be complete" (John 15:6-11). For our joy to be complete we must first recognize the unity we have in Jesus Christ. We are being built into God's temple: "Him who overcomes I will make a pillar in the temple of my God" (Rev 3:12). Yet we also see later in Revelation, "I did not see a temple in the city, because the Lord God Almighty and the Lamb are its temple" (Rev 21:22). We are being built into a unity in Christ that we can only imagine right now.

What a glorious truth this is. I believe developing a friendship with Christ and a better understanding of His forgiveness is the answer for moving into the steps of healing. However, if one denies our Creator and a young earth everything God just offered us for a joy-filled forgiven life is worthless. If you believe in evolutionary philosophies that the earth is old, that means that all the dinosaurs lived millions of years before man ever existed. This also means that dinosaurs died before man existed and, therefore, death is something that is just natural with no meaning or purpose. However, the Bible clearly tells us that death came about by man not vice versa. In Romans we read, "For the wages of sin is death, but the gift of God is eternal life in Christ Jesus our Lord" (Rom 6:23). Even in Genesis 3:14-19 we see that because man sinned death came into the world and all of the universe was cursed. On the other hand, evolution says that death has no meaning and therefore it certainly is not a result of sin and couldn't have come from man because he wasn't around yet. If this is true, then Jesus death can have no joy giving, sin freeing power for your life because then His death has no meaning either. For some reason Christians have a hard time understanding this great truth but evolutionists see this dilemma clearly. Richard Bozarth, and atheist and evolutionist says, "Christianity has fought, still fights, and will fight science to the desperate end over evolution, because evolution destroys utterly and finally the very reason Jesus' earthly life was supposedly made necessary. Destroy Adam and Eve and the original sin, and in the rubble you will find the sorry remains of the Son of God. Take away the meaning of his death. If Jesus was not the redeemer who died for our sins - - and this is what evolution means - - then Christianity is nothing!" Hebrews 9:22 says without the shedding of blood there can be no remission of sins. Without Jesus bloody death having meaning and purpose He cannot logically be your Creator, Savior, or Joy Giver. One needs to first understand the bad news of man's sin in Genesis before he will understand the good news of God's answer to that sin in the New Testament. Without a literal Genesis, I dare say there is no good news.

For those who have experienced great sins in their life they feel a need for forgiveness and renewal; a restoration that cannot take place if the earth is millions of years old.

Understanding that God did create the world and send a Savior for us means that we get to go to heaven. However, many people do not realize that Christ offers much more than salvation to Christians. He also wants us to have pure joy and happiness in this earthly life even while going through struggles. The problem is, how do we get that joy? The answer lies in a deeper understanding of our Creator and Savior, Jesus Christ. If our goal is to just get to heaven and not to have a better understanding of the source of that privilege we may not experience the joy we could have on earth. Too often we treat God as a mean landlord that provides a house instead of a loving Father to live with. When you watch a football game on television, who do you discuss it with? When you go to the lake, who do you visit with? When you go to the movies, who do you go with? If it isn't your spouse it is usually your friend. We share our deepest darkest secrets with those we love, but we also share the most trivial circumstances and happenings with these same loved ones. However, when it comes to our relationship with Christ, we only let Him deal with the big things like, sunsets, cancer or mountains. God DESIRES a relationship with you; one where we share EVERYTHING with Him. Yes, that means confessing our sins, but also our trip to Wal-Mart, sweeping the garage or making dinner, are all jobs that Christ does with you. This may sound trivial but it is what God desires. God is all in all (1 Cor 15:28). That means He is everything in your church life, everything in your home life, everything in your entertainment and everything else in your life. But He can only be that when He is first accepted as Creator and Savior who conquered death with His own purposeful death and resurrection through the cross.

Do we believe that God did all He said He did in the Bible? After all, according to John 1:1-3 the Bible is, in a strange way, Jesus, the Word of God. If we doubt what He said in Genesis, how can we believe Him when He says pure joy comes from knowing His love and forgiveness? If we doubt the miracles of creation how can we believe Jesus turned water into wine? The bottom line is faith. God wants our heart, not just our minds. He wants us to have more than salvation, He wants us to have joy while we journey on this earth. There will be no joy until we recognize God's infinite power to create and save you in a personal way. If God didn't create the world only a few thousand years ago one may doubt His ability in forgiving such a terrible sin one has done. Where is the healing in that?

I used to go through much of my life beating myself because of sins I had done. I would pray, "Please forgive me Lord," but not know if God was answering my prayer. Usually I would later believe He did forgive me but I had to make sure I felt guilty enough for that forgiveness to take place. That was Satan working. Satan does not want you to experience forgiveness and a true joy-filled relationship with Christ. My prayers have changed. I no longer ask God to forgive me of anything. Now I **thank** Him for forgiving me for everything. See the difference? I claim His forgiveness rather than question whether I have it, and Satan hates that. I confess my sin and thank God that it is already forgiven. The very fact that we feel guilty over sins (after forgiveness) suggests that we feel that we have to do something to make that forgiveness complete and that what Christ did wasn't good enough. It suggests we don't really believe God forgave us as He said He does. . . completely casting our sins away as far as the east is from the west. Nothing could be further from the truth.

God tells us that He knew us before He even created the world: "For He chose us in Him before the creation of the world to be holy and blameless in His sight" (Eph 1:4). Right from the start God had a plan to conquer death and provide a Savior for you though you were not yet here (Gen 3:15). The Bible also says that when Christ died He forgave all my sins in advance: "When you were dead in your sins and in the uncircumcision of your sinful nature, God made you alive with Christ. He forgave us all our sins" (Col 2:13). Note, the Bible doesn't say He will forgive but that He *did* forgive. Therefore, as a Christian, every sin was already paid for 2000 years ago. This is why we can boldly thank God for forgiving us rather than asking Him to do so. Because it is already done we only need to accept it. But once again, there is no hope for this restoration if the earth is millions of years old and Jesus' death has no meaning.

Understanding joy all begins with understanding our Creator, the Word of God, Jesus Christ, our Friend. This same Creator was destined to be our Savior before the creation of the world and now desires a relationship with you.

The more we study the Bible without picking and choosing which parts of Jesus we like and don't like (The Word made flesh) the more our relationship will develop. The more our relationship grows the more joy we will experience here on earth as we accept the pure and complete forgiveness of Jesus Christ, our Creator. Yes, Jesus is our Creator as part of the Trinity. John wrote, "Through Him all things were made; without Him nothing was made that has been made" (John 1:3). To deny Jesus as Creator of a young earth means we cannot be healed by Him either. I, for one, am thankful that the earth is young and that He has provided a means of renewal, a fresh start no matter what sin you may have finished. Because the earth is only a few thousand years old, this means Jesus had the power to conquer the curse of death and, therefore, there is nothing too big or too small for our Creator to forgive. I'm also thankful that life on earth can be heavenly with a relationship with Jesus, but even greater yet will be our heavenly heaven in Him.

Outdated Information

There are a few things in this book which are "outdated" but not necessarily untrue. It is important to keep up to date for the sake of credibility as we argue with evolutionists. There are plenty of good arguments we can use that have no answers for an evolutionist so it would better to use them.

The plesiosaur type of creature shown in the chapter on dinosaurs has been investigated by many scientists who have now claimed it to be a rotting shark. Keep in mind that these studies have been done primarily by the pictures that were taken. However, there were chemical studies done on the flesh samples taken of this creature. There were 42 horny fibres taken from the flipper's edge that were stored in an antiseptic solution of sodium hypochlorite. When analyzed, the composition of the amino acids was almost identical to the elastoidin of a basking shark. Because elastoidin is not found in mammals this was considered to be solid evidence that this was a shark.

Even though there is some chemical relationship, the appearance was much different. The horny fibres on the unidentified creature were about 6-10 inches long and attached to the edge of the flippers while in a shark they attach to the inside structures that support the fin. In addition, there wasn't as much chemical similarity as one would think. In fact there was a large difference in some areas of chemical research but this was explained away because they said it could have been from the sodium hypochlorite that the samples were stored in. The basking shark samples could have been put in the same solution but were not. Also, among other marine animals we find similar amino acid compositions furthering the problem in making the amino acid similarity proof of anything.

On board the Zuiyo Maru trawler was a qualified biologist, Michihiko Yano. It was Yano who took the five pictures of this creature and had plenty of time to personally examine it before throwing it back into the water. Most research papers have said that Yano was simply a crew member and not acknowledging that Yano knew what rotting sharks looked like and was scientifically trained in this area. Yano (an eye witness) has insisted that a portion of the photo shows the right anterior fin while researchers simply looking at the photo classify them as two separate fins close together. Yano described a fat-like tissue on the creature that has been dismissed by those only looking at pictures. Yano said it did NOT smell of ammonia as rotting sharks do, but researchers take his term "putrid" and have connected that with ammonia.

Therefore, because of this many creationists still believe this to be a type of plesiosaur. However, because it has become controversial even among creationists when the argument is brought up an evolutionist can simply say that this other creationist has proven this to be false, making you look uneducated. So be wise in using this argument. I believe this was NOT a shark, but I'm being cautious about the whole thing. If you would like further evidence that this is not a shark you may contact us to get a pamphlet going over other physical details from Yano and other research papers.

Many people have shared with me that they have heard Darwin recanted on his deathbed. This is not true, even according to his own wife, Emma, who never liked Charlie's idea of evolution to begin with.

Others have told me women have one more rib than men. This also is false. If you cut off a leg of a man and he has children does his offspring come out missing a leg? It is true that the lower rib will regenerate. Therefore, if God did take out a rib from Adam it could have regenerated back. Further, the Hebrew word used for rib in Genesis actually means "side" and may not have even been a rib. God took a portion of Adam's side to make Eve.

Because Archaeoraptor was a fraud, some have made the connection that Archaeopteryx was also a fraud. This isn't true either. We have a section in this book that describes Archaeopteryx and why it isn't a missing link even though it is a true bird fossil.

Many have shared that NASA found the missing day for Joshua's long day. This is logically impossible because one needs to know how many days there are before you can determine if one is missing. This began back in 1936 by Harry Rimmer. It was taken and made into an urban legend via the Internet today.

Further Evidence of Dinosaur Living with Man

North and South American Indians have recorded many instances of the Thunderbird that bears a strong resemblance of the Pteranodon or the Quetzalcoatlus. In 1699 Captain Juan Mateo Manje was told by the Pima Indians of a great flying animal that would eat Indians. Eventually, they were able to kill this creature. Even the General Don Hernando Cortes is said to have seen the bones of such a creature and sent them back to Spain.

In Illinois there are stories of the Piasa bird. Piasa means, "bird that devours man" and was feared by the Illini Indians. John Russell was a writer from Illinois who researched this story in 1848. He found a cave that this creature supposedly lived in and discovered the floor covered with human bones. In the cliffs of Alton, Illinois, the Indians painted a picture of Piasa that was destroyed in the 1850's when the cliff eroded away. However, the picture had been described by many historians and explorers so that a detailed description fitting the flying dinosaurs remains today.

The Mayans had a sculpture in Veracruz, Mexico that looks like a Pteranodon. In the November, 1968 edition of *Science Digest*, there was an article called, "Serpent bird of the Mayans" where it was said that this animal actually lived from 1,000-5,000 years ago.

Trees Show Evidence of Noah's Flood

In the White Mountains of California grow the Bristlecone Pines. From counting the tree rings these trees are approximately 4,723 years old. This is fascinating when we consider that Noah's Flood occurred about 4,400 years ago. Because research has shown that more than one ring can form in a year when there is warm, moist conditions one can increase the rings about 10% from the actual age of the tree. There are trees that date nearly 10,000 years older than this, however, these dates come from less scientific studies using fossils, etc. In no case were the actual tree rings counted. For example, the Huon Pines of Tasmania, Australia are dated to be 30,000 years old with Carbon dating. I discussed problems with these methods earlier in this book showing that these are unreliable. No Huon tree has been dated over 3,500 years old according to the reliable tree ring counting. Again, this fits nicely with Noah's Flood and a young earth. Even in Chile, South America tree rings show the 2nd oldest tree (Alerce Tree) to be 3,631 years old. The world's largest living tree is a giant sequoia in California named, "General Sherman." It is 275 feet tall about half the size of the great pyramids of Egypt. It was first thought that this tree was 6,000 years old but is now said to be only 2,150 years old. However, this isn't the largest tree that ever lived. In 1872 there was an Australian Mountain Ash that grew to be 492 feet, reaching the top of the pyramids. The main point being, no tree has ever been dated beyond the time of Noah's Flood. This can be no coincidence, but rather further evidence of a young earth and a global flood about 4,400 years ago.

The Geological Column

The geological column has pagan roots. A man named James Hutton (1726-1796) said that the earth was much older than the Bible had said and popularized this theory in his book, Theory of the Earth. This book was published in 1795 among the midst of many revolutions such as the American (1776), French (1789), Spanish (1823), Polish (1831), and Italian (1848). This was an era of Anti-monarchy where people were beginning to reject authority and the Word of God. Hutton used the idea of uniformitarianism, which is that the present conditions of the earth have gone on for thousands and millions of years. Charles Lyell, a Scottish Lawyer, took this idea and turned it into a popular theory in his book, Principles of Geology in 1830. In it he stated that a young earth was based on, "false conclusions, . . . futile reasoning. . . ancient doctrines sanctioned by the implicit faith of many generations, and supposed to rest on Scriptural authority" (p.30). Lyell also said that his goal was to, "free the science from Moses" (*Life Letters and Journals*, John Murray 1881). No doubt, Lyell was motivated to prove the Bible wrong and to rid the idea that the fossils were signs of judgment and wrath of God upon man's sin. I believe Satan wants to remove all evidence of the Flood because he knows it is a sign of a God who judges sin even today.

In the early 1800's the geological column was assigned names such as "Cretaceous" or "Cambrian" and each layer was assigned an age according to a fossil that was found in it. The problem is, this column has never been found anywhere in the world except in the textbooks. Even the H.B.J. Earth Science textbook (1989) tells us, "Unfortunately no such column exists" (p. 326). Clearly, this column is not based on science, but on faith.

To give an illustration of how this works, if one would go to a museum and stand by a fossil you could ask the curator how they knew how old the fossil was. They would tell you they know because of what layer the fossil was found in. Then, if you walked over to the area with this strata layer displayed and ask the same man how they know how old the dirt is they would tell you because of the fossils they find in it. Can you see the circular reasoning?

Our children are being lied to in textbooks and no one seems to be alarmed. Hitler said, "Let me control the textbooks and I will control the state." With textbooks being controlled by evolutionists, our children are being brainwashed much like Nazi Germany. This is why "75% of all children raised in Christian homes who attend public schools will reject the Christian faith by their first year of college" (Video- "Let My Children Go" by Jeremiah Films).

Fetus Similarity with Humans and Animals

For years the idea that the human embryo is similar to that of a fish, salamander, chicken, rabbit and other animals has been widely taught. In fact, it remains in textbooks still today. This is beyond my understanding how such lies can infiltrate our society when it has been proven false for over 100 years. This idea was popularized by Earnst Haeckel who admitted that his "turning point in his thinking was when he read Charles Darwin's Origin of Species" (*Creation Ex Nihilo* March 1996, p.33). Darwin considered the similarity of embryos "by far the strongest single class of facts in favor of his theory" (Icons of Evolution p. 82). In 1874 Haeckel made some drawings to support this similar embryonic development. These pictures appear in many texts today even though they have been proven false. In fact, Haeckel was convicted of fraud by the Jena University Court. Haeckel confessed, "A small percent of my embryonic drawings are forgeries; those namely, for which the observed material is so incomplete or insufficient as to fill in and reconstruct the missing links by hypothesis and comparative synthesis." He also stated, "I should feel utterly condemned... were it not that hundreds of the best observers, and biologists lie under the same charge." (Records from the University of Jena trial in 1875). Walter Bock of Columbia University said, "Moreover, the biogenetic law has become so deeply rooted in biological thought that it cannot be weeded out in spite of its having been demonstrated to be wrong by numerous subsequent scholars" ("Evolution by Orderly Law," *Science*, Vol. 164, 9 May 1969, pp. 684-685). Scientific American said, "Surely the biogenetic law is as dead as a doornail" (Vol. 76, May 1988, p. 273). If it's dead why is it still alive in the textbooks today?

The Merrill Earth Science textbook states, "The embryos of each of these animals have tails and gill pouches." It also asks the question, "Why are fishlike features present in the embryos of reptiles, mammals, and birds?" (1993, p. 451). The Tobin and Dusheck, 1998 text uses embryology to support evolution on p. 381 as well. The 1994 edition of Holt Biology on page 183 compares a chicken and human embryo to show similarities. The 1994 Glenco Biology page 312 compare a pig and a human. The 1998 Prentice Hall Biology on page 223 compares the fish, pig and human. The 1998 Holt Science on page 45 uses this erroneous evidence. The 2000 Biology Concepts and Applications on page 279 compare the bird, reptile, fish and human embryos suggesting similarities to be evidence of evolution. The 2001 Prentice Hall Focus on Life, page 153 shows the turtle and chicken to show common ancestry of man. The 2001 Holt Biology page 288 shows the fish, tortoise, chicken and human to be related. Many other modern textbooks are doing the same and using evidence that has been disproved since the late 1800's.

It is important to note that just because there are some physical similarities in development doesn't mean anything except that we have a common Designer that uses similar design much like an architect has a common design in his buildings. Further, many textbooks show that a frog and a human have similar hand appearances in early stages. However, in humans the skin attaches between the fingers all the way up and as it develops the skin simply begins to go away down the fingers. In a frog the digits actually grow up and out. These are completely opposite growing patterns and cannot show similar origin, only similar design.

Some have even tried to say that genetic similarities show common ancestry. For example, since penicillin has only two chromosomes it may have evolved first. The fruit fly has 8 chromosomes and the tomato has 12. If this is the case, the opossum, Redwood tree and kidney bean must be related because they all have 22 chromosomes. A human has 46 chromosomes and perhaps, after millions of years of evolution we could evolve into a carp that has 100. If we set our sights really high, we might even reach the fern that has 480 chromosomes. Obviously, this is ridiculous. Earlier in this book we discussed how we are 98.6% genetically identical to a chimp and how this didn't support evolution in any form either. Besides, a rain cloud is 100% water and a watermelon is 97% water so I guess they must be related too. (See Kent Hovind's video seminar for more).

Can Creation be Taught in Public Schools?

From the 1800's to 1925 creation was taught in almost every school right from the Bible. As evolution began to creep into the schools in the late 1920's some states passed laws to keep evolution from being taught in the public school classroom. Then, in 1925 the great Scopes trial in Dayton, Tennessee tried to overturn such a law, but they lost. For about 40 years after this many states still had laws on record to forbid the teaching of evolution. Finally, in 1968 the last law was overturned and then in 1980 the law that demanded equal time for evolution and creation was overturned. Because of this, many teachers believe that we cannot teach creation in the public school any longer. This is a lie and a misconception. Even the evolutionist, Stephen Jay Gould admits, "Louisiana passed a law requiring teachers to teach creation if they taught evolution. The law required 'balanced treatment.' It has never been against the law to teach creation. No statute exists in any state to bar instruction in 'creation science.' It could be taught before, and it can be taught now." ("The Verdict on Creationism", *New York Times*, July 19, 1987, p.34). Michael Zimmerman, another evolutionist states, "The Supreme court ruling did not, in any way, outlaw the teaching of 'creation science' in public school classrooms. Quite simply it ruled that, in the form taken by the Louisiana law, it is unconstitutional to demand equal time for this particular subject. 'Creation science' can still be brought into science classrooms if and when teachers and administrators feel that it is appropriate. Numerous surveys have shown that teachers and administrators favor just this route. And, in fact, 'creation science' is being taught in science courses throughout the country" ("Keep Guard Up After Evolution Victory," *BioScience* 37 9, October 1987, p. 636). Eugene Scott of the National Center for Science Education in Berkeley, California said, "The Supreme Court decision says only that the Louisiana law violates the constitutional separation of church and state: it does not say that one cannot teach scientific creationism – unfortunately many individual teachers do. Some school districts even require 'equal time' for creation and evolution." William B. Provine said, "Teachers and school boards in public schools are already free under the Constitution of the USA to teach about supernatural origins if they wish in their science classes. Laws can be passed in most countries of the world requiring discussion of supernatural origins in science classes, and still satisfy national legal requirements. And I have a suggestion for evolutionists. Include discussion of supernatural origins in your classes, and promote discussion of them in public and other schools. Come off your high horse about having only evolution taught in science classes. The exclusionism you promote is painfully self-serving and smacks of elitism. Why are you afraid of confronting the supernatural creationism believed by the majority of persons in the USA and perhaps worldwide? Shouldn't students be encouraged to express their beliefs about origins in a class discussing origins by evolution?" (*Biology and Philosophy* 8 (1993): p. 124. Clearly, things aren't as legally binding as most teachers believe when it comes to teaching creation.

    The fact is, teachers CAN teach creation and even right out of the Bible. In 1963 the ACLU did get prayer out of the schools because it was using the Bible as a means of religion and salvation. However, the Bible can be used as a means of religion, culture and science. The truth is, the ACLU didn't throw the Bible out of school, we did, simply by not being educated as to our rights on this matter. A great book on this topic is <u>Teaching Creation Science in Public Schools</u> by Duane Gish. States can legally require teachers to discuss evolution but they cannot require them to discuss creation. However, teachers MAY discuss creation if they wish, they just can't REQUIRE it. Also, the courts will allow states to REQUIRE discussing scientific weaknesses in evolution. The Bible can point out many of these weaknesses. In the 1963 ruling of the School District of Abiongton Township vs. Schempp the court said, "It certainly may be said that the Bible is worthy of study for its literary and historic qualities. Nothing we have said here indicates that such study of the Bible or of religion, when presented objectively as part of a secular program of education, may be effected consistently with the First Amendment." In Stone v. Graham (1980) the Supreme Court said, "The Bible may constitutionally be used in an appropriate study of history, civilization, ethics, comparative religion, or the like." Also in 1980, the Florey v. Sioux Falls School District case, the Supreme Court ruled, "Permitting public school observances, which include religious elements, promotes the secular purpose of advancing the student's knowledge and appreciation of the role that our religious heritage has played in the social, cultural and historical development of civilization." In 1987 Edwards v. Aguilliard, 482 U.S. 96, the Court ruled, "Teachers already possess the flexibility to present a variety of scientific theories about the origins of humankind. . . and are free to teach any and all facets of this subject. Teaching a variety of scientific theories about the origins of mankind to school children might be done with the clear secular intent of enhancing the effectiveness of science instruction." The California State Board of Education Policy on the teaching of Natural Sciences states, "Discussion of any scientific fact, hypothesis, or theory related to the origins of the universe, the earth and of life (the 'how') are appropriate to the science curriculum." I hope this is enough evidence to show that we are being duped into believing creationism cannot be taught in the public schools. If you would like further information you may also check out the video seminar series from Kent Hovind available on our web site.

Interestingly, the removal of school prayer has had a devastating effect on our society. According to the Education Research Analysts, before the indoctrination of evolution in schools, only 2 to 3,000 words were dedicated to evolution in textbooks. By 1963 there were 33,089 words. From 1963 to 1980 even birth rates for unwed girls ages 10-14 went up 100%. Illegitimate births rose from 5% to 30% from 1960 to 1992. Welfare spending has gone up from 29 billion to 212 billion dollars. Juvenile crimes have gone from 137 to 431 per 100,000 population. Combined SAT scores went from 975 down to 899 (Dept. of Health and Human Resources and Statistical Abstracts of the U.S). One can easily see that the removal of God from our society certainly hasn't helped much. One judge said the Ten Commandments needed to be removed from a school wall because kids might read it and do what it says. Heaven forbid that kids actually obey the Ten Commandments and not steal, cheat, covet, murder etc. If you would like to find out more about this the best resource I have found is David Barton's "America's Godly Heritage" video from Wall Builders Inc.

The Importance of Creation as a Foundation for Morals

The Bible tells us, "All Scripture is God-breathed and is useful for teaching, rebuking, correcting and training in righteousness, so that the man of God may be thoroughly equipped for every good work. In the presence of God and of Christ Jesus, who will judge the living and the dead, and in view of His appearing and His kingdom, I give you this charge: Preach the Word; be prepared in season and out of season; correct, rebuke and encourage--with great patience and careful instruction. For the time will come when men will not put up with sound doctrine. Instead, to suit their own desires, they will gather around them a great number of teachers to say what their itching ears want to hear. <u>They will turn their ears away from the truth and turn aside to myths.</u> But you, keep your head in all situations, endure hardship, do the work of an evangelist, discharge all the duties of your ministry" (2 Tim 3:16-4:5). Unfortunately, even though the Bible clearly tells us it is the Word of God, people have turned to whatever their itching ears want to hear, even if it is a myth.

Today's faith questions are resting upon questions that deal with creation or evolution. People want to know where Cain got his wife and how to fit dinosaurs into the Bible. How did these questions become the foundation of faith?

About 150 years ago the pagan scientists began to tell people that the earth was not young and the Church was challenged by this. What they decided was that as long as the Church was still the foundation for morals and salvation, they could compromise on this issue. This was the first fatal step in separating the Bible from the world.

The question today is this: we believe the Bible is the foundation for morals, but do we believe it is the foundation for geology, biology, chemistry and astronomy? This is the very issue that Clarence Darrow challenged in the Scopes trial. He asked the question, "Where did Cain get his wife?" Because they couldn't answer that simple question, Darrow challenged the historical accuracy of the Scriptures, and thus, challenged the moral accuracy of it as well.

In Sunday School classes across the country we are teaching our children all the nice Bible stories of Daniel and the lion's den, Noah's ark, Jesus and the disciples. However, are we teaching biology, geology and the sciences along with them? Not at all. What message are we sending our children? I believe the message is clear. The Bible is accurate when it comes to morals and salvation, but when it comes to the world issues, you need to turn to the scientists. Bruce Willis says it best, "Organized religion used to hang the whole thing on one hook: If you don't do these things, if you don't act morally, your going to burn in hell. Unfortunately, with what we know about science, anyone who thinks at all probably doesn't believe in fire and brimstone anymore. So organized religion has lost that voice to hold up their moral hand" (USA Weekend Magazine, *Cincinnati, Enquirer*. Feb 11, 2000 p.7). Can you see what he is saying. We are trying to impress morality upon a society who doesn't accept the foundation of that morality because that foundation has been removed from the real world. We look back on the twin tower disaster and people wonder why that happened. Carl Sagan said, "Look at this world out there, all the mistakes, all the mutations, and the death and suffering and disease. Where's the God of love? Where is your powerful God? I don't see a powerful God." Sagan believes in that powerful God now that he is dead (even though that does him no good now) but he wouldn't consider God when he was alive because he didn't believe in Genesis, the foundation of understanding God. Had he known Genesis, he would have understood the curse and fall. You see, we aren't looking at a perfect world anymore. We are viewing a world that has been cursed because of sin. If you don't believe in a literal Adam and Eve, how can you understand original sin? If you can't understand original sin, how can you understand things like death, suffering and terrorism? When Luke traces the genealogy of Jesus he doesn't say, "Now Jesus Himself was about thirty years old when He began His ministry. He was the son, so it was thought, of Joseph, the son of Heli, the son of Matthat, the son of Levi . . . the son of Enosh, the son of Seth, the son of a metaphor." No. Jesus came from Adam, a literal, historical figure. Some try to say that man was made millions of years after creation. NO! Jesus Himself tells us when man was made: "'Haven't you read,' He replied, 'that at the beginning the Creator made them male and female'" (Matthew 19:4). God made man "at the beginning," not "millions of years after the beginning." If we don't start teaching our children Jesus and the Bible as it connects with the real world and sciences I fear we will lose them eternally. The Bible wasn't meant to be a science book, but it is one. Don't lose your connection with reality.

Do You Want $250,000 Dollars?

All you have to do is come up with one scientific evidence of macroevolution and it is yours. The fact that nobody has been able to take this reward should tell you that there is no evidence of evolution. If you think you have any evidence go to drdino.com to get more information on how to claim it. However, I would encourage you to spend your time on something more valuable; the Truth. This Truth is Jesus Christ who said, "I am the Way, the Truth, and the Life. No one comes to the Father except through Me" (John 14:6). Go to the Bible and claim the free gift of eternal life through faith in Jesus. He not only answers where you came from, but where you will be going. Praise God!

Picture references:

1) "Genesis foundation" pg 44 of The Lie by Ken Ham.
2) "Word of God" pg 126 of The Young Earth by John Morris.
3) "Foundations" Transparency # 19 Relevance of Creation by Ken Ham.
4) "Assumptions" pg 21 of The Young Earth by John Morris.
5) "Mind of man" pg 126 of The Young Earth by John Morris.
6) "Castles" Transparency # 21 Relevance of Creation by Ken Ham.
7) "Clearing ground" Transparency #27 Relevance of Creation by Ken Ham.
8) "Drilled cores" pg 79 of The Young Earth by John Morris
9) "Magnetic field" pg 82 of The Young Earth by John Morris.
10) "Battery" pg 11-12 Creation Ex Nihilo, Vol.16 No. 2
11) "Strata" pg 37 Grand Canyon: Monument to Catastrophe by Steven Austin
12) "Tooth" Personal picture.
13) "Speciman ridge" pg 114 of The Young Earth by John Morris.
14) "Log model" pg 103 of The Young Earth by John Morris.
15) "Tree ring" pg 48 of The Young Earth by John Morris.
16) "Carbon build up" pg 64 of The Young Earth by John Morris.
17) "Fossil hat" Back of Creation ex nihilo. June-August 1995. Vol 17, no 3.
18) "Polystrate fossil" pg 101 of The Young Earth by John Morris.
19) "2nd law" pg 217 of What is Creation Science by H. Morris and G. Parker.
20) "Fetus in womb" pg 62 What is Creation Science- H. Morris and G. Parker.
21) "Miller experiment" p 39 What is Creation Science H. Morris & G. Parker.
22) "Feather" pg 67 of Dinosaurs by Design by Duane Gish.
23) "Japanese dinosaur" pg 86 of Dinosaurs by Design by Duane Gish.
24) "Parasaurolophus" pg 82 of Dinosaurs by Design by Duane Gish.
25) "Bombardier beetle" pg 51 of Dinosaurs by Design by Duane Gish.
26) "Evolution is Religion" Transparency # 3 Relevance of Creation Ken Ham.
27) "Stone art" Creation ex nihilo pg 21. Vol. 19:2 May, 1997.
28) "Dinosaur track" Personal picture.
29) "Hammer" Personal picture.
30) "Australopithecus skull" Personal picture.
31) "Mars rock" pg 294 Creation ex Nihilo Tech. Journal Vol. 10 part 3 1996.
32) "Assumptions" pg 21 of The Young Earth by John Morris.
33) "Radiohalo" The Young Earth by John Morris.
34) "Conformity" pg 105 of The Young Earth by John Morris.
35) "Magnetic strength" pg 75 of The Young Earth by John Morris.
36) "Snake" Personal Picture.
37) "Age graph" pg 88 of Methuselah's Secret by Arthur E. Brown.
38) "Ark" Sketch C pg 27 of Noah's Ark and the Ararat Adventure John Morris.
39) "Ark" Sketch G pg 29 of Noah's Ark and the Ararat Adventure John Morris.
40) "Ark" Sketch E pg 28 of Noah's Ark and the Ararat Adventure John Morris.
41) "Ark" Sketch F pg 28 of Noah's Ark and the Ararat Adventure John Morris.
42) "Mystery Object" pg 32 Noah's Ark and the Ararat Adventure John Morris.
43) "Crosses" pg 54 of Noah's Ark and the Ararat Adventure by John Morris.
44) "Cave" pg 52 of Noah's Ark and the Ararat Adventure by John Morris.
45) "Carving" pg 52 of Noah's Ark and the Ararat Adventure by John Morris.

Aerate, Michael J. "Ice Ages, The Mystery Solved," Part III Paleomagnetic Stratigraphy and Date Manipulation. Creation Research Society Quarterly, Vol 21. no. 4 pp 170-181.

Anderson, Kirby (Yale) Personal correspondence with Dr. Baugh of Creation Evidences Museum in Glenrose.

Arizona Highways, pp. 4-11, January 1993.

Austin, S. A., 1991, Mount St. Helens: Geology Education Materials, El Cajon, 61 pp.

Baugh, Dr. Carl, Creation in Symphony Film from Creation Evidences Museum, Glen Rose, TX.

------------------, The Battle, Film from Creation Evidences Museum, Glen Rose, TX.

Begley, Sharon, "Lifting the Veil," Newsweek, June 5, 1995, p.50.

Berner, Robert A. & Landis Gary P., "Gas bubbles in fossil amber as possible indicators of the major gas composition of ancient air" (*Science*: Vol 239) p. 1406.

Blum, Harold, "Perspectives in Evolution," *American Scientist*, Vol. 43, October 1955, p. 595.

Bowser, Hal, "When Elephants Roamed the Range", *Science Digest*, p. 63, June 1983.

Brazo, M. W., and Austin, S. A., 1982, The Tunguska explosion of 1908: Origins, vol. 9, pp. 82-93.

Bray, J. R., 1977, Pleistocene volcanism and glacial initiation: *Science*, vol. 197, pp. 251-254.

Brown, Arthur E., Methuselah's Secret Eagle Publications: Farmington MI 1986, pp 240.

Brown, Walter T, "The continents and the mid atlantic ridge. Pettsburg PN, International Conference on Creationism, Vol. 1, p. 32.

Bruce, F. F., N.T. Documents, p. 14.

--------------------"Continents and the Mid Atlantic Ridge" (Phoenix, CSC, In the Beginning 1989) p. 70.

BSN (*Bible Science News*) 9/90, p. 15.

Buckna, David A., "The Origin of Man: What Does the Fossil Record Show?"

Spring DIALOGUE.

Burr, Chandler, "The geophysics of God" *US News and World Report,* June 16, pp 55-58, 1997.

Campbell, Grant, *Rock Art of the American Indian,* Outbooks, Golden (Colorado), p. 117, 1981. The Moab Mammoth Pictograph", *Scientific Monthly,* pp. 378-379, 1935.

Carington, Richard, "The story of our earth" p 155

Carr, William. Hitler: A Study in Personality and Politics. New York: St Martin's Press, 1979.

Carter, W. E. and Robertson, D. S., 1986. Studying the earth by very-long – baseline interferometry. *Scientific American,* vol. 255(5), pp. 44-52.

C & EN, Oct 11, 1976.

Chambers, Claire, The SIECUS Circle: A Humanist Revolution (Appleton, WI: Western Islands, 1979), p. 3.

Chittick, Donald E., *The Puzzle of Ancient Man,* Creation Compass, Newberg, OR, 1997.

Chronicle Telegram USA, 14 January, 1997.

Clark, Martin E., & Morris, Henry M., The Bible has the Answers, Master Books: El Cajon, 1992, pp.362.

Comptons Interactive Encyclopedia, Version 2.01 VW 1994 Comptons NewMedia, Inc & Compton's Learning Co.

Creation ex nihilo, "Fossil Hat", Vol. 17:3, June 1995, p.52.

*Creation ex nihilo,*17(1)14-17, 1995.

Creation Research Society Quarterly, 1991, 28:29.

Cremo, M. and R. Thompson, 1993. Forbidden Archaeology. San Diego: Bhaktivedanta Institute, p. 214.

Cummings, Violet M., Noah's Ark: Fact or Fable Creation Science Research Center: San Diego, 1972, pp. 352.

Davis, Ed. Alburqurque New Mexico. Personal Correspondence.

Dalrymple, G.B., "40 Ar/36 Ar Analyses of Historical Lava Flows," Earth and Planetary Letters, Vol. 6, 1969, pp. 47-55.

Decker, R., and Decker, B., 1981, Volcanoes: San Francisco, W. H. Freeman, 224 pp.

Denton, Michael, Evolution: A Theory in Crisis, (Adler & Adler: Bethesda MD 1986), p. 270.

Discover, "Up Front," Discover, March 1991, p. 10.

Doell, R. and Cox, A., 1967. Magnetization of rocks. In: Mining Geophysics , vol. II, Society of Exploration Geophysicists, p. 452.

Down, David. "2000 year old battery was forgotten." *Creation Ex nihilo,* Vol 16:2 pp. 11-13.

Dubrov, A.P., "The geomagnetic Field and Life, (New York: Plenum Press, 1978) p. 61.

Ehrlich, Paul, The Population Bomb, pp. 88, 135.

---------------, "World Population: Is the Battle Lost?" Standford Today, (Winter 1968), p. 9.

Eldridge, Niles, *Time Frames*, 1985, p. 52.

Eldridge, Niles, *The Monkey Business* 1982.

E. S. Moore: Coal: Its Properties, Analysis, Classification, Geology, Extraction, Uses and Distribution (New York, 2nd Ed., Wiley, 1940), p. 146.

Fairhall, A. W. and Young, J. A., 1970. Radionuclides in the Environment. Advances in Chemistry, vol. 93, p. 402.

Feig, Konnilyn G. Hitler's Death Camps: The Sanity of Madness. New York: Holmes & Mier, 1979.

Fife, Dr. William, Texas A & M University, Personal Correspondence, July 6, 1995.

--------------------, Texas A & M University, Personal Correspondence, 1994.

Funkhouser, John G., and Naughton, John J.m "Radiogenic Helium and Argon in Ultramafic Inclusions from Hawaii," Journal of Geophysical Research, Vol. 73, No. 14, July 1968, pp. 4601-4607.

Gange, Robert, Origins and Destiny, Waco TX, Word Books, 1986, pp. 162- 164.

Geisler, Norman L., Christian Apologetics, Baker Book House: Grand Rapids, 1992, pp. 390.

Girouard, Michael M. D. Is Life Just Chemistry, ICR film.

Gish, Duane T. Evolution: The Challenge of the Fossil Record. Creation Life Publishers: El Cajon, 1992. pp. 277.

Gish, Duane T., Dinosaurs by Design, Creation Life Publishers: Colorado Springs, Co, 1992, pp 88.

Gish, Duane T. The Fossil Record Film from ICR.

Gish, Duane T. The Origin of Man Film from ICR.

Gould, Stephen J, "Dr. Down's Syndrome." *Natural History*, Vol. 89 (April 1980), p. 144.

Grieve, R. A. F. and Robinson, P. B., 1979, The terrestrial catering record -- 1. Current status of observations: Icarus, vol. 38, pp. 212-229.

G. Richard Bozarth, "The Meaning of Evolution," *American Atheist*, February 1978, pp. 19, 30.

Grosvenor, Melville, B., Quoted by John Morris on the Ark on Ararat, Sandiego, CLP Publishers 1976.

Hall, F. W., "Manuscript Authorities for the Text of the Chief Classical Writers," in Companion to Classical Text, and Bruce Metzger, Chapters in the History of New Testament Textual Criticism.

Ham, Ken, "Creation: Facts and Bias," Video, Master Books.

Ham, Ken, "The Relevance of Creation: A Self-Instruction Program," Master Books, El Cajon, 1988, p.5.

----------- Answers in Genesis film: "What Happened to the Dinosaurs"

Hapgood, C., 1970. The path of the pole. Philadelphia: Chilton.Harris, Laird, R., Archer Gleason L., JR. & Waltke, Bruce, Theological Wordbook of the Old Testament, 47, 862.

Helfinstine, Robert F., & Roth Jerry D., Texas Tracks and Artifacts, 1994, pp 109.

Henry, C.F., Revelation and the Bible, pp. 301-302.

Horner, John R., "Digging for Dinosaurs", 198, p. 131.

Hoyle, F., and Wickramasinghe, C., 1978, Comets, ice ages, and ecological catastrophes: *Astrophysics and Space Science*, vol. 53, pp. 523-526.

---------- "Hoyle on Evolution." Nature, vol. 294, 12 November 1981, p. 105.

H. S. Lipson, FRS., "A physicist looks at evolution." Physics Bulletin, vol. 31, 1980, p. 138.

Humphry, Russel, "Earths Magnetic field is young," El Cajon, CA Impact no. 242, p.2.

--------------------- "Evidence For a Young Earth: Part I" ICR video El Cajon CA.

--------------------- "Radiocarbon, Creation and the Genesis Flood" ICR video El Cajon CA.

Huxley, Julian, What is Science? (New York: Simon & Schuster, 1955), p. 278.

In Search of Noah's Ark CBS special, 1993.

Jacobs, J. A., 1967. The Earth's Core and Geomagnetism, Pergamon Press, Oxford, p. 106.

Josephus, Antiquities, Book One Chapter 1.

Jueneman, Frederick, B., "Secular Catastrophism" Industrial Research and Development, Vol. 24 June 1982) p. 21.

Kelso, A. J., Physical Anthropology, 2nd edition, J. B. Lippincott, New York, p. 142 (1974).

Kemp, Tom, "A Fresh Look at the Fossil Record," *New Scientist*, Vol. 108, Dec. 5, 1985, p. 67.

Kitts, David B. "Search for the Holy Transformation," *Paleobiology*, Summer, 1979, pp. 353, 354.

Klenck, Thomas, "Microwave Oven" (*Popular Mechanics*, Sept. 1989) p. 78.

Larson, Roger, "The mid-cretacious Super Plume Episode" *Scientific American*, Feb 1995) p. 825-885.

Lee, Robert E. "Radiocarbon, Ages in Error," Anthropological Journal of Canada, Vol. 19, No. 3, 1981, pp. 9,29.

Lewis, C. S., Mere Christianity, pp. 55-56.

Life 15(14):60-68, December 1992.

Los Angeles Times, May 21, 1995.

Mao, H. K. & Hemley, R.J., "Optical Studies of Hydrogen" *Science* Vol. 244, p. 1463.

Maddox, Barney T. Human Genome Project, Quantitative Disproof of Evolution, CEM Facts Sheet.

McDonald, K.L. & Gunst, R.H., "An Analysis of the Earths Magnetic Field from 1835 to 1965" (Essa Technical Report, ER 46 IES, July 1967, US Government Printing Office: Washington D.C.) Table 3, p. 14.

Miller, Hugh, "The Old Red Sandstone," Boston, Gould & Lincoln, 1857, p. 221.

Meyerholf, Howard A; Meyerholf, Arthur A.; Taner, Irfan; Morris, Anthony E.L.; Martin, Bruce D.; and Angoes, William B., "Surge Tectonics: A New Hypothesis of Earth Dynamics," Lubbock New Concepts on Global Tectonics 1992), p. 309.

Moore, Ruth; Man, Time and Fossils, 1953, p. 249.

Morris, Henry M., *Creation and the Modern Christian*, 1985.

Morris, Henry M., The Genesis Record, Baker Book House: Grand Rapids, 1993, p 716.

Morris, John D., The Young Earth, Master Books: Colorado Springs, 1994, p.141.

------------------, Noah's Ark and the Ararat Adventure, Master Books: Colorado Springs, 1994, pp 64.

Moses, Phyllis B. & Chua, Nam-Hai, "Light switches for plant genes" (*Scientific American*, April 1988) p. 32.

M. Schweitzer and T. Staedter, "The Real Jurassic Park" *Earth*, June 1997 pp. 55-57.

Mueller, Larry, "A Shock Cure for Snakebites" (*Outdoor Life*, June 1988) p. 66.

------------------, "A Shock Cure for Snakebites" (*Outdoor Life*, July 1988) p. 76.

Napier, W. M., and Clube, S. V. M., 1979, A theory of terrestrial catastrophism:

Nature, vol. 282, pp. 455-459.

NASA, Tech Briefs, Vol 12. no 4, April 1988 (cover).

National Geographic Vol. 136 no. 6 Dec 1969. National Geographic Society: Washington D.C.

National Geographic Nov. 1985. National Geographic Society: Washington D.C. p. 629.

Nature, vol. 227 no. 5258, 1970.

Noorbergen, Rene, Secrets of Lost Races, 1977 p. 26.

Norwich, J., 1968. Sahara. New York: Weybright and Talley.

Nuttall, N. "Mud springs a surprise after 165 million years," *The Times,* London, p.7 May 2, 1996.

Oakland, Roger, "Ancient Man: Created or Evolved" Film

Oestreicher, Alene D., "Worldwide traditions of primordial paradise" (El Cajon, CA, Impact #192).

Organic Chemistry 6:463-471, 1984.

Origin of Life Video, Films for Christ, Mesa AZ.

Osborn, Carl D. MD, "Treatment of Venomous Bite by High Voltage Direct Current." Oklahoma State Medical Association, Vol. 83, January 1990, pp.9-14.

Ostrom, John H., "The bird in the bush", *Nature*, vol 353:19 September 1991, p. 212.

Ovid, 1955. Metamorphoses. Bloomington: Indiana University Press.

Menton, David, "Climbing The 'Ladder of Life' In the Grand Canyon", *Christian News,* April 24, 1995, p. 3.

Metzger, Bruce, The Text of the New Testament, pp. 31- 33.

Parker, Gary E., & Morris, Henry M., What is Creation Science, Master Books: El Cajon, 1987, pp. 321.

Parker, Gary. Answers in Genesis film: Dinosaurs and the Bible.

Patten, D., 1966. The biblical Flood and the ice epoch. Seattle: Pacific Meridian.

Peterson, Dale H. Longevity and the Biblical Record, 1501 S.E 19th St. Edmond OK.

Petit, Charles. Air & Space "Pieces of the rock" April/May 1997 36-41.

Popular Science, New York, Oct. 1989, p. 25.

Powell, Cory S., "Peering Inward" (*Scientific American*, June 1991) p. 107.

Platt, R., ed., 1980. The forgotten books of Eden. New York: Bell.

P. W., Bridgman,: "Reflections on Thermodynamics," *American Scientist*, Vol. 41, October 1953, p. 549.

Raup, David M., "Conflicts between Darwin and paleontology". Field Museum of Natural History Bulletin, vol. 50(1), January 1979, p. 25.

Readers Digest, May 1975, p. 35.

Rees, M. J.; and Carr, B.J.; "The Anthropic Principal and the Structure of the Physical World" Nature, 278, 1987). p. 610.

Rees, Robin, "The force of attraction" (The Way Nature Works, Macmillan publishing Co., New York: 1992, p.14.

Rehwinkel, Alfred M., The Flood, Concordia Publishing House, St. Louis, MO, Renfrew, Colin, Before Civilization, Alfred A. Knopf Publishers: New York, 1974, p. 21.

Ricklefs, Robert E. 'Paleontologists confronting macro evolution.' *Science,* vol. 199, 6 January 1978, p. 59

Roberts, Paul H. (*Nature*, April 20, 1995).

Robinson,, Steven J., "From the Flood to the Exodus: Egypt's Earliest Settlers." Creation ex nihilo Technical journal, vol 9:1 1995, pp. 45-66.

Sagan, C & I. S Shlovski, 1966. Intelligent Life in the Universe, New York, Dell, p. 231.

Salt Lake Tribune, March 19, 1995 p. A12.

Sayce, A. H., (ed.), Records of the Past (old Series), Vol. VII, p. 131f.

Schneour, Elie A., "Life Doesn't Begin, It Continues: Abortion Foes Err in Setting Conception as the Starting Point," *Los Angeles Times*, January 29, 1989, Part V.

Science, vol. 189 no. 4200, 1975, p. 379.

Science 274:1150-1151, 1996.

Science 265:1360, September 2, 1994.

Science News 150:328, November 23, 1996.

Scientific American, June 1983 pp. 86-94.

Shea, J. H. 1982, Uniformitarianism and sedimentology: Journal of Sedimentary Petrology, vol. 52, pp. 701,702.

Sippert, Albert, From Eternity to Eternity (N. Mankato MN: Sippert Publishing, 1989) p. 77.

Sippert, Albert, Evolution is Not Scientific: 32 Reasons Why. (N. Mankato MN: Sippert Publishing, 1995)

Smith, J., 1876. Chaldean Account of Genesis, Scribners, New York.

Snelling, Andrew; Ham, Ken & Wieland, Carl, The Answers Book, Master Books: El Cajon, 1992, pp. 207.

Snelling, Andrew, The Grand Canyon, Film from the Institute for Creation Research, El Cajon: CA.

--------------------, "The Age of Australian uranium," *Creation Ex Nihilo* Vol. 4, No. 2, 1981, pp. 44-57.

Spear, William Jr. Impact #265, July 1995.

St. Louis Post Dispatch, August 24, 1994.

Swinton, W. E. "The Origin of Birds", Chapter I, in Biology and Comparative Physiology of Birds, Vol. I, Academic Press, New York, 1960, p.1.

Sydney Morning Herald, February 28, 1997, p. 11.

Symons, G. J., ed., 1888, The eruption of Krakatoa and subsequent phenomena:

Report of the Krakatoa Committee of the Royal Society, London, Trubner, 494 pp.

Takahata, N., Molecular Anthropology, "A Genetic Perspective on the origin and history of humans." Ann. Rev. Ecol.Syst. 1995. 26:343-72.

Taylor, Ian, In the Minds of Men, TFE Publishing, Toronto 1987 pp. 234-241).

Tryon, Edward P., "What made the world?" New Scientist, 8 March 1984, p. 14.VI: Journal of the Transactions of the Victoria Institute. London: Philosophical Society of Great Britain.

Von Fange, Erich A., Noah to Abram: The turbulent years, Living Word Services, Syracuse, 1994, p 371.

Walker, J.C.G., "Atmospheric Evolution." (*Science*, Vol. 230) p. 164.

West, Ronald R., Ph.D. 'Paleoecology and uniformitarianism'. Compass, vol. 45, May 1968, p. 216.*Weekend Australian*, October 28, 1995, p. 49.

Weiner, Jonathon, Planet Earth (New York: Bantam Books, 1986) p. 31.

William J. Miller: An Introduction to Historical Geology (6th Ed., New York, Van Nostrand, 1952), p. 12.

Williams, H., and McBirney, A. R., 1979 Volcanology: San Francisco, Freeman Cooper & Co., 397 pp.

Williams, Quentin, "How Hot is the Heat of the Earth" (*Sky and Telescope*, Oct 1987), p. 345.

Wilson, Clifford, "Visual Highlights of the Bible" Pacific Christian Ministries, Victoria Australia, 1993, 132 pp.

Young, Davis A., Christianity and the Age of the Earth, 1982, p. 25.

Young, Davis A, "Scripture in the Hands of Geologists," Parts One and Two, The Westminster Theological Journal, Vol. 49, Vol. 1 Spring, 1987, pp. 1-34, and Vol. 2, Fall, 1987, pp. 257-304.

Zimmer, Carl, "The Ocean Within" (Discover, Oct. 1994) p. 20.

----------------, "Location, Location, Location," (*Discover*, Dec. 1994). p. 32.

A

Abortion, 7, 14, 15, 21, 65, 129, 130
Abraham, 10, 31, 41, 128, 138, 162, 164, 166, 168
Adam, 13, 14, 15, 21, 26, 40, 41, 62, 115, 125, 138, 157
Ahora Gorge, 146
Ancient Man, 41, 125, 126, 128, 129
   longevity of, 138
   used more of brain, 128
Ape
   jaw of, 94
Ararat, 5, 126, 140, 141, 146, 148, 149, 150, 153, 177, 179
   dangers of, 146
   size, 146
Archaeology, 4, 5, 125, 160, 175
Archaeopteryx, 3, 72, 89
   and the Hoatzin, 72
Ark, 5, 43, 92, 140, 141, 144, 145, 146, 147, 148, 150, 152, 153, 175, 177, 178, 179
   Albert Shappell, 149
   archaeology, 153
   Ed Behling, 147
   Ed Davis, 146
   eyewitnesses, 145, 148, 149
   George Green, 148
   Jacob, 148
   John Morris, 150
   Pentagon, 150
   size, 145
Austin, Steve, 47, 48, 53, 121, 174
Australopithecus, 94, 95, 96

B

Bible
   and archaeology, 160
   authors of, 169
   finished, 168
   historical, 159, 161
   inspired, 168
   Scriptural evidence of, 162
Biogenesis, 65
   amino acids, 68
   Stanley Miller's experiment, 66
   whats needed?, 65
Bombardier Beetle, 81
Bronze age, 30
Brown Recluse Spider, 136
Burdick track, 86

C

Carbon dating, 38

accuracy of, 55
and Noah's Flood, 55
catastrophes affects on, 55
process of, 55

Catastrophies
and fossilization, 57
Carbon dating, 54
Tunguska, 44

Cave Men
hunters?, 34
in Bible, 33
technologically advanced, 31
use of electricity, 32
who were they?, 30

Christ, 3, 6, 7, 11, 12, 15, 18, 19, 20, 30, 38, 62, 80, 117, 126, 127, 130, 141, 147, 158, 159, 161, 162, 163, 167, 168, 169, 170, 180

Clark print, 85

Clothing, 13, 14, 32, 128

Coal
extent of, 47
fossils found in, 48

Comets, 4, 49, 115, 178

Complexity of Man
brain, 156
DNA, 156

Cro-Magnon, 94

D

Dating Methods, 24, 43, 55, 75, 83, 105, 106, 108, 112, 117
and archaeologists, 112
and the end times, 108
C-14, 55, 56, 57, 109, 110, 111, 112, 117, 128, 132
contaminated by water, 107
embarrassments of, 105, 108, 110, 111
for sedimentary rocks and fossils, 105
igneous or metamorphic rocks, 106, 108
Uranium/Lead, 106, 107, 108, 110, 182

Day of Creation
24 hours, 38
according to Hebrew scholars, 39
hebrew meaning, 38
logical explanations, 40
why 24 hours denied?, 39
why six days?, 39

Death
came after sin, 38

Different races
all same color, 35

Different Races
all from Noah, 36
all same blood, 36

from evolutionary standpoint, 36
genetic answers, 37
Dinosaur, 70, 75, 76, 78, 79, 81, 82, 83, 86, 87, 88, 89, 90, 91, 92, 99, 112, 138, 145
    Brachiosaurus, 82, 88
    did they evolve into birds?, 88, 89
    footprints, 83
    in Scripture, 79
    Maiasaura, 88
    out of place fossils, 83, 85, 86, 87
    Oviraptor, 89
    Protoceratops, 88
    sitings, 77, 78
    T-Rex, 89
    twisting of evidence, 76
    what do we really know, 87, 88
    why we don't hear they are found with humans, 76
Dinosaur Extinction, 90
    Bible, 91
    by atmospheric conditions, 91
    by flood, 91
    by hunting, 92
    Chicxulub, 90
    comets, 44, 90, 91
DNA, 66, 67, 99, 156
Dragons, 80
    in the Bible?, 81

E

Earths Age
    according to archaeology, 41
    according to Ussher, 41
    why it is made hard to determine, 40
Earths Magnetism, 24
    higher at time of Christ, 29
    rapid reversals, 29
    reversals, 24
Ed Behling, 147, 150
Ed Davis, 146, 150, 152
Electromagnetic Field, 61, 91, 111, 116, 117, 134, 135, 136
    and snake bites, 136
Enoch, 51, 138
Evidence Against an Old Earth
    absence of soil layers, 124
    amount of Helium in the air, 116
    archaeology, 125
    comets, 115
    electromagnetic field, 116
    Meteoric dust, 114
    moon dust, 114
    population, 99, 130
    salt in the sea, 121

soil erosion, 122
the sun, 118
winding of galaxies, 115

F

False Prophets, 169
Fathers, 12, 13, 75, 108, 125
Feathers
　evolution of, 74
Firmament, 29, 91, 111, 131, 132, 133, 134, 135, 138, 140, 144
　higher air pressure, 133
　higher oxygen, 133
　less carbon, 132
　metal, 131
　no radiation, 132
　pink light, 132
　tropical climate, 134
Flight
　evolution of, 74
Fossilization
　of humans, 99
fossils
　no transitional forms, 59
Fossils
　always fully formed, 69
　and the Grand Canyon, 71
　conditions needed to form, 58
　content of entire record, 100
　dating rocks, 76
　in relation to Noah's Flood, 58
　index, 69
　intrusions/redeposited, 76
　living today, 70
　polystrate, 59, 70
　time to form, 57

G

Genesis, 3, 6, 7, 10, 12, 13, 15, 21, 26, 27, 28, 29, 30, 34, 36, 38, 39, 40, 41, 49, 57, 62, 68, 79, 87, 89, 90, 113, 117, 125, 126, 129, 131, 134, 140, 141, 144, 145, 154, 157, 163, 164, 167, 168, 177, 178, 179, 180, 182
Genetics
　98.4% same as chimp, 65, 98
　and one human cell, 67
Gentile, 19, 20, 22, 164
Gentry, 112
George Green, 148
giants, 126, 143, 144
Gibbon, 94, 96
Gould, Stephen, 59, 64, 72, 177, 179
Gradualism, 43

Grand Canyon, 3, 43, 46, 71, 72, 108, 123, 146, 180, 182
Great Commission, 3, 18

H

Haley's Comet, 115
Ham, Ken, 7, 10, 20, 36, 88, 92, 96, 125, 177, 182
HBO, 133
Helium, 116, 176
Hominidae, 94
Homo Erectus, 94, 96
Homo Sapien, 93
homosexuality, 11, 14
Homosexuality, 7
Hydrogen, 132, 179

I

Ice age, 23, 26, 28, 29, 45, 48, 49, 50, 51, 100
    cause, 49
    exposing land bridges, 29
    historical records, 51
    in the Bible, 51
    not global, 49
    short period, 48
    when was it?, 50
Iron Age, 30

J

Java Man, 94, 96
Jehovah, 162
Jesus, 6, 10, 12, 19, 22, 61, 68, 141, 147, 158, 160, 161, 162, 163, 164, 165, 166, 167, 168, 169
Josephus, 41, 131, 161, 178

K

Kei Moris-Tomato Plant, 134
Kelso (quotes), 93, 94, 178

L

Languages
    common after flood, 36
    get less complex, 36
    no link to animals, 36
London Artifact, 87
Lucian, 161
Lucy, 93, 95

M

Mammoth, 51, 92
Marriage, 12, 14
Methuselah, 41, 138, 174
Miocene Age, 105
Morris, Henry, 40, 41, 80, 141
Morris, John, 25, 26, 28, 29, 112, 146, 150, 177
Moses, 20, 132, 168, 170, 179
Mt. St. Helens, 48, 52, 53, 71, 174
    Coal formation, 47
    Spirit Lake, 52

N

Nasa, 132
Neanderthal, 93, 94, 96, 139
Nebraska Man, 97
Noah, 5, 7, 25, 26, 27, 30, 36, 41, 43, 44, 47, 48, 49, 53, 55, 56, 57, 58, 72, 75, 90, 91, 92, 99, 107, 108, 116, 123, 128, 140, 141, 144, 145, 147, 148, 150, 152, 153, 168, 175, 178, 179, 183
Noah's flood, 25, 43, 47, 58, 72, 75, 90, 108, 116, 123
    and carbon dating, 55
    where did the water go?, 144
Noah's Flood
    source of water, 28

O

Ontogeny recapitulates Phylogeny
    Mongoloid idiocy, 64
Ontogeny Recapitulates Phylogeny, 63
    "gill slits", 64
    "yolk sac", 64
    abortions, 65
    and the human "tail", 64

P

Pangea, 23
    Biblical significance, 26
    days of Peleg?, 27
    during flood?, 26
    movement of, 23
Paul, 19, 20, 32, 39, 117, 129, 160, 161, 168, 169, 170, 176, 181
Peking Man, 94, 96
Pliny the Younger, 161
Pornography, 7, 11
Primordial Paradise, 131, 170, 180. *See* Firmament
Prophecy, 163, 169, 170
    list of, 163
Protoavis, 73

Punctuated Equilibrium, 74
Pythagoras, 31, 161

R

Race, 35, 36
Racism
   Hitler and evolution, 36
   stems from evolution, 35
Radiation, 8, 28, 29, 91, 132, 138
Radio Halos Show Instant Creation, 113
Ramapithecus, 94
Rehwinkel, 7, 75, 181

S

Saber Toothed Tiger, 137
Sarah, 138
Schneour, Eli, 14, 182
Snakes, 136, 137, 146
Socrates, 161
Spirit Lake, 48, 52, 53
Stone Age, 30, 32
   technology not needed, 32
Suetonius, 161

T

Talmud, 162
Taylor trail, 85
Technology, 31, 110, 126, 128, 156
Thallus, 161
Thermodynamics
   first law, 61
   how evolutionists explain, 62
   second law of, 62
Tower of Babel, 27, 28, 29, 30, 32, 34, 37, 80, 127, 128
   cause of division, 30
   hinders technology, 32
   origin of races, 34
   possible cause plate tectonics, 28
   relates to stone age, 30
Tree Shrew, 93

U

Uniformitarianism, 43

V

Vestigal Organs, 64
Volcanoes, 45, 46, 108

Krakatoa, 45
Mt. St. Helens, 46
Tambora/Sumbawa, 45
Von Fange, Erich, 27, 32, 51, 56, 75, 128, 183

Y

Yellowstone Park, 52
   relation to Mount St. Helens, 52
   Specimen Ridge, 52

About the Author

Brian Young is the founder and director of Creation Instruction Association. He served as principal and teacher of Christian Schools for ten years before the Lord led him into full time Creation ministry. Brian has been speaking on creation for 11 years and he goes into jails, nursing homes, schools, churches, and even out on the streets. He speaks throughout the country on issues dealing with evangelism, the Bible and the creation/evolution debate. He also publishes a quarterly newsletter called *From the Beginning*. Other books he has authored include: The Stars: God's Word in the Sky, Genesis: Yesterday's Answers to Today's Problems, and Revelation: All of God's Word Revealed. To set up a seminar or to find out more information about the C.I.A. visit the web at www.creationinstruction.org.